The Conscience of a Majority

OTHER WORKS BY BARRY GOLDWATER

The Conscience of a Conservative
Why Not Victory?
Where I Stand
An Odyssey of the Green and Colorado Rivers
Face of Arizona
People and Places
Arizona Portraits, Volumes I and II
Journey Down the River of Canyons

THE CONSCIENCE

OF A MAJORITY

BY BARRY GOLDWATER

Prentice-Hall, Inc., Englewood Cliffs, N.J.

Grateful acknowledgment is made for permission to reprint:

A column by John Chamberlain of February 4, 1970, copyright © King Features Syndicate.

A portion of Jack Anderson's column released December 10, 1969. This reprint was made available in the public interest only by Bell-McClure Syndicate and the author, Jack Anderson, and is not intended as an endorsement of any policy.

The letter to the Editor of the *Washington Post* under date of December 25, 1969, by Raymond Nakai, Chairman, Navajo Tribal Council.

Portions of a column by Richard Harwood and Laurence Stern which appeared in the November 19, 1969, issue of the *Washington Post,* copyright 1969, The Washington Post.

Portions of Stanley Penn's piece *Shape of the Future—Computers Will Bring Problems Along With Their Many Benefits,* published by *The Wall Street Journal* on December 20, 1966 and subsequently published in Dow Jones Books *Here Comes Tomorrow.*

An editorial which appeared in the *Washington Evening Star* on April 4, 1970.

Second printing........September, 1970

The Conscience of a Majority
by Barry Goldwater

ISBN 0-13-167726-8

Library of Congress Catalog Card Number: 71-128518

Printed in the United States of America *T*

Prentice-Hall International, Inc., London
Prentice-Hall of Australia, Pty. Ltd., Sydney
Prentice-Hall of Canada, Ltd., Toronto
Prentice-Hall of India Private Ltd., New Delhi
Prentice-Hall of Japan, Inc., Tokyo

To the children
of the
Space Age Generation

Contents

Introduction   *1*

PART I   *The National Conscience*
CHAPTER I.   *Early Stirrings: The Forgotten American*   *9*
CHAPTER II.   *1964 in Retrospect*   *29*
CHAPTER III. *The Awakening: The Revolt of the*
              Middle American   *45*

PART II   *The Failure of Liberalism*
CHAPTER IV.   *Isolationism Again*   *71*
CHAPTER V.   *Money, Liberals and Defense*   *99*
CHAPTER VI.   *The Legacy from Big Labor*   *116*

PART III   *The Communications Media*
CHAPTER VII. *The Press*   *137*
CHAPTER VIII. *The Networks and the News*   *167*

PART IV   *The Shape of the Future*
CHAPTER IX.   *Tomorrow's Leaders*   *193*
CHAPTER X.   *Saving the Earth*   *212*
CHAPTER XI.   *The Great Challenge*   *233*

Introduction

IT HAS NOW BEEN TEN YEARS SINCE MY FIRST POLITICAL BOOK, "CON-science of a Conservative," was printed. In that decade, tremendous events have occurred—some tragic, some inspiring, some monumental —and they have been accompanied by enormous changes, some so great that the President of the United States saw fit to rank them in relation to Creation itself. But man himself has not changed. He is still the complex, material and spiritual being who incorporates in one nature all the elements of love and hate, unselfishness and greed, kindness and cruelty, that he has always possessed.

The nature of man and the application of political philosophies to his nature provided much of the substance for the "Conscience of a Conservative."

That book presented to American conservatives a challenge which dared them "to demonstrate the bearing of a proven philosophy on the problems of our time." It stressed the fact that despite signs of a conservative revival among the people of the United States, the radical ideas that were promoted by the New Deal and the Fair Deal under the guise of liberalism still dominated the councils of our national government.

Very simply, the "Conscience" was an attempt to bridge the gap between theory and fact. It was an attempt to examine and answer the question of why the American people—admittedly oriented to conservative principles—had been unable to translate their views into appropriate political action. Or as I put it in that earlier book:

1

"Why should the nation's underlying allegiance to conservative principles have failed to produce corresponding deeds in Washington?"

In those days it was my firm belief that there was a deep and broad feeling for a reapplication of conservatism to American life. I sensed that far from being something which we could take for granted, individual freedom in the United States not only needed defending but needed to be defined, promoted and presented in a new light and against a different background if it were to become alive and meaningful once again to the American people.

Perhaps the heaviest impact of the "Conscience" fell in the domestic sphere. Recognizing this, I later, in 1962, wrote a sequel devoted to international relations and the application of conservative principles in the conflict with Communism. That volume, "Why Not Victory?" became Part II in what might become a trilogy on the subject of conservatism and its relationship, effect and guidance on the American people.

It might well be argued that in foreign policy there is no such a thing as a liberal approach or a conservative approach, and I might well agree with this until I think of the definition of conservatism that has always guided me, namely, "The solutions of the problems of today can be found in the proven values of the past."

If we look at foreign policy in this light, then I think history can well dictate to us that our foreign policy must be built upon strength, that it must be built upon a determination to meet commitments we have honorably made with our allies, that it does not mean that we assume the role of policeman of the world, nor does it mean that we engage in every dirty little war that comes along.

Foreign policy built upon the historic use of the built-in strengths of our instruments of policy—namely, propaganda, politics, economics and the last instrument, war itself—can keep peace. Doubters of this thesis need only look at the incidents in the Formosan Straits, Lebanon and Cuba, wherein aggressive Communists backed down in the face of resolute determination on the part of the United States. Those who would say otherwise should also learn something from Vietnam and our refusal to seek victory there.

My newest volume will carry on with that message and attempt to show that the wisdom of our forefathers, who provided us with the foundation of a constitutional government of checks and balances, is perhaps the surest footing we have for the upcoming years wherein this nation retains its world leadership and the responsibilities, risks and dangers of that leadership.

The future can be as frightening as it is hopeful; as terror-ridden as it is exciting; as positive as it is negative. It all depends upon our attitude and our commitment and our dedication as we embark and move along toward the challenges of tomorrow, which are also the challenges of today. The maintenance of individual freedom is the common denominator. It has always been man's greatest challenge and will forever fall in that category.

If we base our efforts on the past, if we use the past, if we treat what has gone before merely as prologue, as something that we learned for the primary purpose of making us equal to the tasks that lie ahead, we will proceed firmly and surely.

Probably the major reason why I have attempted to write this book to add to the library of conservative publications is that the utter and complete failure of so-called liberalism makes it again necessary for the people of this country to do some real thinking and searching for a philosophy and an application of that philosophy which in their opinion will solve the problems of today and prevent the problems of tomorrow. The gigantic size and influence of the Federal Government, against which conservatives have been warning for many years, has now grown almost completely out of hand.

But we have not solved the problems of welfare, nor have we cut the welfare rolls down as was the original aim of this program. We have not solved the problems of 30 percent of our farmers, and they find themselves today in as bad or worse condition than they were in when the Federal agriculture program first started. The Postal Department is a shambles. The transportation systems of America (ground, that is) are in equal disrepair. The overpowering ability of the Federal Government to act as a tax collector has practically destroyed the revenue sources of local, county and state governments. We are in a war whose policies, strategies and tactics have been dictated by civilians with little knowledge of warfare and small regard for the lifetime experience and wisdom of military people.

This, then, is the situation we find today as we consider the future and the resources which we possess to make the most of it. It is for this reason that I like to think that I direct my remarks in this book more to the young people of our nation than to any other segment of our population.

There is a gap in this country between the old and the young,

just as there has always been and always will be. But I disagree
with those who speak about a "generation gap."

If a breach does actually exist in the attitudes of our differing
age groups, it is more of an "understanding gap"; or if you want to
put it another way, it is a "lack-of-understanding gap."

Perhaps our trouble lies in paying too much attention to current developments. With the direction our government has been
taking in the past 30 to 35 years, and with the rapid and dramatic
changes which have taken place in our way of life, we seem to have
ignored the long view. We have forgotten that the young people
of today are living totally different lives, in radically altered circumstances, than we did when we were their age.

For example, an entirely new and different situation exists in
our educational system. There is a fresh difference in the amount
of free time available for today's young people.

Our children have a far greater understanding of what is
transpiring around them and what is taking place in their world
than did the children in my generation at the same age or even ten
years older.

When I speak of the young, my reference is not to people in
their thirties or even in their late twenties. I am speaking of teenagers and those yet to reach that wonderful stage of life more than
of any other group. It is with these youngsters that I find the most
fascinating thought processes. I find in visiting with these young
people that a lot of what they actually talk about today is what I
think of as conservatism.

Naturally, they don't describe it this way. Some, I am sure,
would hotly deny my premise and go right on to say they want to
"do their thing."

My generation did not use that phrase, but it is a good phrase,
and it encompasses precisely what I have always felt was true American conservatism.

And I would certainly hope that young people who might
read this book will find as a result a greater readiness to agree that
their concepts are the concepts of freedom that conservatives have
long held dear. I would hope they would come to realize that not
all the older people in our beloved country are unaware of or in-
sensitive to changes that have taken place in their life styles. It is
my humble belief that the young people of today, if they make
the attempt, can apply all of the lessons and the principles and the

traditions of conservatism to the new way of life they are embarking on at this time. The proven and lasting values of the past, as propounded by responsible conservatives throughout this country, are the same principles that have been applied successfully to all the problems of man down through the centuries of history.

And there perhaps has never been a time in history when they were more applicable than they are today. Events such as the Cambodian operation and moves by liberal forces which resulted from that action underscore heavily the premise I attempt to set forth in the chapter entitled "Isolationism Again." By the same token, new outbreaks of student unrest following the tragic deaths of four students at Kent give special importance to the fundamentals which I stress in the chapter on "Tomorrow's Leaders" and in other parts of the book concerning the requirements of an ordered society founded on justice.

From the oldest recorded history of man down to the precise moment of the present, the application of conservatism has been the process of individuals "doing their thing" in an atmosphere of freedom.

Only when this activity is carried out without regard to the rights of others does it depart from the precepts of conservatism.

Man is free, and man wants to remain free. But freedom can never include the right to abuse others or the property of others.

So with all these thoughts in mind, I proceed with a deep feeling of debt and gratitude to my long-time associate and writer, Tony Smith; to his secretary, Judy Armstrong, who so laboriously has taken down the countless bits of dictation that Tony and I have applied to this project, and to all of the members of my staff who have put up with the strange attitude that people sometimes assume when they get into the business of writing a book.

The introduction is complete, so let's get on with "The Conscience of a Majority."

PART

I

The National Conscience

I

Early Stirrings: The Forgotten American

There are literally scores of millions of Americans who are either outside the organized pressure groups or find themselves represented by organizations with whose policies they disagree in whole or in part.

These millions are the silent Americans *who, thus isolated, cannot find voice against the mammoth organizations which mercilessly pressure their own membership, the Congress, and society as a whole for objectives which these silent ones do not want. They, thereby, have become the "forgotten Americans" despite the fact that they constitute the majority of our people.*

This description of the Silent Majority of Americans about which we read and hear so much today did not come from a speech by President Richard M. Nixon, nor did it come from a speech or a statement by Vice-President Spiro T. Agnew, nor did it come from *Time* magazine's description of the Middle American to which it gave the 1969 Man of the Year Award, nor was it taken from any of the many long articles in magazines and periodicals and newspapers throughout the nation about the rising importance of the so-called "Silent Majority" or "Forgotten Americans."

Rather, this description came from a statement which I wrote and had inserted in the *Congressional Record* of January 11, 1961. It was a statement of "Proposed Republican Principles, Programs and Objectives" and was an attempt by me to translate into a political guidebook, if you will, the findings that had struck me in my travels throughout the length and breadth of this country in the late 1950's and during the 1960 presidential campaign. I found in my talks with men and women, young and old, of all colors, races and creeds and religions, a vast restlessness, a vast unhappiness—a feeling that was almost universal, which said that the individual by himself and unorganized was virtually helpless to achieve what he really wanted to achieve—that is, economic well-being, a rising standard of living, improved education, cultural development, dignified human treatment in social and economic relationships.

In other words, I found this feeling of inadequacy on the part of those Americans most deserving. I am speaking of the Americans who quietly go their way working, saving, praying and doing their bit to help their fellowman without necessarily taking any great part in or adding any great voice to the development of public policies having to do with social welfare and with economic conditions and so forth.

Many of these so-called Forgotten Americans belonged, as I say, to organizations; but they looked to those organizations for help in areas for which they were formed to help. In other words, a labor union member looked to his union to help him negotiate with his employer and help him achieve a higher wage level and better working conditions. However, he didn't necessarily want to turn over his entire life and his entire future to the dictates of that union. What that statement of principle was designed to do was give voice to a clear and growing need which I perceived in our society for a greater sense of individual responsibility and obligation and an opportunity for the individual to perform in his own behalf. It was an attempt to give individual expression or to say to the Congress at that time that there are millions of Americans who are not satisfied with this pressure group representation at every level of government, who are not satisfied to have others speak for them, who would of their own right like to voice their own opinions on a few of these things.

If you will, it was an expression of protest against the tendencies to classify more and more Americans as mere holes on a computer card. It was an attempt to come to grips with what I regarded as a dehumanizing trend in our society. I, therefore, set forth principles and proposals as a fundamental guide for government action, especially on a Federal level. And it was done as a means of giving voice to the suppressed views and feelings of millions of Forgotten Americans who, even then, constituted a substantial majority of our society. As I attempted to describe it in that statement:

> *It recognizes that those private activities which are essential to the successful functioning of a modern society have tended to become institutionalized in huge, organizational units which, themselves growing larger with each passing year, continuously narrow the area in which the individual may act freely, decisively and effectively.*
>
> *The fundamental problem which confronts the Republic is to find the means to protect individual freedom, action and responsibility without hampering or destroying those processes and techniques which a modern industrial society must employ if it is to survive and develop.*

Say what you will, in the light of what happened in the years following the development of that statement, I feel that I had accurately read the pulse of the American people. Perhaps I had believed it to be beating more rapidly than it actually was. In fact, I sincerely thought that the American people, the Forgotten Americans, that is, had almost reached the point of rebellion against this process of dragooning. In that I was wrong. It was to take additional years for that American to come into his own and to gain proper recognition.

I took occasion at that time to point out that in the Eisenhower years the individual Americans had amassed enormous private savings and insurance and had reached an all-time high in putting aside funds for their future life. I also warned that many of the Welfare State extension programs that had been proposed in the 1960 Democratic Convention Platform would destroy or threaten the savings that these people had been able to put aside. As my statement put it:

> *The Democratic Party Platform is an ominous threat to the financial security of the American people, the overwhelming majority of whom now possess substantial savings, insurance and pension rights. It threatens not only those who are on fixed income at the present, but the*

future of every family which through thrift and present sacrifice has sought to make provisions for the future. The reckless and spendthrift promises of the Democratic Platform could be carried out only by means of a program of Federal spending so tremendous as to require either an enormous increase in taxation or a policy of deficit spending leading to uncontrolled inflation.

I must remind the reader this statement was made in 1961. What happened after that was an unexampled period of Federal extravagance, and the result we see today. It is represented in the additional burden being carried by the Silent Majority and being carried unhappily. It is the burden of what we predicted in 1961, an enormous increase in taxation and an uncontrolled condition of inflation. The deficit spending also entered in. This became a permanent fixture of the Democratic administrations which followed.

I warned in that statement that irresponsible spenders would yield to the siren song of further government borrowing to promote further government spending. I said that an unbalanced budget and growth in the national debt would follow as inevitable sequences of this policy. One prophetic statement included in that policy declaration read as follows:

Inflation will run rampant, the purchasing power of the American dollar will melt away like snowdrifts in the spring sun and our hard-working and thrifty people will watch in stupefied dismay as the value of their savings, their insurance, their pension funds diminish each day, ultimately perhaps to vanish almost entirely.

My contention then was that the people were getting sick and tired of this trend even before the Kennedy Administration with all its new programs came into office.

What has happened since then is, of course, history. However, it is important to understand that what this nation desperately needed in 1960 and for the years of that decade was a system of priorities. They needed to know what was most important, what was second most important, what was third most important. They never got an answer.

The administration, under the late President John F. Kennedy, sent thousands upon thousands of words to Congress in special messages—all of them labeled "crisis" or "must." Everything that came from the White House was a priority program, a crash program, a must program, something that had to be done—and done immediately—in the best interest of our citizens.

But they never told us which was the most important. They never told us which was the least important. Consequently, the Congress of the United States, and the American people generally, were confronted with a whole nation full of alleged crises. It was like a man being caught in a room full of flies but armed with only one fly swatter. In other words, this nation did not and does not have enough money to do everything that every liberal do-gooder and politician would like to see done. There are some things that people should be made to do for themselves. There are some things, many things, that individuals want to do for themselves. Their own dignity, their own respect for themselves and for their abilities and skills require that they be permitted to look after their own welfare in many important aspects.

I don't know what would happen if it was put to the American people flatly that the Federal Government would like to take over all responsibilities and do everything for them and make them nothing but ciphers in the whole scheme of things. I think if it were put that way, the American people would make their wishes fully and abundantly clear. I believe they would vote for self-expression, for the maintenance of opportunities for man to exercise his own God-given capabilities and skills.

I believe that the average American, the Silent Majority, if you will, believes the government's place is important in that government should protect, government should insure him justice and order in a well-organized society. It should also provide him with protection and defense in the international sphere.

However, I do not believe that the average American, the forgotten American, the silent majority, wants Uncle Sam to take over every facet of his life and work. I think that is the great lesson that we are learning today. For three and a half decades the New Deal, the Fair Deal, the New Frontier, the Great Society, all the liberal political movements have been offering Federal financing as the end-all answer—the panacea, if you will, for every problem that ever came up to confront the American people. Federal spending for housing, for health, for education, for civil rights, for equal employment opportunities, for urban renewal, for rebuilding cities, for revamping farms, Federal spending was the answer always. It was the answer to every problem ever to arise when the liberals were in control of the government. And we have had, as I say, three and a half decades of liberal performance. We have had between 30 and 40 years of these kinds of panaceas. We have had all this government expenditure, billions upon billions upon billions of dollars, to solve all of these problems. Yet today we are confronted with a greater mass of domestic problems than any nation this world has ever seen, has ever heard of, before.

And why is this? Why is it that we have housing problems? This was all to be taken care of under programs that FDR proposed in the 1930's, under programs that Harry Truman proposed in the 1940's, etc., etc. You can go right down the list of domestic problems. You will find, for example, that the liberals are the ones who are most vocally concerned about civil rights. Why is it then that racial strife and the really difficult problems of discrimination that have confronted this nation were never foreseen before they happened, were never understood fully before they came upon us full-blown, were never adequately provided for until they forced themselves upon the legislative mind and the human conscience of the people running this government?

In this, I am merely touching the high spots of what I think has been the failure here of an approach to any and all of our problems over the past three and a half decades. I say the liberal answer has failed, and I say the proof is staring every American squarely in the face. And I believe this failure is the root cause of why we have today a silent majority, of why we have today a heavy percentage of youthful unrest and dissatisfaction which is finding its expression in many unhappy ways, including the taking of drugs, the protests on campuses, and so forth. In all of this liberal organizational activity aimed at any and all social and domestic problems, the individual is most often ignored. He is there just to be manipulated. He is there to be submerged, to be swamped, to be treated as something you can mold into a social pattern.

Up until now, this has been a fairly easy process. The average American, the silent American, has lacked the time, the energy, the resources, and sometimes the courage, to "buck" the machine, to oppose the organization's leadership and bureaucracy. The old expression "you can't fight City Hall" has had its application here.

But there are times when all of these admonitions, all of these fears, doubts, uncertainties get washed away by the urgency of events. And I believe that today we are seeing the average American get a real noseful. I think he is ready to be heard; I think he is already being heard; I think this is the meaning of the 1960's. I think it started in the late 1950's and early 1960's.

As I attempted way back there in early 1961 to come to grips with the uneasiness and unhappiness which I felt was building up in the vast majority of unheard-from Americans, I pointed out that one of the big factors was the reckless spending of government money and the consequent threat to the hard-earned savings of the American people. This found its expression in many ways. As a matter of fact, it found its expression in the elections of 1960. Republicans carried all areas of the country, for example, where people lived who had retired on fixed incomes. This specifically showed, I believe, that that class of Americans was worried, was afraid, was frightened by the Democratic promises of reckless spending. They had every reason to be afraid, as the present cost-of-living index so eloquently demonstrates. Another aspect of this concern, also mentioned in my 1961 Statement of Principles, was the subject of law and order. On this, my Statement of Principles had this to say:

> *One of the finest pillars upon which American society rests is the proposition that law and order are an absolute essential for the preservation and improvement of our democratic way of life. A profound respect for the law and abhorrence of disorder and anarchy are deeply ingrained in the American character.*

I believe today that this deeply ingrained aspect of the American individual has been greatly disturbed. Not only people who have a strong sense of law and order, but also average citizens who never before gave it much thought are disturbed. They have begun to regard the attack on all elements of authority, whether it be parents, school administrations, the police or the military, as a threat to society as a whole. They deplore the fact that anybody in any position of authority is today almost completely liable to be designated as a "pig" by some malcontents. And I believe that the average person, the one who hasn't particularly made a fetish about his concern for law and order, is becoming alarmed. I believe he sees what can happen if we disregard laws and if we no longer obey laws which we personally dislike for any one of many high-sounding reasons. I believe he understands that we are tampering with the very fabric of an ordered society.

For without the police, without people of authority, without the exercise of authority, in a nation of 204 million people you would have nothing but the law of the jungle. Anarchy has no place in the United States. I believe everyone is beginning to understand this. Perhaps the example of anarchy in the courtroom, as disgracefully shown in the so-called trial of the Chicago Seven on charges of fomenting a riot at the time of the Democratic National Convention, did as much as anything to shock the American people into a new awareness. The shouts and curses of the defendants coupled with acts of defiance and disrespect on the part of their attorneys made this one of the most disgraceful experiences in the history of American jurisprudence.

Several things set the Chicago trial apart from earlier examples of courtroom disruption, such as those that occurred during the Sacco-Vanzetti murder trial of the 1920's and the explosive trial of eleven Communists before United States Appeals Court Judge Harold R. Medina in 1949. Most serious of the Chicago departures was the participation in the disruption by the defense attorneys. It perhaps is not thoroughly understood by the layman, but a lawyer, regardless of who he represents as a client, is at all times regarded as an officer of the court and, as such, bears a special kind of responsibility in the working of the judicial system.

In the trial of the Chicago Seven, the defense attorneys were so contemptuous that one of them, William Kunstler, was sentenced to four years and thirteen days in prison on 24 counts of contempt. Another defense attorney, Leonard Weinglass, drew one year, eight months and five days on 14 counts of contempt. Unfortunately, the press spent most of its time and space declaiming on the length of these sentences and pointing out that Judge Julius Hoffman had imposed the most severe contempt citations on record. The American public would have been better served if the communications media had devoted its space to the frightening reasons why it was necessary for a reputable United States judge to impose such severe sentences. Nobody seemed especially interested in what could have happened to American jurisprudence if Judge Hoffman had not taken the sternest possible action to punish a deliberate attempt by defense attorneys to defy the law. More and more responsible judges are becoming worried by the growing belligerence and contemptuous attitude on the part of defense lawyers in political cases. As Second Circuit Appeals Judge Irving Kaufman put it, "When lawyers don't play by the rules, a trial does not work." This is especially true when lawyers appearing in political cases are radicals and rebels in their own right and, consequently, refuse to act as officials of the courts.

And this extension of street-corner anarchy into the halls of justice has started many thoughtful and concerned legal experts on a search for better methods of control. It is unthinkable, of course, that courtroom anarchy should be permitted to continue. For if we do not have obedience and decorum in the nation's courtrooms, it will be the end of the courts; it will be the end of the dispensing of justice; it will be the end of individual liberty and the end of government as we know it.

These are the life and death stakes that were involved in the proceedings at Chicago; but to judge by the liberal press, you would have thought that they were just routine maneuvers in another petty confrontation between pacifists and legal authorities.

By the same token, some other courts are being derelict to the cause of justice in another fashion. This stems from an overweening concern for the rights of the accused criminal and an almost psychological fear that some accused criminal may not be given all of his constitutional prerogatives.

All of this concern for the accused has another side effect. It produces a lack of concern for the person offended against. It shows a lack of concern for the great silent majority whose rights to protection and safety have been infringed upon by the criminal. As one American news magazine put it in an article entitled "The Troubled American": "Suddenly the focus is on the citizen who outnumbers, outvotes and could, if he chose, outgun the fringe rebel. After years of feeling himself a besieged minority, the man in the middle—representing America's vast, white, middle-class majority—is giving vent to his frustrations and his disillusionment and his anger."

The revolt, if I might call it that, of the troubled American has been a long time coming. As I have attempted to prove in these pages, it was seen way back. It was recognized in 1960 and 1961, not only by myself, but by many people. I just happen to have the document in which I put down the thoughts I had and the predictions I had to make with reference to this.

Recognition of those early stirrings, I might explain, was not confined to politicians and civic leaders. The organized church—or at least that large segment represented by the Catholic Bishops of the United States—was also beginning to show concern for the submerging of individual freedom. In fact, in their annual statement of November 20, 1960, the bishops pointed out that:

"This history and achievements of America stand as a monument to the personal responsibilities of free men. Our institutions and our industry, the fruit of the American sense of responsibility, have in the past inspired, guided, and helped many other nations of the world. If our future is to be worthy of our past, if the fruit of America's promise is not to wither before it has reached full maturity, our present preeminent need is to reaffirm the sense of individual obligation, to place squarely before ourselves the foundation on which personal responsibility rests, to determine the causes of its decay and to seek the means by which it can be revived."

The bishops' statement then goes on to call for a renewal of the sense of personal responsibility, initiative and individual obligation. It deprecated the inordinate demand for benefits to be secured through organization pressures. It criticized the placing of an excessive and constant reliance on the United Nations and asked for an objective evaluation of the moral aspects of UN activity.

In the same statement the bishops lamented a widespread, cynical reaction to revelations by the Senate McClellan Rackets Committee of dishonesty, waste and malfeasance in labor relations. It spoke out against the growing conformity and mechanizations and the favored treatment increasingly being given to those anonymous, organizational men while reasserting the worth and dignity of the individual.

In their own way, the bishops were expressing the fact that in the very nature of organizations is the inevitable tendency to oligarchy and suppression of personal responsibility. They recognize that such suppression is possible even in organizations which are benevolently motivated towards humanitarian goals. It was also recognized that the good of an organization tends many times to become the predominant consideration while the individual member grows more rapidly anonymous, an increasingly helpless automaton unable, and eventually unwilling, to exercise free choice and personal responsibility. Thus, the bishops declared:

"A fresh evocation of the principles and practices of personal responsibility can revivify our society and help to stem the seemingly inexorable march toward the automation of human beings and the steady loss of that freedom which is man's distinctive attribute. It will cure the mental lethargy and inertia which permit organizations to usurp, mainly by default, the rights of their members. It will stimulate a self-reliance which will automatically restore the balance between freedom and security. It will reject unwarranted pressure from groups that seek unjustly to aggrandize their power and will restrict them to their lawful ends."

I must admit it has taken the troubled Americans longer than I had expected for them to become part of the public scene, and believe you me, they are a part. Whether you like it or not, they are no longer silent. They are being heard from. The TV networks in this nation heard from them in a big way when Vice-President Agnew had the temerity to point an accusing finger and ask an important segment of American industry to stand up and examine itself to find out if it was performing its role in the American scene correctly.

The silent American gave voice as an aftermath of the Agnew blast. He gave voice in telephone calls to the network stations, in telegrams, in letters to Congressmen, in public statements; and I believe he was heard from earlier than that. I believe he was heard from at the polls when President Nixon was elected. I believe that he expressed himself then in favor of the man who came down most squarely and most solidly on the side of limited government, reduced government spending, adequate measures for peace, and enforcement of the law through every conceivable means possible. I believe that the American, the silent American, has reasserted and is reasserting the traditional values of this nation.

The conservatives have always talked about the proven values of the past and about the great worth of experience. They like to point out that on statues in front of the National Archives Building here in Washington are written the phrases, "What is past is prologue" and "The past is prologue; Study the past." In other words, the American conservative has long felt that we were exercising a departure from traditional values and accepted principles, things that had worked in the past. And I believe that the American people, the great American silent majority, now agree, even at the risk of being described as "square" and as being "old fashioned" and "out of it" and "not with it" and whatever other expression you want to use.

I believe the great majority of American people are reasserting the traditional values that have characterized American patriotism for many years.

If you don't believe me, look at the automobile windows on American cars. You'll find flag decals all over them. Generally, you'll find a nationwide crusade being organized to restore prayers in the schoolrooms, to ban sex education, to curb pornography. Another phenomenon is the great rise in the popularity of Vice-President Agnew. Throughout the 50 states, cars are blossoming with Agnew bumper stickers such as "The Spiro of '76."

The uneasy mood has also spawned a coast-to-coast surge to law-and-order politics. In one city after another, you will find in the political offerings candidates who use law and order as their actual campaign platform. Think about that. It is amazing to think that in this nation, this nation conceived on a basis of laws and of ordered justice and of freedom of the individual and of freedom of choice and of freedom of speech and freedom of assembly, that the very guardians of freedom—the police, the authority, the people who make sure the majority has a chance to exercise those freedoms —come under such attack that a man actually adopts as a political platform a concept of support for law and order.

I suggest that this is a sign of the time; this is what the silent Americans are talking about; this is what the conscience of a country is all about. Most Americans have the right attitudes and the right reactions, and I think that they are opposed to what has gone on, what has been allowed to grow up in the permissiveness of the liberal approach and in the great reach for change.

This great reach for change for the sake of change has no relationship to progress. Change for the sake of bettering the human plight is an important change; that is progress. But change for the sake of change can very often be change for the worse.

Some years ago, liberal politicians began to suggest that now is the time "to think unthinkable thoughts." It was anything but. It was time to forget unthinkable thoughts and start thinking about the real values, the cherished values, the traditions and principles that had made this nation strong and that had made its people great. It was a time for a return to patriotism. But the liberals persisted, with a lot of help from the communications media; and somewhere along the line, the "unthinkable" became the "acceptable." The idea of change for the sake of change became synonymous with "good."

A pattern began emerging that eventually could bring about the destruction of our free society. The "unthinkable" says automatically that because of "changing times" we not only must alter our old methods of living, but we also must change all of our previously held attitudes. Thus, you find a vicious and growing attack directed at every tradition, every standard and belief—no matter how fundamental it might be to an ordered society of freedom and justice—that has existed long enough to be regarded as old-fashioned.

This concept says that "change" must be made regardless of the laws, the courts, the churches or any other obstacle. It panders to the current hue and cry, the latest so-called "crisis," the newest demands of special groups—all without weighing the consequences, or the good of the greatest number of our citizens, or the fundamentals of human freedom.

Just apply the idea of "unthinkability" to any area of government, society or religion, and you'll begin to see what we're up against.

In foreign affairs, of course, the "unthinkable" is to downgrade the United States while finding virtue and honor in her enemies. It is to urge surrender in Vietnam, to stop "isolating" the poor, misunderstood Chinese Communists, and to cut back our military commitments all over the world, including Europe, to the peril of the Atlantic Alliance and the Pacific.

In military affairs, the "unthinkable" argues for unilateral disarmament, destruction of our nuclear arsenal, virtual abandonment of the Strategic Air Command, and the substitution of judgment by "Whiz Kids" and computers for that of experienced and knowledgeable military commanders.

In fiscal affairs, the "unthinkable" goes under a title of its own, the "new economics." Although the trend began many years ago under determined liberal assault, the total, official disregard for fiscal responsibility began with the propaganda deriding "economic myths" and something they called "the puritan ethic." Since then, we have been treated to a steady stream of "unthinkable" and unsound economics.

Almost overnight, constant government deficits became a measure of economic health, and balanced budgets became a danger to an expanding economy. We were told that government had found a formula for sustained prosperity without economic dislocation. The basic ingredient, of course, was government spending as measured as a percentage of the Gross National Product. And today the results are coming in with every new cost-of-living index. Inflation is here, and the complete fallacy of the "new economics" is being proven in a way that burdens every American taxpayer with skyrocketing prices and higher taxes.

In the field of religion, the "unthinkable" once was a Supreme Court denying school children the privilege of praying in their classrooms. Today, the "unthinkable" says "God is dead" and the Ten Comandments no longer have any validity.

In the area of law enforcement, the "unthinkable" (compared with past standards) is the idea of obeying only the laws you consider just. It is the official toleration of civil disobedience so long as the cause is considered righteous. It is the finding of ready, generalized excuses for instances of mass rioting, violence, and vandalism; it is the assumption that most law enforcement agencies are basically "brutal" and unjust. It is the excessive attitude of concern by some groups and judges for the "rights of the accused" to the exclusion of the rights of the community.

Charles E. Whitaker, former Associate Justice of the United States Supreme Court, put it bluntly in a magazine article when he pointed out that "toleration of some crime encourages all crime." In this country we have been tolerating many kinds of crime in the name of justice. As a result, we have a condition bordering on anarchy in many of our cities—where the safety of law-abiding citizens has virtually disappeared in the flood of murders, rapes, armed robberies and felonious assaults.

On the college campuses—on one campus in particular, the University of California at Berkeley—the "unthinkable" took the form of demonstrations for the right to display publicly a filthy four-letter word, all in the name of "free speech."

The advocates of "unthinkability" also make special targets of the built-in instruments of democracy. Many of them argue that the Constitution was designed for use 200 years ago and claim that it is outdated because it places too much restriction on the use of power by the Executive Branch. The same argument has been directed against our historic system of checks and balances as it applies to Congress. The drive, here, is aimed at streamlining the Legislative Branch of government to do away with the few remaining methods by which a responsible minority can restrain an arrogant, power-hungry majority.

I am struck with the unhappy realization that the concept of "change" as it is advocated by today's liberals is becoming a sickness. It no longer looks to the consequences. It no longer respects the confines of decency and taste. No institution, be it church, school, or the United States Capitol, is sacred or even respected. Patriotism is something that the arch-liberal laughs at. He regards love of country and respect for the flag as examples of old-fashioned nationalism—or as forms of disloyalty to the United Nations. He derides what he terms "superpatriots" and talks glibly of a "higher patriotism" which calls upon him to oppose his country's policy in a time of war.

We might pause here to consider just what an unthinkable thought actually is. To the average person it means something reprehensible, something that is really inexpressible, something that cannot be voiced in front of children or in mixed society. In other words, the mere fact that the intellectual community may think it is time for Americans to think unthinkable thoughts does not necessarily guarantee that those thoughts will be any better than what we had been thinking before.

The reason they are unthinkable thoughts is that they have been considered and rejected by thinking people. There is no reason to believe that the level of mental activity, the level of thinking, is any higher today than it was in the past, in those hoary old days of McKinley, back in the days to which the liberals like to consign the American conservative.

No, the thinking processes of man do not change that much. I am inclined to believe that the thoughts that occur to many of our leaders today, at least many of our most vocal citizens, are still unthinkable, still unprintable, still inexpressible, and should be forgotten.

However, there still seems to be an attitude among some people that we must change for the sake of change, that we must think unthinkable thoughts because these are the only ones left, that we must act in unactable ways, that we must go against all the traditions and the mores and the customs of the past. The purpose here is shock value alone. The liberals' concept of unthinkability runs something like this:

It's unthinkable to consider treason or fault your own country; so then think it and do it. It's unthinkable to consider walking around Wall Street without any clothes on; so think it, even do it. And it's unthinkable to take the law into our own hands and to obey only those laws which we feel are right for us. It's unthinkable; so think it, perhaps do it. And it is unthinkable for the average, well-educated young American to take harmful drugs like LSD, "speed," "goof-balls," and all the rest of it. It's unthinkable; yet think about it and do it. It's unthinkable to run down the guardians of law and order. It's unthinkable to go up to a policeman and call him a pig; so think it and do it. If it's unthinkable, it has shock value. Therefore, if you want to catch public opinion, if you want to attract the TV cameras, if you want to get your name and picture in the paper, the thing to do is not only think unthinkable thoughts but do unthinkable things.

So much for the liberal approach as expressed by the new left. The dreadful thing is that some people believe it is the correct course.

This is the very sorry path to which I believe we have come. It is a very sorry situation when actual leaders in America can suggest that the only way we are going to make headway, the only way we are going to right the wrongs that have gone before us, is to flout law and order and to flout authority and to destroy ordered justice. This is what we're really talking about, ordered justice, or the rights of the majority of our people to have an element of security and protection. We are talking about the rights of the majority, not the privileges of the minority. In other words, most of what we hear today is coming from the vocal and ill-directed minority. What we are not hearing, but what we are going to hear more and more, is the voice of the silent majority. And believe you me, when the silent majority begins to speak at full strength, it will be heard loud and clear. It already is beginning.

Now this harking back to the early days of the last decade is not designed as an exercise in retrospection. It is not designed to show that the author has any special powers of political prophecy, nor is it intended to play the old game of "I told you so" for those who study the questions of political movements and political candidates.

I must confess that the "I told you so" school of human behavior does exercise a peculiarly strong pull on political candidates, especially those who have been defeated for nationwide office such as I was in 1964. However, nothing is to be gained through vindictiveness or through spitefulness. Rather, as a true conservative, I am attempting to use the past merely to expose the lessons learned in that past to show how those lessons may be made applicable to the problems we face today and to the challenges we face tomorrow. No, I hark back to the year 1961 for a very specific reason. It is to show that the conscience of this country had its early stirrings many years ago. It is to show that the majority of our people had begun to suspect that the easy answers of the liberals to the problems that beset our nation were not the correct answers. It was to show that many years back this nation began to develop a consciousness of the individual which today I believe is finding its expression in that phenomenon which the President refers to as the "Silent Majority," and which other Americans refer to as the "Forgotten Man," and which most publications refer to as the "Middle American." I believe the consensus that we are witnessing today had its early beginnings many years ago and that some people in public life fore saw them at that time. I think any man who traveled as far and as wide across this nation and spoke to as many diverse groups of people as I did in those years of the late 1950's was bound to recognize that there was a vast restlessness moving in the land, that there was something that was trying to break through, that there was something going on in the ranks of America's silent majority.

It is this phenomenon which I detected and which I say was perfectly obvious for any discerning politician to detect in the Statement of Principles which I wrote in 1961. My purpose here is not to emphasize that ten years ago I was correct about some things. No, it is not that at all. It is to show you that this great national feeling which is now resulting in positive expression at the polls and throughout America generally did not have its beginning in any one specific issue or event.

There are many among us who like to ascribe this entire attitude of the silent majority or the middle Americans to a white backlash. They would like us to believe that it is all the result of gains made by the black man in our society. Others would like us to believe that it all is the result of selfishness on the part of corporate interests. Others would like us to believe that it is all the result of air pollution. Some would like us to believe it is all the result of arbitrary and brutal forces of law and order. Still others, of course, would like us to believe that the whole thing is the result of weariness and frustration over the war in Vietnam.

My purpose here is to show that it was none of these things in particular. Actually, all of them played a part. But the overall discontent was a general dissatisfaction with the status quo as handed down to us from the Democrat liberals. The liberal answers with their lack of results were no longer enough to satisfy the American people. Thus, the early stirring of our American conscience was beginning at the start of the last decade and its growth has been progressive ever since.

Actually, my candidacy for the presidency in 1964 was itself a product of this early stirring of the national conscience. Ask yourself, if you are politically minded, how a man with as little political experience as I had, coming from a state as small as Arizona, could in the short space of one and a half terms in the United States Senate suddenly become a national factor in the political scheme of things. As the politicians would say, it "wasn't in the wood." Actually, I was not widely known until the late 1950's; and I never became heavily financed in the fashion of political candidates as we have been used to considering them. I, myself, am not a wealthy man in the light of political fortunes such as those owned by the Rockefellers and the Kennedys and so forth. I am very frank about my financial status. It was published in 1964 when I was a candidate for President. The figures then, as given by my banker, showed that my wife and I together had a fortune that ran roughly at $1.5 million. When you compare this with the super-millionnaires of today, the people whose fortunes run between $50 million and $500 million, you can see how my personal fortune could not possibly have been the source of my political advancement.

No, it was something more. I know that this word is not entirely acceptable to all people in political life, but if there ever was a "groundswell" working on the part of a particular candidate, I believe I witnessed that. I had nothing to do in the early 1960's with the bumper stickers that showed up urging "Goldwater for President" or "Give us Barry" or any of the other devices such as the chemical formula "$AU\ H_2O$" (for "gold" and "water"). These bumper stickers and the newspaper stories and predictions that showed up in the early 1960's predicting the Goldwater candidacy in 1964 were none of my doing. Some of them were inaugurated by people of whom I had knowledge or whom I had known; but certainly none of them was activated on orders, direct or indirect, from me or from any of my close political advisors or my close friends. No, this was part of the stirring. I believe this was part of the attempt to find a way out of the mess with which the liberalism of three decades had surrounded the American individual. I suppose I became a catalyst in this respect because of my long advocacy of conservative principles. Basically, I argued against the expansion of Federal Government. I argued for Federal thrift, fiscal responsibility, cutting back the power and the spending of the Federal Government. I argued for constitutional rights, for a strong military, for all the things that the liberals of our day were busily undercutting or going against.

In other words, my position perhaps was more directly opposed to what many Americans were beginning to find onerous and irksome in public policy. I have heard it said that I brought to my political stance something called "charisma." If so, it is something that defies my efforts at explanation. Perhaps it has something to do with a quality of concern for others that I have always felt and which I have not earned in any special way. Perhaps it was just given to me by God or by my parents, but I honestly like people. I enjoy people. I welcome their views, even when they are directly and vehemently opposed to my own.

This feeling is what took me across the length and breadth of this country, week after week, year after year, from the time that I became a United States Senator. I liked people. I wanted to know what they were thinking, and I pride myself on believing that the rapport was established through which I could get at some of the things that were deep down and were bothering these people.

That 1961 Statement of Principles is an expression of what I found in the people I met and with whom I talked. It was an attempt to draw a blueprint actually in political terms for my own political party, because I felt then as I feel now that the Republican Party has the only answer and is the only political vehicle that can take the silent majority, the forgotten Americans, out of their unhappy state.

In this I was entirely correct. I believe that this feeling on my part was transmitted to many Americans through appearances that

I made on television, through personal contacts, through magazine articles and newspaper stories, through all the media. I think this attitude of concern for the people and concern for their problems and my habit of speaking out on them led some people to think I had an excess of political courage. It was not courage. It was common sense, at least the way I saw it from my Far Western vantage point. My Far Western vantage point told me that if you want a nation to thrive economically, you have to place that nation's government on a sound economic basis. Budgets were drawn up to be balanced. Surpluses were made to be valued. Deficits were made to be avoided. These things were very simple. But in the 1960's we were in the hands of a new breed of politicians who were busily attempting then as they are today to try and convince the American people that the old values, the old traditions, the things that they have always believed in and lived by, are somehow wrong because they are old.

This goes against the grain; this violates something deep down in the conscience of the individual American. I believe today it has reached down deep enough to find expression through a silent majority which more and more is insisting upon being felt, upon being a factor, upon being a determinate in the development and evolution of our public policies.

Now, as I have tried to point out, my elevation to the position of a candidate seeking the presidential nomination of my party was a direct result of pressures from below. I have called it a groundswell for lack of a better word. I do know this: that from all directions, the pressure came—from big people, from little people, from old and young, and from all segments of our society. And I must say that as far as grass roots political movements go, I believe that the conservative revolution, of which I happened to be something of a symbol, reached an astounding peak the week before the assassination of President John F. Kennedy. If there has been more political steam built up behind a set of principles and ideas in our history, I certainly have never heard of it and certainly never saw it. But with the assassination of President Kennedy, the steam went out of all things political in this nation. This was the inevitable aftermath of a horrible event, the assassination of a young and promising President, and it just so happened that the buildup behind my candidacy had more political steam to lose than anything else then existing in this heartbroken nation.

CHAPTER

II

1964 in Retrospect

VERY EARLY IN THE LAST DECADE, I FOUND MYSELF BECOMING A political fulcrum of the vast and growing tide of American disenchantment with the public policies of liberalism.

There was no question here of which came first—the chicken or the egg. The restiveness of the American people—the early stirrings of a national conscience in search of better ways and means to attack our public problems—was certainly not of my individual making. It is true enough that I sensed it early and sympathized with it publicly, but I did not originate it. The circumstances surrounding the people's recognition of liberal failures in almost every field did the job.

In a sense I was caught up in and swept along by this tide of disenchantment. In all events, I joined it and helped give expression to a new public attitude which the die-hard, knee-jerk liberals did not credit then and will not understand even now. My program, if you could call it that, was a conservative response to a growing national demand. It was my firm belief that there was a deep and broad market for an application of conservative principles to American life. I felt the people were hungering for a time-tested philosophy of unquestioned quality. I sensed that, far from being something which we could at long last take for granted, individual freedom in the United States not only required defending but needed to be defined, promoted and presented in a new light and against a different background if it were to become alive and meaningful once again to the American people.

At that time, however, the liberals in control of the government had become so accustomed to having their own way that my suggestions calling for a firm foreign policy, fiscal sanity and a society of law and order were looked upon as almost radical departures from accepted and existing policy.

We had actually moved so far down the road to collectivist liberalism, with all its Keynesian and Fabian trappings, that serious proposals to heed the lessons of history were quickly dismissed as the work of crackpots and kooks.

To the average liberal it was unbelievable that there could be in this country a new respect for capitalism, the free-enterprise system and patriotism. These had too long been the subject of ridicule and discrediting by liberal politicians for any of them to understand that a fresh generation of Americans was not only looking ahead to the future, but studying also the past and what had worked in those days.

But all of a sudden, the road to rebellion on many college and university campuses led in the direction of seeking conservative answers to vexing and persistent public problems. Despite the best efforts of the ADA, the Democratic National Committee and liberal spokesmen everywhere, the word "conservatism" became respectable and relevant again in the early 1960's after long years of serving as the undeserving butt of left-wing ridicule. Strangely enough, in the early part of the last decade, the strongest expressions of revolt against the establishment were to start a conservative group, join the Young Americans for Freedom, or subscribe to the conservative magazine *National Review* or the weekly newspaper *Human Events*. Young Americans were becoming sick and tired of being "brainwashed" by liberal professors, authors and commentators. They could look around them and see the chaotic fruits of three and a half decades of liberal policy, and they had every right and reason to seek better answers and a more meaningful rationale.

I mentioned the evolution of a personal program of advocacy in the early days of this rebellion against liberalism. I covered some of it in the document I quoted in the previous chapter. But if I had to itemize in very general terms, I would say that that program expressed warnings that unless this nation altered the basic course it had been following since the middle 1930's, we would be in very serious difficulty on three major fronts:

1. In the handling of our foreign relations with respect to the

Communists generally, and particularly in our handling of the situation in Cuba and Southeast Asia.

2. In the area of fiscal affairs, where the escalating trend in Federal deficits would lead to a period of critical inflation.

3. In the handling of our free society of ordered justice, where years of permissiveness at the highest levels of government and the encouragement of permissiveness by the courts were leading to an incredible increase in the crime rate on our city streets.

Of course, nothing was done in the wake of the 1960 presidential election to alter the near-disastrous course we had been following in this area of public life. Senator John F. Kennedy was inaugurated as President, and the liberals quickly began to interpret his paper-thin victory over Vice-President Nixon as a mandate from the people for new and bigger spending programs, continued wishful thinking in the conduct of our foreign policy, and an extension of permissiveness in all areas of our domestic life. And, of course, it was along these three lines that the nation found itself in a state of genuine crisis in the later years of the decade. And as we came up to the national election of 1968, the crises called "Vietnam," "inflation" and "crime" led the Hit Parade of national issues, and it was on the basis of the action he promised in these three areas that President Nixon won his election to the White House.

But let me go back a bit now to the events in the middle 1960's leading up to my unsuccessful campaign for President of the United States.

By the time any of my people began to think seriously about the Republican nomination for President in 1964, I had been able to isolate some of the more abrasive problems which were feeding the groundswell of discontent throughout the country. A large part of it was directly attributable to the inhuman vastness of the Federal bureaucracy itself. Where once only large corporations and small businessmen felt themselves being tied hand and foot by governmental red tape, the same feeling had begun to affect the individual citizen as well. More and more Americans found themselves grappling with paperwork involved in social security questions, in complicated income tax forms, and in long and seemingly meaningless census forms. The less fortunate among our citizens were introduced to the complexities and irritations attendant to the welfare and assistance programs. As government grew and extended its control and impact over the lives of individual Americans, a meaningless but persistent irritation grew apace. And it was an irritation which ultimately would find its outlet in the revolt of the middle American.

In these months between 1960 and 1964, my speaking schedule took me into every state. I appeared on all kinds of programs: educational, business, academic, and even union. I made a special attempt to visit as many schools and universities as my time would allow. And the more I saw of my fellow Americans, the more I became convinced that my concerns were becoming their concerns; that my fear of unlimited government organization was becoming their fear of big government; that my fear of fiscal irresponsibility, of unbalanced budgets, of unlimited Federal spending, was becoming their fear of a government that refused to order its income and spending in a reasonable fashion; that my fear of unwise moves aimed at placating an aggressive Communist enemy were becoming their fears of a threat which had moved as close as 90 miles from the shores of Florida.

Looking back on this period, it seems strange to me how often conservative Republicans correctly anticipated a solid nationwide protest against the prevailing policies of accommodation in foreign affairs and permissiveness at home. I think back to the days preceding the Congressional elections of 1962, for example. Many Republicans for more than a year previously had been pointing to the aggressive sword-rattling regime which Fidel Castro had built up in Cuba and calling attention to the threat that Russian military involvement on that island presented to the United States. And throughout that campaign and the months that preceded it, the liberals of the Kennedy Administration were vehement in their insistence that a Communist Cuba presented no threat to the United States and that Russia and the Soviet Communists were interested in reducing world tensions and in developing a meaningful policy of peaceful coexistence. Senator J. William Fulbright, Chairman of the Senate Foreign Relations Committee, said at the time that we had nothing to fear from Cuba, even should the Russians introduce a formidable and sophisticated modern weapons system on that island. Then, of course, in October of 1961, came the nerve-wracking and world-shaking incident we now remember as the famous "Cuban Missile Crisis."

In this situation, a Democratic President, who had encouraged his fellow liberals to "pooh-pooh" the threat of an aggressive Soviet enemy, found it necessary to go on nationwide television, declare

what amounted to a national state of emergency, and issue an ulti-
matum to the Soviet Union to remove its nuclear missiles from the
island of Cuba immediately. As a suddenly alarmed nation literally
trembled in front of its TV sets, a Democratic President placed this
nation on a collision course with a Communist enemy whom only
weeks before he had been hailing as friendly and benevolent. The
fact was that President Kennedy, despite all the wishful thinking
in and about him on the subject of accommodation with the Soviet
Union and doing business with a mellow and jovial Nikita Khru-
shchev, was suddenly confronted with the stark fact that one move—
the installation of missiles on the island of Cuba—had almost succeeded in drastically altering the balance of power in a divided world
so that it would be heavily weighted on the side of international
Communism.

As I said, conservative Republicans in this instance were proven
100 percent correct. Yet many, like Senator Homer Capehart of
Indiana, who had warned repeatedly of the Communist danger in
Cuba, were defeated for reelection in November of that year.

In trying to define and itemize the disenchantment growing
up in this country, I repeatedly encountered the problem of governmental confusion on a scale so huge that people felt powerless
to do anything about it. We were all aware that the huge Federal
budget which Democratic Congresses pushed through in those years
contained many special projects for many special groups in many
special regions for many special political purposes. But we were
also becoming aware of a new type of boondoggle, one that seemed
to serve no purpose except to explain away a new reason for the
expenditure of taxpayers' money. Week after week, new items of
budgetary cost crept up in the public print. Some of them involved complex research projects into the habits of certain kinds
of monkeys. Other examples were equally as meaningless and downright ridiculous. About the only rationale that seemed to hold them
all together was a rationale that said to the average American taxpayer, "Here is another example of Federal bureaucracy running
wild and feeding on itself for the purpose of growing ever bigger
and more unmanageable." A full recital here of the kind of boondoggle research projects that had sprung up during the liberal years,
many of which still exist today, would not only frighten and anger
the casual reader, but I believe it would actually leave him awe-
struck.

These were the kind of irritants that were pushing the American people toward a demand for new leadership. These were the kind of irritants that sent a young Congressman, William V. Roth, Jr. (R-Del.), on a one-man search for Federal assistance programs in 1967. It proved far more than a one-man job; however, Congressman Roth is to be congratulated for the tenacity of his endeavor and the shock value of its results. For by September 17, 1969, Congressman Roth was able to tell the Senate Subcommittee on Intergovernmental Relations that his two-year investigation had shown the following:

1. That no one knew exactly how many Federal assistance programs actually existed in the Federal Government. Roth's own collation showed that as of September 17, 1969, there were 1,315 such programs and that this was 225 more than his listings for 1968.

2. That the present maze of government assistance programs is so confusing that those who are intended to benefit very often do not know what programs exist, where to get aid, whether they qualify for help, or how much money is available.

3. That there has been no centralized planning or management of Federal assistance programs in the Executive Branch and that there can be no consolidation of programs without a comprehensive sorting out of the ones now in existence.

4. That one government agency is not fully informed as to the operations of sister agencies, even though their activities are often interrelated.

5. That Federal programs are most beneficial to wealthy states, communities and colleges that can afford professional staffs to search out programs, but handicap the smaller states and communities.

6. That of the 1,315 assistance programs, there are 51 business and economic development programs in 14 agencies; 19 civil rights programs in 6 agencies; 165 education programs in 14 agencies; 62 pollution and natural resource programs in 9 agencies; and 33 water resources and conservation programs in 8 agencies.

Even this last breakdown does not accurately reflect the magnitude of the problem which confronts determined economizers in the Federal establishment. For example, the 165 education programs referred to include only programs which help classroom instruction. Actually, there are more than 455 programs in 27 agencies that can potentially benefit educators or educational institutions with problems such as housing, research and manpower training.

Congressman Roth proved what many early investigators had also found and many other interested citizens had long suspected, that the very programs which were intended to solve problems have helped to create new problems. The amount of good that should come from billions of taxpayers' dollars had been drained off into exorbitant administrative costs and wasteful procedures, with too few dollars finally reaching those they were meant to help.

Another very direct cause of discontent in the public conscience in 1964 was the whole problem of crime in the streets. Everywhere I went this question was raised, and everywhere I went in the 1964 campaign I attempted to point out this growing permissiveness in our society as an issue. My discussions having to do with public morality and crime met with universal approval. However, I sensed in the people a disinclination to think that the Johnson Administration would not come to grips with the question of law and order in a very direct and meaningful way. It was as though the people could not quite believe that a national administration would go along month in and month out appointing new commissions to study the problem; go on month after month trying to convince themselves and others that the growing crime wave in this country had deep sociological reasons for which society as a whole was responsible; go on month after month refusing to give executive sanction to bills passed in Congress to strengthen the hand of law enforcement officials and permit the use of electronic surveillance devices in the war against organized crime. Nevertheless, the problem grew, and the newly elected President and his Attorney General, Mr. Ramsey Clark, continued to equivocate. The problem has now grown to a point where newspaper columnists are writing about "moral monsters" in our American society. Mr. John Chamberlain, a syndicated columnist for King Features, had these interesting words to say in his offering of February 4, 1970:

> *When Barry Goldwater, running for President in 1964, started talking about crime in the streets, he thought he had a good issue. But he was just four years ahead of his time.*

Today as the candidates for office in 1970 begin their campaigns, there is a race to preempt the tag of being the most unequivocal enemy, in any given district, city or state, of the moral monsters who seem to be swarming over the land. And as the campaigns warm up, the unthinkable will be thought, the inadmissible will be admitted, and the unspeakable will be spoken. Mafia characters will be dragged out into the cold light of day, the police will start going after vandals, timid school superintendents will do more than admit to themselves that they have a terrifying drug problem on their hands and parents who have been trying alone to cope with the trouble with their rebellious offspring will find themselves attending mass meetings to consider their predicament. . . .

The very fact that the children of big time politicos have been victimized by drug pushers is bound to make the crusade against moral monsters a popular issue for anyone who can prove that he has been a pioneer in combating the spread of juvenile crime. When a newly elected New Jersey governor, a major candidate for the gubernatorial nomination in California, a New York state Democratic aspirant to succeed Governor Rockefeller in Albany, and a Hartford, Connecticut, city manager all have to confront the fact that their own offspring have been arrested for drug possession, it pretty well defines what is bound to be issue number one for the coming election year. The Fagins who organized the drug pushing will be everybody's major enemy.

In addition to the growing problems of a huge bureaucracy, uncontrolled government spending, and a crime wave in the streets, there was also the question of a frustrating and unpopular war in Southeast Asia.

This was the situation by the late summer or early fall of 1963, when it became obvious that groups working on behalf of a Goldwater presidential bid were making serious headway in the drive to gather delegate support in the Republican National Convention. However, even with the encouraging reports which came in almost daily from the field, I continued to have grave doubts about the ability of this group of relatively young people in politics to overcome the power long held by the so-called Eastern Establishment in the Republican Party. Until this time, I had made no definite commitments, either direct or implied, to anyone on the subject of my possible candidacy. I was still extremely reluctant to make the effort. However, as time wore on and the grass roots groundswell grew and the issues took on greater importance from a conservative point of view, I began to look upon the opportunity of contesting with my old friend John Fitzgerald Kennedy with greater enthusiasm. In fact, the prospect was never more exciting than in the period immediately preceding the tragic event which was to make such contest forever impossible. What this country had not had for a long time, in my humble estimation, was a thorough and honest search of the issues and a presentation of solutions and alternative solutions by candidates of fairly divergent political philosophy. If you will, it was my feeling that this country should be presented with "a choice, not an echo."

President Kennedy, I knew, would be willing to go to the hustings with me and lay out before the American people just what we both saw as the issues confronting our nation and the possible solutions available to the American people offered by our two political parties. By mid-October of 1963, my enthusiasm for such a contest had reached the point where I had, in a tentative way, discussed the possibility of becoming a candidate with long-time members of my staff and close friends and associates in politics. In the meantime, Denison Kitchel, a prominent Phoenix attorney and state Republican official, had agreed to serve as my campaign chairman in my effort to become reelected to the Senate from Arizona. Dean Burch, a Tucson attorney who formerly had served as my administrative assistant, also joined the team.

And as the prospect of a national bid for the presidential nomination grew, Messrs. Kitchel and Burch came to Washington to work more closely with members of my staff and to become acquainted with the mechanics involved in the flourishing "Draft Goldwater" movement which had been put together by Texas Republican Peter O'Donnell, and New York publicist and political advisor, F. Clifton White. Then came that fateful day in November of 1963 when we were all astounded by news reports from Dallas, Texas, that President Kennedy had been assassinated. At the time I was en route to Muncie, Indiana, via Chicago, accompanying the body of my mother-in-law, Mrs. Anna Johnson, who was to be buried in her family plot in Indiana. My nephew, Mr. Ray Johnson, Jr., brought me the news. At first, like everyone else, I was unable to believe it or take it in, but later the news reports we received along the way confirmed our earlier information.

It is only natural that many people tried to read political implications into my attitude at that time. I can only say that politics were completely wiped out of my consideration. I had served with Jack Kennedy on the Senate Labor Committee in a very close relationship, even though we disagreed on many issues. I had a deep appreciation of his ability, and I enjoyed his sense of humor; and in the months and years that we worked together, we had enjoyed many humorous as well as serious exchanges. Not too long before his assassination, I had visited him in his White House office to plead the case of a routine appointment on one of the Federal regulatory agencies, and when I came in, he got up from his desk and said: "Barry, if you want this seat, I will give it to you gladly."

Of course, we both chuckled at his allusion to many published reports that I was among those who might be considered for the Republican presidential nomination. I recite this little episode to show that our relationship was friendly and easygoing. Thus it was that my reaction to his assassination was one of profound shock. In fact, it took me many days to realize that such a thing could happen in our modern age and in our civilized society. And during that time I decided definitely that I would not seek the Republican presidential nomination. The death of John Kennedy had removed much of the zest which I had foreseen in a presidential contest. In addition, it was quite obvious that should I succeed in obtaining the Republican nomination my opponent would be Lyndon Baines Johnson. And while I hold him as a personal friend, I was certain in my own mind that he would not engage in a serious, down-to-brass-tacks campaign aimed at a fundamental classification of the issues for the American people. I felt that he would refuse to discuss anything that was not of an immediate advantage to himself as a candidate or to a segment of the Democratic Party that he commanded. My knowledge of Lyndon Johnson told me that we could never go before the American people and present the alternatives and the choices that would have been possible had Jack Kennedy lived and had I been named to oppose him in the presidential elections. I made no particular secret of this feeling. My wife Peggy and my staff, as well as Mr. Kitchel and others closely identified with the national effort in my behalf, were fully aware of my thinking at that time.

As I say, this decision was reached in the immediate aftermath of a national tragedy which had touched me personally. However, in the weeks that followed, new arguments kept arising, and I must admit that I found it more and more difficult to hold out against them.

One involved the obvious fact that many young people throughout the country, and especially in the Republican Party, were counting heavily on a conservative bid in the forthcoming elections. The second argument said that if I did not capture the Republican nomination, it would go to either Nelson Rockefeller, Pennsylvania Governor William Scranton, or Michigan Governor George Romney. To me and to my supporters this would only mean that win, lose or draw in the presidential contest, the Republican Party leadership would be irrevocably lost to the extreme liberal wing of Republicanism, and the conservative element, which then held a majority of the party, would be left with no place to go in a presidential campaign. By Christmas of 1963, I had pretty well decided (1) that I would not want to deprive the youth of my party and of this country the chance to work with, and win or lose with, a card-carrying conservative candidate for President, and (2) that this was no time to surrender the Republican Party to the liberal minority with such a powerful voice in the communications media and especially in the Eastern half of the nation. The final decision was made in my home in Scottsdale, Arizona, the day after Christmas, and we began preparations at that time for announcement on January 3 of 1964.

This was the starting point of the long and arduous trail which took me through a back-breaking primary campaign in New Hampshire and an equally back-breaking primary campaign in California and which took me to the presidential nomination in San Francisco and to the hustings of America in the campaign of 1964.

It is not my intention here to dwell on the details of that political effort. If anything, it is a subject for later, more exhaustive treatment if I ever become one of those Americans who decides that he has enough to tell the American people to write his memoirs following the completion of his public career.

Here it is enough to record that I have no regret. And while there certainly were things done that I would do differently if the occasion were again to arise, still I do not think changes would have altered the outcome of that election. I was confronted with the plain fact that the American people, with their profound and admirable sense of fair play, would insist on giving Lyndon Johnson a full term in office—a fair chance to show that he deserved the office which he stepped into in the wake of an assassination tragedy. I do not think that any one factor was more responsible than another for my defeat. But I came away from that contest with a deep feeling of gratitude. I was, and am today, extremely proud of the great honor that my party bestowed upon me, and I enjoyed the tremendous privilege of meeting hundreds of thousands of my fellow Americans in all parts of our great country.

If I have one genuine regret, it was that my first impression of how such a campaign would go proved correct. I have today a real regret that the American people were not permitted to hear a dialogue between two candidates who had different solutions to offer for the outstanding problems of our times. I especially regret the fact that President Johnson never agreed to discuss seriously and honestly with me the course of action which this nation would be forced to follow in Vietnam. The President knew and I knew during that campaign that our country was in a shooting war in Vietnam. President Kennedy had sent troops to that country in 1962. True, they were sent as "advisors," but they carried with them orders to shoot back if they were ever attacked. In such a jungle war, this eventuality was bound to happen; and the minute those orders were given to our troops, everyone concerned knew that we were in a war.

My regret is that President Johnson did not join with me in explaining the situation and the possible courses of action which would have to be followed by any American President who was interested in this nation's responsibility and in the honorable fulfillment of its commitments. Rather, President Johnson was satisfied to leave the impression in the minds of voters that Senator Goldwater wanted war and the escalation of war, while he preferred peace and deescalation of hostilities.

And I might say LBJ had very little difficulty, with the aid of the Democratic National Committee and his campaign public relations people, in creating a caricature of Goldwater which was so grotesque that, had I personally believed all the allegations, I would have voted against my own candidacy. In this, the Democrats' course of action was simplicity itself. All my opponents had to do in the general election campaign was to rehash and emphasize and under-score at every turn the completely false and ridiculous charges that had been hurled at me by other Republican aspirants in the presidential primary campaign. They could and did quote at great length from allegations by Governors Rockefeller and Scranton and their supporters to the effect that Goldwater was an extremist and a radical who favored the use of nuclear weapons in Vietnam and who would work to abolish the social security system if he ever became President.

The campaign against me was based on one element—fear. People who had known me for years and who had understood and approved of nearly all of my public positions began to have questions about my intentions as a result of this nationwide barrage of scare publicity.

Strangely enough, public opinion polls, which showed me running a very bad second in the presidential race, consistently showed a majority of Americans supporting the conservative concepts and principles which I had always advocated. A majority of Americans were shown repeatedly to be in favor of limited Federal power, a reduction in government spending, the development of balanced budgets, and a policy of firmness and strength in dealing with our adversaries in the field of foreign affairs.

Thus, it can be seen that the tide of disenchantment with liberal nostrums was still running strong but was derailed by a campaign based on fear where my presidential candidacy was concerned.

My point here is to show that my resounding rejection at the polls in 1964 was a temporary departure in a strong conservative trend which was running in public attitudes. The most mistaken observers in the country were those who gleefully proclaimed that Goldwater's defeat had marked an end to the conservative revolution in America. It was nothing of the kind, and this fact became fully apparent to the strategists for Richard M. Nixon in the early days of the 1968 presidential campaign.

While liberal columnists and commentators were busily reciting the death rites for the GOP and lamenting the possible end of a two-party system in the United States, interested political investigators began to notice that historic and significant changes had been wrought in the Republican Party as a result of my candidacy.

These observers took a hard look at the GOP, past and present. They saw that after decades of winning prior to 1930, and years of losing after 1930, the Republican Party had simply dried up at the roots. They found that the foundation of the party in the Eastern, Midwestern and Plains states had disappeared entirely in some areas and had eroded badly in many others.

But they also discovered that the Goldwater cause had brought tens of thousands of new people into our party throughout the nation and provided the GOP with a badly needed transfusion of new blood at the grass roots.

Perhaps the most important thing about this transfusion was that it came from young and energetic people and from segments of the population which, heretofore, had not been noted for their contribution to the nation's political organization. Although these new troops were not at first successful, their vigor and enthusiasm strengthened the sinews of the Republican Party and completely revitalized the party's structure throughout the country. These new recruits stuck with it because they were motivated by ideas as well as ideals. They worked their way up in the party organizations; they became Republican leaders and candidates; they became precinct leaders, county chairmen and state officers. And by 1966, they were giving our party great national victories that had a vital bearing on our ability to win the White House in 1968.

Those who bemoaned the so-called "Goldwater disaster" in 1964 overlooked the fact that my defeat had another side to it. To be specific, my campaign broadened the base of the Republican Party nationally in a way that had never happened before. Where Republican presidential candidates before me had numbered their financial campaign contributors in the tens of thousands, my campaign counted them in hundreds of thousands. When Richard Nixon ran for reelection in 1960, financial contributions to his campaign ran between 40,000 and 50,000. The best count ever made of the individual contributions to my campaign four years later put the total at around 661,500.

In addition, our party had organizations and the nuclei of organizations in hundreds of areas where they had never existed before. This was not only true in the South, where the phenomenon was spectacular, but also proved to be the case in many large metropolitan areas which had long been almost the sole preserve of the political liberals.

Nationally, too, our party leadership presented a better ideological balance. The more than half a decade since the turn of the century had seen Republican strength among the voters shift from the Atlantic seaboard and Northeastern states to the Midwest, the West and the South. Despite this shift, however, the great majority of the party's most influential leaders resided in Atlantic and Eastern states—this notwithstanding the fact that our greatest potential for new votes was in other areas of the country.

If nothing else, my nomination dispelled the long-held belief in the omnipotence of something that had arisen in the days of Thomas E. Dewey and had always been referred to as the Eastern Establishment. In party conventions, where conservative leaders like Senator Robert A. Taft of Ohio were repeatedly defeated, the blame was always laid at the doorstep of the Eastern Establishment.

Interestingly enough, when I became seriously interested in the nomination, many of my closest advisors predicted that our biggest and most determined opposition would come from that quarter. As a result, early in the campaign my staff set out to identify the leaders of the Eastern Establishment only to find that the powerful structure which had dictated two Dewey nominations and two Eisenhower nominations no longer existed as a viable political directorate. As my press secretary, Tony Smith, observed in one of our strategy meetings: "If the Eastern Establishment still exists, it exists only in the names of Governor Nelson Rockefeller, Senator Jacob Javits and their political backers. Its influence right now scarcely extends beyond the borders of New York State."

And this was one of the early developments of the campaign— the discovery that the powerful Eastern Establishment no longer existed as the cornerstone of liberal Republicanism except in the memory or the imagination of political columnists and commentators. If there was one thing that the drive for Republican delegates proved in 1964, it was the fact that the liberal element of the party had no national cohesiveness and was inclined to come apart at the seams in anything approaching a political confrontation with the conservatives.

As an aftermath of the 1964 campaign, then, it became apparent that if our party was to succeed, a redistribution of leadership more in balance with the party's grass roots strength would have to be made. Part of this redistribution, of course, came about naturally in the wake of the presidential campaign. It was quickly completed in the years that followed by Richard M. Nixon, who was to prove himself to be one of the cleverest political strategists in our nation's history.

I like to think, and I believe I am justified in this belief, that one of the direct results of my candidacy in 1964 was to attract new young leaders to the Republican banner. I have every reason to believe this is especially true throughout the Southern states, where Republicanism was coming into its own for the first time since the Reconstruction. However, it is a mistake to confine the development to any one section of the country. My mail proves to me daily that the events of 1964 were responsible for bringing to our political party fresh new leaders in every state in the union. Occasionally, I get a letter from someone who says: "Back in 1962 I wrote and asked you what I could do to aid the cause of conservatism in American politics, and you advised me to join the Republican Party and work within that framework to achieve my goal. I just want you to know that I took your advice and am now chairman of my county's Republican committee and helped turn in a sizable majority for President Nixon in the 1968 campaign."

I like to think that the events of the last decade turned our party, organizationally, into a national party again for the first time in many years. If my efforts, including my defeat in 1964, contributed to this cause and furthered the awakening that we see today in the revolt of the middle Americans, I am profoundly grateful. Because I believe what is transpiring in the majority conscience at this time in history is essentially a rededication to the principles and policies which made this nation great enough to become leader of the entire free world.

III

The Awakening: The Revolt of the Middle American

A FULL AWAKENING OF THE MAJORITY CONSCIENCE TO THE REALITIES of politics in a new era is now in progress.

It presages seismic changes in public attitudes toward problems which confront the American people.

In other words, the early stirrings which I described in the earlier chapters and which were evident in various degrees throughout the 1960's are now breaking through the surface of American politics. In the years ahead they will be punctuated by conservative and Republican victories at the polls. I don't pretend that from here on there will be an unbroken stream of GOP successes in national, state and local elections; but I believe an unmistakable trend in that direction was begun in 1968 and will become more pronounced in 1970 and 1972.

One of the characteristics of this national awakening which many people call the revolt of the Middle Americans is the refusal of liberal spokesmen to believe or comprehend what is taking place. They console themselves with the thought that all major political upheavals in American history have come from the left-hand side of the political spectrum, and they confidently expect this to continue. However correctly these liberals might be reading American history, they are overlooking the obvious facts which exist in American society today. They have overlooked the fact that technology and progress have transformed the mass attitudes in this country to the point where they are now concentrated in the center and thus to the right of the political philosophy which this nation has followed for the past three and a half decades.

Thus, today *Time* magazine can lead off its essay for March 16, 1970, with the flat assertion, "Liberalism is a fractured philosophy; that is one of the most obvious and most important facts about the American political scene."

To make the insult more binding toward the favorite philosophical approach of this nation's self-appointed thought leaders and literary geniuses, the weekly news magazine charges liberalism backers with its own "crime of crime"—not giving sufficient weight to changing conditions. The architects of change for the mere sake of change were found guilty of the final sin of "not changing." As *Time* magazine put it:

"Conservatives, or just cool pragmatists, in the Nixon Administration are attacking, one by one, the most cherished liberal beliefs and programs. Both the beliefs and the programs are suddenly seen to be vulnerable because their backers clung to them too uncritically, too long, without sufficient regard for changing conditions."

Another strong indication of liberalism's decline is found in a Gallup poll of April 17, which found that the American people, by the ratio of 3 to 2, preferred to be labeled as "conservatives" rather than as "liberals." The sampling of 1,528 adults in 30 localities showed 52 percent preferred the label "conservative," 34 percent preferred to be known as "liberal," while 14 percent held no opinion. And on April 18, the Gallup poll reported that the U.S. public favored the appointment of conservatives rather than liberals to the Supreme Court by a whopping margin of 5 to 3. In this sampling, based on interviews with 1,551 adults, 49 percent preferred conservatives, 27 percent preferred liberals and 24 percent had no opinion.

And the interesting thing is that the majority of Americans have moved into the center and to the right in their attitudes at the very time when a new brand of leftist radical is pulling the Liberal Establishment, as such, further to the left.

This is the meaning of a silent majority which unmistakably shows its support for the relatively conservative policies of the Nixon Administration, which shows its appreciation for the candor and honesty of a Vice-President who speaks out unafraid and who applauds the return to a feeling of patriotism in our foreign affairs.

This is the meaning of the high popularity rating given to a

President who was elected with a razor-thin majority and whom the liberals confidently predicted would fail miserably in his handling of public affairs during the first year of his administration.

This also is the meaning of a rising public outcry against an obvious and pronounced liberal bias in the communications media.

The new Liberal Establishment has been defined by political students as a loose confederation made up of like-thinking segments of the communications media, the academic community and university "think tanks," the wealthiest of the tax-free foundations, some corporate conglomerates, and some segments of the organized church. I find no reason to argue with this definition of the so-called Liberal Establishment. The whole leftist ideology in this country has long been supported by these same groups with the addition of some leaders of organized labor.

It is this establishment, however, which today is wallowing in a long-held belief in its own self-righteousness and a complete confidence in obtaining the political support of a majority of this nation's voters in the near future.

From the beginning of this upheaval, this reawakening of a majority's conscience, the liberal community, especially the communications branch (i.e., the press, radio and television news teams), has indulged in an almost unbelievable brand of wishful thinking. Let me give you an example. When this groundswell first began to gain national stature, when the dissatisfaction with the liberal status quo first began to bubble to the surface in colleges and universities and suburbia, the national news magazines set out to explore and define what they termed "the conservative revolution." That is precisely what it was, but the description held only long enough for the liberal opinion-makers in this country to recognize its inherent danger to their entire approach to public affairs and governmental problems. They switched so rapidly that it was almost unbelievable. In 1962, for instance, a CBS news team came to see me and asked for my cooperation in the development of a documentary film which was to be two and a half hours in length and which was to be entitled "The Conservative Revival." I cooperated to the fullest extent possible for a busy member of the United States Senate and a major spokesman for the conservative wing of the Republican Party.

I intend to go into this whole episode in considerable detail in a later chapter in this book devoted to television handling of the news, but for the purpose here let me say that in a few short weeks the intention of this television network to produce a documentary on the conservative revolution was watered down to a half-hour presentation entitled "Thunder on the Right," in which sincere and responsible conservatives, myself included, were lumped together with all kinds of racists, bigots and kooks from the Far Right. I point this out merely to show how quickly a major television network leaped to the opportunity to pervert and actually attempt to divert a strong movement which was running in the political attitudes of the American people.

Almost overnight, the Far Right became a major threat to everything Americans hold dear—at least that was the impression portrayed by the news media. Groups which are very seldom heard of today—like the Minutemen and the John Birch Society—were held out to thinking Americans as major threats to the freedom which we all hold dear. The strong tide running to conservatism was deliberately made to appear like a strong tide running in the direction of Fascism in the view of the news media.

Liberal spokesmen all performed on cue during this period when a little-known candy manufacturer named Robert Welch (founder of the John Birch Society) came up with a suggestion that former President Eisenhower had Communist tendencies. It was used to smear the entire conservative movement in this country. Talk about guilt by association. The very people who deplored and decried this practice in the case of domestic Communism and the era of Joe McCarthy used it unashamedly to equate any conservative with the ridiculous and extreme views of radicals on the right of the political spectrum. During the days when I was being considered as a Republican candidate for President of the United States, I don't think I appeared at more than three or four press conferences out of literally hundreds where I was not asked if I wanted to disavow the political support of members of the John Birch Society. It did no good to explain over and over again that I did not feel that any aspirant for national political office had the right to disavow or foreclose support from any duly qualified American voter. I could explain ad nauseam that while I would not specifically disavow support from the Far Right, at the same time I did not seek it nor do anything to encourage it. I said the same thing about the Communists in this country, and I could never quite understand why my acceptance or disavowal of support from the Far Right was so much more important to political writers than whether my Democratic opponent expected to accept or disavow support from the Radical Left and Communists dedicated to the violent overthrow of the United States Government. For years liberal Democrats had blandly accepted support from Communist figures without raising any editorial eyebrows.

Perhaps three and a half decades of unqualified voter support for the leftist nostrums of the New Deal, the Fair Deal, the New Frontier, and the Great Society have lulled liberal spokesmen into a false sense of security. Mr. Kevin P. Phillips, a special assistant to the Attorney General and author of a perceptive new book called "The Emerging Republican Majority," has put his finger on this condition in a way that the liberals steadfastly refused to do. In a recent speech to the Yale Political Union, Mr. Phillips recalled that political revolutions of the past, those associated in history with Jefferson, Jackson, Bryan and Roosevelt, all came from the left and have nothing in common with the slow-moving middle American revolt which is presently taking place. He explained it this way:

> *Past political upheaval in the United States has not come from the left but from the people. In the past the elites engendering popular revolt were economic elites, landed or industrial elites committed to economic conservatism. Thus, popular change had to come from the left.*
>
> *No more. Technology and economic growth have raised the old working class constituency to a new affluence, enlarging the old middle class into middle America.*
>
> *And at the same time a separate and antagonistic new Establishment has grown at the top of American society. This is the historically unique Liberal Establishment. In the past, establishments were toryhoods of no-change; landowners, industrialists, people whose affluence was rooted in stability. But this is no longer where the fast action is. The new establishment is liberal, a toryhood of change, people who make their money out of plans, ideas, communications, social upheaval, happenings, excitement.*

How often have you heard the Nixon Administration described as colorless and dull? If this is the hallmark of the present national regime, it is assumed by deliberation. It might even be called the "badge of identification" with the silent majority. It is an outgrowth of the reawakening of conscience in this country which is demanding an end to phony excitement and change for the sake of change and to government by street mobs.

The new Liberal Establishment described by Phillips differs radically from those we have known before in that it does not enjoy populist support. As Mr. Phillips points out, the new liberals are to the left of prevailing American opinion, to the left of the Oklahoma dustbowl, to the left of Levittown, to the left of Main Street, U.S.A. Believe it or not, the Liberal Establishment of 1970 is far outside the mainstream of American thinking, desires and life. The average middle-class American has had it up to his eyebrows with the excesses of liberalism. He is fed up with purposeless change and the calculated destruction of recognized values and standards. And, again as Mr. Phillips put it, he is fed up with "fashionable liberal bigotry toward the Irish, Italians, Poles, Suburbanites and blue-collar workers." Mr. Phillips made the point in which I have believed for many years, that the liberal values today are not the values of progress. They are the values of progress perverted, progress altered and changed for political reasons. And for the first time in history, the correction can only come from the middle American on the right.

Mr. Phillips describes the awakening American conscience as an oncoming political revolution. He correctly identified the target as "establishment liberalism, the phony revolution of the glossy magazines which mock Nixonism and middle America as cottage cheese and Sears Roebuck." In identifying what he terms a self-proclaimed coalition of futurism, humanism and progress, Phillips said:

"It is Scarsdale, Park Avenue, Wall Street, the Episcopal Church, the major metropolitan newspapers, television networks, the best suburbs and universities, the Beautiful People. If the list is familiar, it should be. These are the places and institutions that have attacked virtually every great popular political movement that America has produced. Some of them are now attacking popular conservatism and the Nixon Administration. They laugh at Vice-President Agnew like their forebears laughed at social security, Harry Hopkins and the WPA."

Perhaps President Nixon has come closer than anyone else in attempting to define the era into which an awakened American conscience is taking us. He called it an era of New Federalism and believes its roots will not rest in the large cities, as did other eras in our political development. Instead he believes with many conservatives that the new movement will grow in suburbia, the American heartland of the Midwest and the booming territories of Florida and Texas, Arizona and California.

President Nixon is today being accused of following a "Southern Strategy." I say "accused" because of the way the press and the news media in this country have treated the American Southland. Its mere inclusion in the plans of any national movement make that movement almost automatically something evil with racist overtones. There is very little tendency in the press to consider the Southern states as comprising an important and integral part of this Republic, these United States. To follow any political strategy which includes the South as a major factor becomes almost automatically the reason for the press to accuse.

The phrase itself, so far as I know, was originated by columnist Joseph Alsop in 1962 or 1963 and aimed accusingly at the efforts of Goldwater politicians. It didn't matter that the so called Southern strategy at that time wasn't even a strategy; it was simply a fact of political life. However, it was a fact of political life which infuriated liberal Democrats and especially those who liked to make a political issue out of the subject of civil rights and problems involving the American South.

Those editorialists who use the phrase "Southern Strategy" in a derogatory sense are, in essence, telling the American people that a political strategy involving 26 percent of the people in this nation is somehow wrong.

On this I know what I'm talking about because my inclusion of the South in a problem of applied political science aimed at obtaining the Republican presidential nomination in 1964 made me the nearest thing that a free American politician can come to the status of political "criminal" to the communications media and the political columnists of this country. It might be easier for candidates approaching a problem in national vote-getting if the South were disenfranchised. It might even qualify for liberal obliteration. I used to be accused of having said that it would be a good thing for the future of this country if the Atlantic seaboard were to be sawed off and allowed to float out to sea. I must admit to having given voice to this sentiment at one time during my political career. Of course, it was said in a humorous, tongue-in-cheek vein which my critics never bothered to explain. And it was a reference to Eastern financial interests rather than the political context in which it is very often repeated today. Even so, I readily confess that I have been impressed for some years with the unrealistic provincialism shown by the Liberal Establishment along the Eastern seaboard on political matters as well as financial pursuits. Throughout the entire liberal era, these liberal "elite" politicians acted as though the West didn't exist and the South was something to be ashamed of in public but to be used on election day so long as it remained solidly in the Democratic column.

One is bound to wonder today whether the New York liberal, when he assails President Nixon for making a political appointment from the South, isn't harboring a secret desire to saw off the United States along the Mason-Dixon Line and let the Southland drift off in the direction of Cuba.

In the Senate cloakroom I have a lot of fun with my liberal colleagues, especially concerning their views of the South. I must say that many of them are soft-pedaling their habitual scorn of states like Alabama and Mississippi since the question of forcing integration became a problem in the North. A sign of the times, I believe, was the action of Senator Abraham Ribicoff (D-Conn.) in supporting the Stennis amendment to the Education Authorizations Bill on the grounds that the North should be treated to the same restrictions as the South when it came to the question of integrating school systems.

The Southern strategy, in its most elementary form, is a perfectly logical and reasonable acceptance of the fact that the South has a growing population which votes in national elections. My own Southern strategy, if it can be called such, was a question of seeking votes in areas where they abounded most numerously.

But the whole idea of a two-party South which is rapidly becoming an actual fact is another part of the middle American revolt. It deserves more than casual consideration in this chapter.

Much of the early Republican spadework throughout the South is attributable to the efforts of one man in particular. He is I. Lee Potter, long an important leader of the Republican Party of Virginia, who inaugurated through the Republican National Committee an organizational campaign known as "Operation Dixie." In the late Fifties and early Sixties the efforts of Mr. Potter and his helpers went far toward breaking down the barriers to the development of a two-party political system south of the Mason-Dixon Line.

There has been a change. This change has been a long time coming, and the first cracks began appearing in presidential voting. Republican candidate Thomas E. Dewey made surprising inroads in the South in the elections of 1944 and 1948, polling one-third of the total popular vote in the area embraced by Alabama, Arkansas, Florida, Georgia, Kentucky, Louisiana, Mississippi, North Carolina, Oklahoma, South Carolina, Tennessee, Texas and Virginia.

It may be that this was the beginning of a revelation to many Southerners. For in getting their feet wet in presidential elections, they gradually began to understand that it was possible to vote Republican without being hit by a bolt of lightning and without being branded "Yankees."

When the Republicans begin to spawn strength in county commissions, in state legislatures, in the county judiciary, as is now happening, there can be little doubt of the fundamental nature of the change.

The significance of this change extends far beyond a regional border, however; and there is, therefore, a great need today for a proper understanding of this emergent political phenomenon in the South. Unfortunately, it has been singularly lacking in post-election statements of party officials and "think pieces" offered by some of the nation's political reporters and analyzers. Their solutions, almost without exception, deal variously with the candidates or the weight of a single issue or the concurrence of a temporary crisis.

One of the common explanations for growing Republican strength in the South asserts that the GOP is making its gains through appeals to extreme segregationists. This is a theme popular with Northern Democrats and with some Northern Republicans who are annoyed at the conservative nature of the Republican trend. And no analysis could be more absurd on its face. Republican influence in the South is growing in direct proportion to the South's moderation on the race issue. It is located in the urban areas, where a new view is emerging, while the Democratic strength is more and more being confined to the rural communities, where the race issue has undergone little change.

Any arguments which attempt to localize the cause of Republican strength in the South simply ignore not only the process but also the causes of what is happening throughout the Southern states of our country. They miss the point that the South is, and has been for some time past, undergoing a profound evolution of political and economic thinking and acting. They fail to take into account the vast changes which have taken place in the South over the past two decades.

But perhaps the greatest mistake made by the newly risen "host" of experts on Southern politics is the belief that the Republican trend is something new.

This, of course, is utter nonsense. The Republican trend in the South has been developing over a period of years and has kept pace with the evolutionary process of change. In effect, it amounts to a political flowering of a new society. It is the expression of progress toward a two-party political system in a section of the country which long confused traditional political practice with its own welfare. Call it an awakening, if you like. But you must remember that it has been a gradual, slow-paced awakening which has gone on for a long time and only showed up in a relatively massive way in recent elections.

The very deliberateness of the process attests to its soundness and marks its lasting qualities. Make no mistake about it, Republicanism is in the South to stay. If it were the overnight development that many commentators and politicians would like us to think, then I believe we might be justified in looking for a single reason for Republican strength.

But this is not the case. The changes which are now finding political expression in the South have been going on for years. They are attuned to new economic and commercial developments and attitudes. They have roots in the new industrialization of a part of the country which, from its earliest settlement, has existed in an agricultural economy and society. They are related to the growing importance of business activity and concern for the interests of the business community. They are tied in with the steady and growing expansion of urban communities and cities and the declining influence of the rural areas.

And this last point is of particular importance. Republican strength is greatest in the urban areas of the South. These areas are growing in numbers and in importance. Recent Supreme Court decisions on reapportionment make it certain that the urban areas of the South will become increasingly important in statewide elections. And, as Republicans gain in these elections, so will the political sinews of the party organization. More and more patronage at the state and local levels will fall into Republican hands and become the framework for lasting political organizations at the "grass roots" of the South.

It is the South itself that is changing, not the approach of political parties to the South. A new and vigorous middle-class society is developing in the wake of industrialization and heavier emphasis on commercial attitudes.

And because of this, it is particularly significant that Republican strength in the South is emerging in a city environment. It shows that a new and different kind of conservatism is rising to displace the old, rural traditional—almost hereditary—conservatism of the Democrats. It is primarily an economic conservatism stemming from the growth in business activity, the increase in per capita income, and the rising confidence of the South in its own ability to expand industrially and commercially. And it is a brand of conservatism which sees Democratic Party policies of inflation and nonproductive, reactionary devices, such as unbalanced budgets and deficit financing, as parts of the old pessimism which once gripped their region.

In the Republican Party the South therefore sees a welcome trend away from centralized control of government and an emphasis on local responsibility and individual freedom.

The Republican Party in the South is based on truly progressive elements. It is manned by young, energetic and imaginative Southerners who are standing up in the nation and looking about them with a kind of pride and optimism and hope which hasn't been seen since before the days of the Reconstruction. These are the new, vigorous Southerners who have adopted the full scale of modern technology without sacrificing respect for and belief in the essential underpinnings of history. Having adopted this modern technology, they are following through with a realistic political outlook that is unwilling to be taken in by the reactionary devices and mechanisms of government extravagance and the other manifold varieties of economic fallacy which have become the standard program of the Northern Democrats.

Consequently, I believe the South has become an area of new opportunity and therefore new challenge for the Republican Party. And it has become an area which will demand and obtain an increasingly strong voice in the conduct of Republican Party affairs.

What we do with this opportunity can affect the future of the Republican Party and the nation for many years to come. By the same token, what we might fail to do—through some mistaken interpretation of what the growing Republican trend in the South actually means—could have long and lasting effects.

In this I strongly disagree with some members of my own political party who have evidenced a timidity—almost a reluctance —to take full advantage of the enlightened trend toward Republicanism and economic conservatism in the South.

Politically speaking, the South and Southwest are the areas which offer the greatest potential for the development of increased Republican strength in the nation. The South and Southwest regions have been steadily adding votes to the national total for Republican candidates while some Northern states, such as New York, have not gone Republican since Dwight Eisenhower was our candidate for President.

What's more, the South has put to shame many states which we used to regard as solid Republican areas. The strength throughout the South and Southwestern states has been growing by leaps and bounds while GOP strength in other areas has shown continued slippage.

But while the South is important, the revolt of the middle American is far more than a regional phenomenon. It is so compelling that the liberals among today's politicians and editorial commentators are working overtime to invent an opposition based on semantics. Some of these inventions are downright ludicrous when the history of the liberal movement in this country is adequately understood. Take the word "polarization," which has become almost a rallying cry for politicians and news commentators who oppose the changing political atmosphere. Interestingly enough, the word "polarization" seldom was heard in American political discussions prior to the inception of the Republican Nixon Administration. And it seems to have been promoted with especial vigor since the President called attention to the Silent Majority and Vice-President Agnew began giving voice to some of this majority's pet peeves.

It will be recalled by those who remember the early days of the New Deal that the liberal community in this country virtually invented the concept of polarization. The entire political approach of the left-wing Roosevelt Administration in those days was based on polarizing the attitudes of the so-called "have nots" against the so-called "haves." Through every conceivable public relations device then available, the liberals identified themselves as the sole champions of the "have nots." They polarized public thinking to the very best of their abilities on behalf of men and measures which could be identified with the disadvantaged portion of our population. Needless to say, the category which the New Deal championed was the vast majority. By methods of polarization, these liberals managed to make symbols of evil out of anything which contributed in any way to the capitalistic forces of an American economy that blew up in the Depression of 1929, even though the disaster was not caused by American economics. The persons of wealth were called "Bourbons" and "Economic Royalists" and otherwise characterized in a fashion calculated to engender the dislike if not actually the hatred of the so-called "have nots."

Actually, to the proponents of democracy, those of us who believe in a Republic and believe every free man should have the right to formulate his own opinions and to express them freely, no fault could be found with these deliberate and entirely successful efforts at polarizing American thought and dividing the nation. Those politicians and spokesmen who felt they were promoting the correct remedies for the economic and social ills of this nation had every right to mount their campaigns to polarize thought in this direction. Many were men who felt they were right and who set out to sell their idea to a majority of the American people.

This is the meaning of that word which liberals use so facilely —"dialogue." The purpose of meaningful debate, whether it be in the halls of Congress, in the houses of the state assemblies, in the council rooms of our municipalities, in the meeting halls of our Parent-Teacher Association, or wherever free Americans meet to discuss and debate and argue their views, is polarization. The object of stating a point of view is to polarize enough support in favor of that point of view to make it official policy.

The fact that the liberals themselves were the political force which first refined the art of polarizing political thought makes their use of this argument especially phony. The desire, of course, is to keep the silent majority completely silent until it stops demonstrating its support for and belief in the policies of conservative Republicanism. Any majority in this nation which is not oriented to the left-hand side of the political spectrum is a threat to liberalism as we know it today. It is a majority which the liberals never want to find voice. This is, of course, what particularly bothers them about Vice-President Agnew. Without fail, every time Mr. Agnew tees off on another "sacred cow" of liberal ideology, loud voices are raised to accuse, try and convict him of the political crime of "polarization."

For example, Senator Edward Kennedy, while deploring Mr. Agnew's description of a group of impudent snobs as "impudent snobs," charged the Vice-President with trying to "pit Americans against Americans." Other liberals, including Republican Senator Charles Goodell of New York, repeatedly charged Mr. Agnew with "dividing the nation."

All of a sudden, it seems, dividing the nation becomes a crime. I don't know what the liberals thought John F. Kennedy or Lyndon Johnson or Hubert Humphrey were doing when they took to the campaign stump and proposed policies with which a clear majority of the American people disagreed. Perhaps John D. Ehrlichman, Counsel to the President, identified it best when he said that polarization happens to be the cliché of the moment. He said, speaking of Vice-President Agnew's controversial statements, "I don't think it is illegitimate for someone in his situation to help bring a balance into communications." He added:

> *It seems to me a sort of desperation defense to say that the Vice-President is polarizing people when he says the press is unfair. It's like charging a lawyer in a lawsuit with trying to polarize the jury for his clients.*
>
> *In this country there is a constant contest for support on issues. Politics is the art of polarizing. People are constantly asked to decide for candidates A or B or to vote for or against a bond issue.*

This argument, of course, is not lost on the liberals. They understand polarization better than any other group in America. They also recognize that it has a reasonable ring for public consumption; they realize that most responsible Americans can bring themselves to deplore the pitting of one American against another without thinking through the full meaning of this easily mouthed phrase.

Even President Nixon, who got to the White House by polarizing more voters on his side of the ballot in 1968 than Humphrey was able to polarize on the Democratic side of the ballot, is not excused by the liberals. Mr. Nixon's crime, it seems, was to speak out for the vast "Silent Majority" of American citizens who have shown through every means possible that they support his policies. In fact, the President's crime has even been given a name. David Ginsburg, a Washington attorney and well-known liberal who served as executive secretary of the Kerner Commission on Civil Disorders, describes it as "the Forgotten American-Silent Majority theme."

Ginsburg has established himself as something of a "high priest" in the ranks of those who once hailed but now abhor the process of "polarization" because it no longer supports their views. In dwelling at length on this subject in a meeting before the Pittsburgh Communications Foundation, Ginsburg was quoted as defining the Silent Majority theme as "an explicit appeal to all the resentments of race and class that infuse the culture of the white working man." Thus, Mr. Ginsburg, in one fast paragraph, infused the President's speech of November 3 on Vietnam with cultural and racist overtones because he made reference to the Silent Majority.

Not to be outdone, former Vice-President Hubert Humphrey insisted the Nixon Administration is waging a deliberate campaign of polarization.

"I personally doubt," said Mr. Humphrey, "that our country has seen in 20 years such a calculated appeal to our baser interests. I disagree with those who would create an atmosphere of suppression and call it patriotism."

Where Ginsburg placed his emphasis on alleged racial injustice, Humphrey concentrated his attack on the administration's attitude toward anti-war demonstrators. However, both men objected strenuously to the administration's attempt to mobilize opinion on behalf of issues and policies which its top officials believe to be in the best interest of the American people.

Ginsburg complained that President Nixon is "making the forgotten American feel sorry for himself without offering him a helping hand." He argued that a conspiracy of sorts exists in over-all administration action. As he put it, "The President's Southern strategy, the Vice-President's attack on the media, the Attorney General's characterization of the anti-war demonstrators—they are all part of the same thing. We don't recognize it for what it is because we have not seen anything quite like it before."

What Mr. Ginsburg actually is saying is that the liberals have never before encountered public officials with the courage to consistently criticize the "sacred cows" of liberalism. He certainly can't mean that he has never before seen a national administration which opposed three or four pet theses of its political opponents. If so, he must have slept through the past three and a half decades when Democratic liberals ruled the roost and shouted down—in the finest exercise of vocal "polarization" ever seen—anything that happened to be suggested by a Republican of conservative, traditional leanings.

It strikes me that we have come full circle in our political development when those liberals who gained their political ascendancy by pitting the so-called "have nots" against the "haves" and by making bloc appeals to minority and racial groups are beginning to complain that somebody is beginning to pit Americans against Americans on behalf of sound constitutional government, economic sanity and peace-promoting policies in foreign affairs.

Another semantical pitch mounted by frustrated liberals is a bold attempt to discredit President Nixon for taking action on behalf of the American people. Crazy as it seems, the crime in this context is called "preemption." It is now becoming fashionable for leftist newsmen and politicians to refer to President Nixon as the "Great Preemptor."

Thus do the American liberals express their unhappiness over a Republican president who shows a proper concern for domestic problems that afflict 204 million American citizens and never were solved by the liberal administrations that went before.

You might think, to hear them talk, that all issues of a domestic nature having to do with welfare or humanitarianism were the exclusive property of the liberals and the left-wing Democrats. To credit the crime of preemption, you must accept the premise that only the liberals have any right in this country to concern themselves with questions of health, education, welfare, employment, urban renewal and pollution. It is as though the leftists feel that their long-term utilization of domestic problems for political, vote-getting purposes staked out for them an exclusive claim against which no Republican should ever dare to move.

The liberals were particularly upset by the President's strong leadership in the matters of crime prevention and environmental welfare. They charged him repeatedly with preempting ground that they had previously staked out in the fields of air pollution, water pollution, noise pollution, and many other types of pollution which are rapidly making life more difficult and more uncomfortable on the planet Earth.

The mere fact that the liberals did not stand up and cheer when President Nixon assumed the kind of leadership which they failed to provide, but which is absolutely essential if we are ever to come to grips with such grave problems, is sufficient, of itself, to show that their concern is largely motivated by political considerations.

To American officials seriously worried over the crime rate on our city streets, over the rising costs of health care, over what is happening to the environment that surrounds us all, the President's assumption of firm direct leadership should have been cause for celebration. Certainly such officials or politicians could find a better use for their time and energy than running around accusing President Nixon of "preempting" issues which the Democrats have previously regarded as their own personal preserve but which they had not succeeded in alleviating.

A lot of the anger which gives rise to semantic attacks involving words like "polarization" and "preemption" stems from the fundamental fact that President Nixon is not performing in office the way the liberals and the Democrats and many of the so-called intellectuals in our society so confidently predicted. These critics expected the President to either take no action at all on outstanding domestic welfare problems or to move in a direction which would cause him to fall on his face politically.

The skill and determination which Mr. Nixon has brought to all of the problems confronting this nation both at home and abroad can only be marked down as a tremendous political surprise to his outstanding critics in the press, radio and television industries and other places where liberals abound and give air to their opinions. Virtually none of the President's outspoken critics expected his popularity to be running in the 60 percent and over area one year after he took office. Indeed, many anti-Nixon liberals thoroughly believed that by this time in the new administration Mr. Nixon would be listed as one of the least popular of all Chief Executives ever to serve in the White House.

About the best the liberals can do after charging the President with "preempting" their issues and "polarizing" American opinion in behalf of his policies is to complain that he is not proposing enough money for domestic programs. For example, former Secretary of Health, Education and Welfare, John Gardner, who today heads up the Urban Coalition Action Council, is running around the country warning that dire consequences will follow unless additional billions are pumped into programs for housing, health, education, job training, etc.

Like many other liberals, of course, he is perfectly willing to stand by and let the Democratic National Committee accuse President Nixon of not coming to grips with the problem of inflation. Gardner and all the rest of them know the connections between excessive Federal spending and constantly rising prices in the supermarket. But they never let this interfere with their grandiose ideas for promoting their own pet welfare projects at the taxpayers' expense.

The conscience of a majority, like that of a man, concerns itself with the pursuit of good. It is first pricked and then disturbed by evident injustice, unreasonable human distress and by all kinds of preventable suffering and trouble.

In the United States in the 1960's, the national conscience got plenty of exercise. For it was during this decade that the liberal chickens began coming home to roost. All of a sudden, the Federal henhouse was full of problems. After years of so-called liberal progress, the nation found itself plagued with the deepest kind of social, economic and cultural problems.

Heading the list was racial discrimination in a society which prides itself on brotherhood, followed closely by pollution and poison in an age of wide horizons, detergents and antibiotics. Another problem pushing the leaders was lawlessness and crime in a time when the educational processes of the nation should have reached a new peak of efficiency and at a time when the art of reasoning had been elevated to a level of intellectual sanctification by the liberals. There also were the claims of poverty in the midst of affluence, and housing shortages in a nation that had proven its ability to reach and walk on the moon.

It was, I believe, the realization on the part of the American people that the problems of the sixties were being heightened to a level of rhetorical crises for patently political purposes that brought on the revolt of the middle American.

What I am saying is that the conscience of the majority recognized fully the need for erasing discrimination and bigotry, but it resented the demands of politicians that the correction be made in line with their own particular prescriptions. Most Americans understood in their hearts that it would take more than mechanical devices, such as civil rights acts of Congress and forced desegregation orders from the Supreme Court, to remedy this deep and troublesome problem in American society.

I believe they agreed with the thesis which I repeated over and over again in the campaign of 1964—that is, that discrimination will not be abolished nor full equality of the races attained until it happens first in the hearts of men.

Many times I have bemoaned the fact that it is impossible to enact moral legislation. If this were possible, my name would head the list of sponsors on any proposed bill to make man forever noble, forever unselfish and forever loving toward his fellowman. This idea of brotherhood has got to be the core of any understanding that we can ever bring about between the oppressed and discriminated-against minorities of our country and the powerful and affluent majority.

Force is not the answer, whether it be by act of Congress, by court ruling, or by a local police chief. Force does nothing but engender counter-force. By the same token, anger—no matter how righteous, no matter how justified—is likewise not the answer; for anger stems from aroused temper and negative emotion. It does nothing toward the end which we all desire—an understanding between men who must live together on this planet regardless of their race, their color, their religion or their cultural and social heritage. Introducing anger into the search for such reasonableness begets nothing but counter-anger, and counter-anger brings fresh levels and greater intensity of the original anger. Escalation of negative emotion and disruptive human relations is obvious and has been proven many times over, in many communities and in widely differing situations. But men still resort to this means of expressing their attitudes, although I hope and believe that the passing years are beginning to bring a lessening of this emotionalism.

This certainly is true in the case of the government's relations with our Indians. For this is a question which has been on the national conscience for many, many years. And I believe the reawakening of that conscience in the decade of the sixties has done a whole lot to clarify this situation.

For one thing, people are beginning to understand that there is no such thing as "an Indian problem" in this country. The matter is a question of a great many problems to which no single approach can be used with complete effectiveness. It must be understood that the Bureau of Indian Affairs lists 263 separate eligible tribes and this figure excludes some 300 native Alaskan tribes that are not considered eligible for government benefits.

Each of these tribes has a different culture and language, and each of these tribes is extremely proud of its individualism—this is, of its background, culture and religion. They do not want to see these completely changed because they are not convinced that the white man's way is necessarily best. And it is this conflict of attitudes and this indecision about approaches to future developments that constitute the largest single stumbling block in the way of proper education for the Indians.

But the new awakening of national conscience is having a beneficial result where the Indians are concerned. It is channeling more attention, stronger efforts and more money into the campaign for proper training and education.

My own state of Arizona supplies one of the best examples of the multi-faceted problems which are involved with the American Indian. Arizona has almost 40 percent of the Indians of this country, ranging from tribes of around 25 persons to the Navajo Tribe which numbers over 100,000. These Indians, comprising fifteen separate tribes in Arizona, speak three different basic languages. Each of these tribes has its own religion and its own culture. They do not like to see their children taught to believe that the white man's culture and the white man's religion are superior. This produces a fundamental conflict.

However, in the course of educational processes, some Indian youths prefer to take on the white man's way and the elders do not object. But they do not like the idea of the white man's methods and the white man's thinking being forced upon their young.

Only recently have our so-called governmental experts become aware of this attitude and begun to give the tribes themselves a larger share of the responsibility for developing curricula and teaching.

In all the years of liberal welfarism, it never seemed to get through to the social engineers in our government that the Indian problems are as many as they are different. Some tribes live in areas isolated from the white man's cities, his railroads, his airways and even his highway systems. Others live close to or even in the middle of areas populated by the white man and covered with his modern technological devices and gadgets. It has not been possible for the government to devise a single approach to these problems in the past. Every effort has failed right from the beginning, when the legendary "pipe of peace" was first smoked between Indian warriors and representatives of the Great White Father in Washington.

Perhaps the whole matter which is too often summed up in an easy phrase entitled "the plight of the American Indian" is best understood by the Indian leaders themselves.

There has been a growing tendency of late—just as there has been repeatedly in the past—for some of our younger politicians to appeal to the Indian by arguing that the tribes have been victimized for years and that they can solve all existing problems with one great program. I have seen this happen many times, and it always makes me amused to see how much wiser is the average Indian leader than these hot young crusaders who believe every conceivable human problem can be met and overcome through the mere passage of a liberal program calling for new expenditures of Federal money. The really important fact is that the Indian, through vast experience, knows that the problems that bother him can only be solved by himself. I am not saying he doesn't feel some help will be needed from Uncle Sam. Experience has taught him this too. But the big problem where the Indians are concerned is the problem of making available to all Indian youths as much education as they and their families want them to have. I can remember the time just ten years ago when I knew of only two Indians in my state who held college degrees. This year, one small tribe alone has forty youngsters in college and the largest tribe has over 1,000. In the latter group, at least 50 master's degrees and five doctorates are coming up this year.

One of our difficulties today is in comparing life on the Indian reservation with our own way of life in an affluent society. It is an oversimplification to count the electrical appliances and luxury items and decide that the Indians are badly deficient. In one sense it is true, and in another it must be remembered that many Indians like their way of living. But the big lesson is that you cannot lump all Indians into one group. Nor can you appraise all Indian attributes and aspirations as a whole. Some Indians are fond of the white man's ways. Some are not at all sure they approve nor want the white man's ways. Some are sure they do not want everything that we have in the way of culture, religion and material possessions.

But we are learning very rapidly that education is the one big key to a better way of life for the American Indians. And we are commencing to approach this problem in the only way it can be handled effectively—with maximum Indian help and participation.

The middle American senses what is generally needed in the area of race relations. I suggest he identifies this need with Christian brotherhood. And I suggest he bristles with anger and resentment and opposition when he is *told categorically* what must be done. I believe this is a fundamental error which the liberal politicians of this country have made. I believe it is complicated and compounded by intemperate appeals to minority groups—appeals based on the contention that society as a whole owes reparation for injustices which have existed for many decades in the relationship of the races in this country.

And this brings me to one of the root causes which I detect in the demise of liberalism. I believe it is popular disgust with the continuous insistence that society must shoulder a mass responsibility and a mass guilt for everything which is not perfect in the human condition at this point in the history of our country. It's pretty hard to convince a man who has worked hard all of his life, lived according to his own moral precepts, and paid ever-increasing taxes to support the social engineering and paternalism of the liberals in government that he is today responsible for slums, ghettos, poverty, discrimination and crime in the streets. The average American is especially sick of liberal contentions that today's criminals, especially the young brutal types who commit murders, forcible rape and muggings, are somehow the victims of society's failures.

This whole question of collective guilt is a liberal device which has long outlived its usefulness. It never did have validity with responsible citizens who performed their work, fulfilled their civic responsibilities, and added to the forces which add up to good in our society.

I believe the idea of collective guilt began first, i.e., I believe it got its first big forward push in liberal philosophy and literature, right after World War II when we were led to believe that the American people were collectively responsible for the bombings of Hiroshima and Nagasaki and the deaths that resulted in those Japanese cities from the initial usage of atomic bombs. For years, in the aftermath of World War II, the American public was treated to the spectacle of scientists beating their breasts and lamenting the fact that they had played a part in the development of what was believed to be the ultimate weapon.

You would have thought, for example, that nuclear fission would never have become a reality without some members of the scientific community who worked, at government's request, in the old Manhattan Project which developed the A bomb. To hear some of them talk, you would have thought that it was a foregone conclusion that mankind would make use of their particular work to blow itself up and that the perpetrator of that work bore an individualistic, personal responsibility for anything that might happen. During all this lamenting and self-criticizing and assigning of guilt to all people who were part of the government which developed the A bomb, the fact that our enemies were working on the same device was overlooked. But those who felt especially guilty never considered what their portion of the responsibility would have been if they had refused to help develop the A bomb and if, because of their refusal, Adolf Hitler had perfected it first. It is easy to imagine what might have happened to the Western world if Mr. Hitler had gotten the A bomb. And it is just as reasonable to ask why anyone who helped the Nazi madman to gain such an advantage should not be held forever guilty and responsible. This places a different emphasis on the whole idea of responsibility for destructive weapons.

By the same token, it has become fashionable in liberal circles today to overlook a youthful criminal's responsibility and claim that a society which permits the existence of broken homes and slum conditions is to blame for that boy's crimes.

One occasionally wonders, when he has been doused with another outpouring of this sociological slop, what happened in the early days of this country when poverty was much more widespread than it is today, when slums and ghettos constituted the major portion of our cities, and when the word "affluence" was so rare that it was almost never heard in American conversation. Where, one is compelled to ask, did society's responsibility lie in those periods?

This whole line of argument—the liberal contention that individual responsibility can somehow be submerged and overlooked in a sea of collective guilt and mass social dereliction—adds up to the average American as an enormous "cop out." The American citizen who is afraid for his wife to go out on the street after dark has had a noseful of this overweening concern for the so-called rights of the accused. He has had it so long that he is insisting today upon a society of ordered justice wherein law and order are devised first and foremost for the protection of the innocent majority.

PART

II

The Failure of Liberalism

IV

Isolationism Again

AMERICAN ISOLATION, BOTH AS A NATIONAL ATTITUDE AND AS A POLICY of government, is not new in the United States. It certainly did not begin with the present agitation to withdraw from the Vietnam conflict and to turn our backs on international commitments which now involve possible military action elsewhere in Asia and definite action in the NATO countries. Nor did it begin with the strong resistance to entanglement in Europe's struggles in the 1930's, when organizations such as America First were formed in a vain effort to keep this country's head in the sand and away from Europe's involvement with the Third Reich, Adolf Hitler, Mussolini and, of course, World War II itself.

The concept goes back before even the post-World-War-I sentiment which led this country to forego membership in the League of Nations and to reject officially Woodrow Wilson's strong desire for our partnership in what was then a new breed of internationalism.

Actually, the concept of isolationism is as old as the Republic. It was our desire to be isolated from the British powers of taxation and oppressive, unrepresentative governmental rule of the colonies that led us to the Declaration of Independence and the Revolutionary War.

And it was an extension of this same feeling that led to the evolvement of the Monroe Doctrine which, in effect, was a sort of

Western Hemispheric isolationism and warned foreign powers to maintain a "hands-off" attitude where the Western Hemisphere was concerned.

In these early days, of course, the accident of geography strongly abetted our desire for, as well as implementation of, a policy of American isolationism. We were protected, both east and west, by large, hard-to-cross oceans. We were not especially friendly with Mexico at the time, but the relationship with our neighbors to the south certainly constituted no kind of threat. Our neighbors to the north shared with us many cultural, economic and linguistic ties which made Canada a natural ally.

In other words, we were ideally situated to the erection and maintenance of a policy which would become known as "Fortress America." However, the geographic factor was not long to withstand the progress of technology. A time would come when the development of fast-flying planes and instantaneous communications would have the effect of drawing us into more intimate relationship with the rest of the world. When World War II broke out, there still existed in this country a strong manifestation of isolationism, and the technological advances, many of them then on the drawing board, had not impressed themselves upon our national conscience. At the very outset of World War II, a majority of Americans honestly held to the belief that it was none of our argument and that we could indefinitely avoid involvement by the mere process of remaining aloof.

Thus, when the storm clouds gathered in Europe presaging a titanic struggle between the forces of the Fascist Axis powers and other nations of Europe, we were not aware, as a nation, of the worldwide ramifications the struggle would entail. We adopted a policy of neutrality. The Congress of the United States even wrote this neutrality into the form of legislation. And this proved a stumbling block for the job of moving this nation into a state of preparedness when it began to become evident that it would be extremely difficult for us to remain completely unentangled with World War II. Indeed, the evidence was never entirely clear to all Americans.

But it began to become apparent that we had grown more and more international in many nonpolitical ways. Our large companies did business in many foreign countries. Our melting pot population had many strong cultural and family ties to other countries. Our art and literature easily crossed every type of national boundary. In other words, our commerce, our social consideration, our cultural achievements (art, literature, etc.) had gone around the world, had become global in nature, and were beginning to exert heavy pressure on the government of the United States to become involved in a global sense also.

As a matter of history, we eventually were forced into repeal of the Neutrality Act. It became to our advantage to lend aid and comfort in the form of lend-lease shipments to the enemies of the Axis powers for security reasons of our own. And, of course, the process of our total involvement was completed in several hours' time on December 7, 1941, when the Japanese carried out their attack on Pearl Harbor.

There was no question of isolationism during World War II. In fact, the mere mention of the word carried an ugly and completely unfavorable connotation. We were in war up to our ears against a totalitarian force which was out to rule the entire world. We were involved deeply and intimately and personally with our allies—the British, the French and the Russians. We lost all vestiges of that old status which we used to call "Fortress America." Instead we became, in name and in fact, the "Arsenal of Democracy." Not only did our new internationalism—breech-born by the grim lesson of Pearl Harbor—bring us into the war, but it gave us a new sense of our relationship with a responsibility to the other nations of the world.

This same sentiment, of course, prevailed in the post-war period and placed us in the forefront of the powers which joined together to form the United Nations and adopt the charter which we all hoped could be used as a framework for maintaining peace in the world in future years. That same sentiment, plus the obvious threat of international Communism, led us to formulate the Marshall Plan and the expenditures of billions upon billions of dollars in foreign aid to assist, not only in the rebuilding of war-torn Europe, but in a vast effort to produce viable economies in many areas of the world which were known generally as the undeveloped nations.

Thus, without even seeking the role and, indeed, not actually realizing its full importance, the United States became the world's Number One power. We, of course, in the early post-war days were the sole world possessors of the atom bomb and a nuclear capacity.

And this alone set us apart from other nations, in particular the Soviet Union.

The role of world leader was new to the United States—at least it was new in a peacetime context. As I remember our earlier history, the Twenties and the Thirties stand out clearly in my mind as being two decades of relative quiet so far as our interests, as citizens, in the activities of other countries were concerned. In fact, even the rise of dictatorial tyrants like Hitler and Mussolini did not disturb this quietude until Europe was at war, and even then it did not move us to rapid action. We actually did not, as a united nation, regard World War II as our own concern until the sneak attack by the Japanese on Pearl Harbor.

These were the days of actual isolation for the United States. It is difficult today to understand just how complete this isolation was. It can best be understood, I think, by merely mentioning the fact that in 1927 the entire world celebrated an important and historic event. It was the memorable occasion when a young aviator named Charles Augustus Lindbergh made the first flight across the Atlantic Ocean. Previously, the only connecting link between Europe's ferment and North America was by ocean liners, most of which took five days to a week to make the crossing one way.

And even though Lindbergh paved the way for air transportation which would eventually enwrap our world and bring us all much closer together, this did not happen overnight. It took many years to develop the kind of speedy transportation which came into being in the post-World War II period.

In this period, too—the 1920's and 1930's—we were at best a second- or third-rate power. In terms of military strength alone, we were probably even further down the list. Our Armed Forces had been allowed to decline in the wave of pacifism that swept the English-speaking nations in the 1920's. Militarily we were pitifully weak when the threatening and aggressive shadow of Adolf Hitler fell over Europe. Many of our people began to stir uneasily when Hitler's air-supported ground armies overran most of the European countries, when the British were pushed to the sea at Dunkirk, and when England itself became a target for Nazi bombers and the threat of invasion hung grimly over Winston Churchill's homeland. But the home front drive for involvement never gained proper strength in those early days because we were constantly being reassured by President Roosevelt, who repeated over and over that

American boys would not fight in foreign wars. Another complicating factor was the attitude of the small but noisy group of American Communists and their followers, fellow travelers and dupes.
These far leftists, who had shouted warnings about Adolf Hitler's
rise, who had supported the Communists in the Spanish Civil War,
and who agitated continually for American involvement against the
Axis, changed their tune completely when Hitler suddenly and un-
expectedly signed a pact with the Communist leader, Soviet Premier
Josef Stalin. Strangely enough, the level of agitation for American
involvement on behalf of the British fell noticeably in this country
during the time of the infamous alliance of totalitarian tyrants Hitler and Mussolini and Stalin. This was because United States Communists had been compelled to switch gears. The agitation for
American entry into World War II on the side of the Allies did not
pick up its old tempo again until Hitler characteristically double-
crossed Stalin and invaded the Russian homeland.

This period was one of great soul-searching and confusion on
the part of America's leaders as well as its citizens. President Roosevelt had ceased to promise that American boys would not fight on
foreign shores and had begun to work through various channels to
support the Allied cause. We moved from an isolated, peace-loving
nation, whose people had once taken seriously the Geneva Disarmament Conference and the Kellogg Peace Pact, to a nation preparing
reluctantly and inexorably toward participation in the second world
war of the century. Through the efforts of President Roosevelt and
with the strong urging of Winston Churchill, the United States repealed its Neutrality Act, embarked on an extensive lend-lease program to help supply Russia and Great Britain, and began a partial
mobilization of its own resources through enactment of a new Se-
lective Service law and an ambitious program of aircraft and ship-
building and the calling up of some National Guard ground units
which used wooden equipment and paper weapons.

Thus ended those comfortable days when I, upon taking the
oath of office as a Second Lieutenant in the Army Reserve in 1930,
was moved to wonder why I even bothered. I remember thinking
that I would never be called upon to go to war and that the training
I would receive would be merely a carry on of my four years of
ROTC.

And although we had slowly but surely been moving in the
direction of involvement, I don't believe the majority of our people

honestly believed that our participation would ever go beyond that of supplying the sinews of war for others to use. Then suddenly we awoke to the realities of a world which had been changing more rapidly than we understood on December 7, 1941, when the Japanese pulled their sneak attack on Pearl Harbor and sunk or disabled most of the ships in the American fleet.

Overnight we became a nation totally committed to the winning of the war against the Axis, and we began right then an all-out drive to produce the equipment and the men to get the job done as quickly as possible.

Three words were entered in the long list of time-honored and patriotic slogans which had moved Americans to supreme efforts and their finest hours. "Remember Pearl Harbor" became the rallying cry which would rank with those old sayings of the past such as "Remember the Maine," "Fifty-Four Forty or Fight," "Don't Give Up the Ship," "Make the World Safe for Democracy."

Pearl Harbor sounded the death knell for any remnants of isolationism which existed in this country. The "America Firsters" literally disappeared overnight, and we devoted our energies and our concern to matters of global strategy.

As I pointed out earlier, we went into this conflict as an inferior power in the world's strategic balance, and we came out of this war the undisputed leader. Aside from possession of the world's most terrifying weapon and the tremendous military victories which we achieved, we were also the country which dominated the air. And history teaches us that the country controlling the popular mode of transportation in any given era has always been the country which leads the world. This axiom can be traced way back into ancient times when dominance of the Mediterranean and control of inland waterways were such vital factors in the balance of power. Later the oceans themselves became the lanes of transportation and the lanes of world power. There was the time that the Straits of Gibraltar were the key and were first controlled by Portugal, then Spain and finally England.

It must be recalled that by proper use of seapower, Britain was able to maintain a relatively peaceful world for nearly 200 years. This was the period of the "Pax Britannica" when the mere possession of the world's most powerful fleet was sufficient to discourage aggressors and prevent war.

And, of course, we came out of World War II holding undisputed air superiority over the entire world.

It was on the strength of this that we later developed the Eisenhower-Dulles policy of "Massive Retaliation." This, in effect, was merely a posture which served notice on the world that we would never strike first but that if we were ever attacked, we would retaliate in such a massive way as to utterly destroy the attackers. This policy was an effort to make the best use of our tremendous power. At that time there was not a nation in the world that did not understand the dimension of our authority through military might.

This was an era, too, when little-known treaties began to take form. They resulted from the Eisenhower Administration's belief that we would be in a better position to maintain world peace if we had concrete and written understandings with our allies as to just what we would do with our military power if they became involved in trouble. Consequently, treaties were negotiated and ratified with the North Atlantic Treaty nations and with the NATO organization itself, all of which definitely would commit the arms of the United States to war if its treaty partners got into trouble.

Other treaties were negotiated, including the one in Southeast Asia (SEATO), which further committed our nation to possible armed conflict in the future under certain specified conditions.

Then we stumbled into the Vietnam war. I use the word "stumbled" advisedly because I feel our involvement there resulted from a number of miscalculations and mistakes having to do with the whole problem of our role as a guarantor of freedom in a world threatened by Communist aggression.

President Eisenhower had made a commitment to South Vietnam following the Geneva Conference. It should be remembered that the United States did not sign the pact made at the Geneva Conference, principally because we were unhappy with the indefinite provision made by that conference for a future election to determine when or if the two Vietnams, North and South, would be united.

Regardless, the President did give the word of his office and the word of this country that we would help South Vietnam if its government ever was threatened. And when this contingency did arise, President Eisenhower dispatched advisors to teach and counsel South

Vietnamese soldiers, sailors and airmen in the arts of modern warfare. This was the status of our forces in Vietnam until President Kennedy in 1961 ordered 16,000 men to be sent to Vietnam in the role of advisors but with orders that would permit them to return enemy fire if the occasion arose. I believe this was the actual beginning of our long and frustrating military involvement in Southeast Asia. And I believe it was the first major mistake of our Vietnam adventure. Because what we did, in effect, was go to war without an attendant commitment to see it through to victory. Had President Kennedy, instead of sending a rather small token force of combatants, sent the entire strategic air fleet and United States Navy, I think the government of North Vietnam would have gotten the message and the war would have ended almost before it began.

During the years immediately following World War II and until fairly recently, say the last decade, this nation's commitment to the concept of internationalism was solid and unassailable. But I must say where military operations against Communism were concerned, some very interesting qualifications arose, especially among the so-called arch-liberals in and out of this government. For example, when we correctly went to war in Korea in June, 1950, the Far Left in this country was not only surprised but shocked and disgruntled. In retrospect it seems apparent that the Communists had taken to heart some declarations by American officials to the effect that our line of perimeter of defense ran through the Mariana Islands of Saipan, Tinian and Guam. They had some reason to believe that anything to the west of the Marianas could be challenged without fear of American intervention. The reasoning seemed to be that our internationalism stopped short of the Philippines or Korea and that the nation's war weariness was sufficient to make us ignore a threat to Asian freedom from international Communism.

Thus it was that the North Koreans moved precipitously and without warning across the 37th Parallel into non-Communist South Korea with every expectation of victory through American default. The North Koreans were ready and equipped. Behind them stood the arms and manpower of Red China, and behind the South Koreans stood nothing but water.

The factor that wasn't counted on in this situation was the strong attitude of President Harry S Truman. In characteristic directness, President Truman recognized a clear threat to freedom and ordered American troops to intervene. In effect, Mr. Truman was saying that the United States of America was accepting its share of responsibility for freedom against the tyranny and aggression of Communism in the same fashion that it had some years earlier accepted its share of responsibility for freedom when it was threatened by the forces of Fascism.

American Communists were extremely unhappy at this intervention. And many non-Communists of liberal and leftist persuasion shared this unhappiness. Over an extended period of time, General Douglas MacArthur became at one and the same time the hero of the Far East and the enemy of the left-wing forces in the United States. Almost before we knew it, General MacArthur was being pictured in some segments of the American press as a "man on horseback" determined to grab as much military power as he could and whose secret aim was to turn the Korean conflict into World War III by forcing a confrontation with Red China beyond the Yalu River. Actually, what General MacArthur sought was permission to cross the Yalu River and destroy the airfields and supply dumps of the enemy, which was busily engaged in the business of killing American fighting men.

The powerful influences at work in the country on the left-hand side of the political spectrum won the day in this argument. They managed to have General MacArthur replaced, to prevent American miliary forces from crossing the Yalu, and to give this country something that it had never had before and which had never existed in the long history of mankind—the concept of limited warfare.

To my knowledge the restriction placed on General MacArthur and the miliary commanders who followed him in Korea was the first time any American military force had ever been confined in its pursuit of an enemy. Because the Korean War finally cooled off, or at least its major hostilities brought to a halt, some misguided American politicians were encouraged to believe that the concept of a limited war and a halfway victory could be usefully employed again. And it is that experience, I believe, that we have to thank for the long, heartbreaking, expensive, nonconclusive war in Vietnam.

The concept of limited war is, of course, a contradiction in terms. Throughout history war always has been the final resort of diplomats unable to arrange nonviolent settlement of international disputes. War, by its very nature, is a total thing. Once resorted to, it is a process of overcoming your enemy. The idea that such a process can be limited would have astounded the great military experts of history. Von Clausewitz, Britain's Wellington, and our own George Washington would have been convulsed with laughter if anyone in an official capacity had ever seriously suggested such an approach to the art of warfare.

So how could such a fallacious concept become operational in the American military establishment? I can understand its appeal to civilians and even the fact that it might prove provocative, simply as a subject of debate, among some statesmen. But to men trained in the business of national defense and military operations, the concept is nothing short of a denial of everything they have been taught —both in their classes and by the experience of history. So when we get around to wondering about the adoption of such an inconclusive approach to military action in the United States, I think we have to look to and blame the great power that civilians such as former Defense Secretary Robert McNamara and his army of civilian assistants and computer-minded "whiz kids" exerted over the American military policy during the past decade.

When you have an academic-minded man of no experience in the business of defense and weapons and military strategy heading the Department of Defense, you have to expect theory rather than practical solutions. This is what happened when Robert McNamara left the Ford Motor Company after a very brief experience in the business community and was placed in charge of the world's largest military organization. It was inevitable in the impractical academic atmosphere of so-called "cost effectiveness" with which McNamara surrounded himself that the half-war experience in Korea would be dusted off and brought into being. As I have pointed out, wars have never been fought in a limited way nor can they ever be fought effectively if victory is not expected. If victory is not expected, a nation should never go to war. This is true because in such a circumstance the national goal becomes obscured. It becomes impossible to convince military men they should sacrifice and fight and bleed and perhaps die for a limited objective which their own commanders have a hard time defining. By the same token, when you have no goal such as victory, it becomes impossible to sell your nation and its people on the need for combat.

This is what has been happening in Vietnam. We made a major mistake by becoming heavily involved in Vietnam without clearly reaching a determination to win. I have already stated my belief that the theory of limited war came from the Pentagon in the period of Secretary McNamara, but I must say that it was compounded and extended by President Johnson's desire to please everyone.

For example, if President Johnson had escalated the war all at once and made a determined push to win, I am convinced that the war would have been ended before his term of office was up. But he chose a piecemeal brand of escalation while insisting that he still endorsed the idea of limited war, and nothing was accomplished but tremendous expense, higher American casualties, and an ever-deepening frustration on the part of the American people. Johnson tried to keep both the "hawks" and the "doves" happy, and he made neither group happy nor did he accomplish what needed to be done in Southeast Asia.

It is a shame that President Johnson did not pursue in the middle 1960's the course of action which he urged on the Truman Administration in Korea back in the days when he was a member of the Senate. His views were outlined emphatically in a speech on July 12, 1950, in which he urged all out American action to defeat Communist North Korea. Let me quote from Senator Johnson's July 12th speech:

"There is no way out short of total victory. . . . Shall South Korea be remembered as a slaughter house of democracy—or as a graveyard for aggression? . . . Words are useless; criticism is wasted; delays unthinkable."

President Johnson at that time argued strongly against the kind of temporizing which characterized his 1964 campaign pledges not to "escalate" the war in Vietnam. As he so correctly and dramatically put it: "So long as we continue to rely upon words—not upon actions—to win this struggle in South Korea, we are as guilty of a crime against freedom as the executioners who fire the bullets in the faces of our sons."

Of course, it was not until 1965 that Mr. Johnson, as Commander-in-Chief of the U.S. Armed Forces, went very much beyond words in Vietnam. And, of course, well into 1968, he was still holding out of bounds some sources and routes of Communist military supply.

When he was a Senator urging action upon President Truman, Mr. Johnson complained that the opinions of our Joint Chiefs of Staff—the opinions of our highest military advisors—were being

"straitjacketed in a maze of bookkeeping and accounting procedures." And, of course, this is exactly what former Defense Secretary
Robert McNamara, with Mr. Johnson's support, did to the Joint
Chiefs of Staff during the entire course of Mr. Johnson's administration.

Perhaps it was prophetic, but I can actually place a date on the
time when I got my first strong whiff of the new isolationism which
we have seen grow and flower in the past few years. On August 28,
1964, I issued a statement from my presidential campaign headquarters in which I commented on President Lyndon Johnson's acceptance speech to the Democratic National Convention. I did not
see the President deliver his speech on television, but I read the text
of it the next morning. I remember that a heavy strain of national
self-sufficiency ran through that text. In fact, I was so impressed with
this evidence of an administration planning to turn in on itself after
the style of the old "Fortress America" type of isolationism that I
made this the theme of my public statement.

My statement to the press said:

> *Lyndon Johnson's acceptance speech was a clear with-*
> *drawal from leadership in international affairs. It was per-*
> *haps the most isolationist acceptance speech in modern*
> *American history.*
>
> *Not once did it mention directly the challenge to*
> *Communism or the many brushfire conflicts that Com-*
> *munism has ignited around the world. Not once did it go*
> *to the heart of the problems that are splitting our alliances*
> *apart, splitting the world apart, and putting this nation,*
> *everyday, on the brink of crisis.*
>
> *The eyes and ears of the entire world were turned to*
> *that acceptance speech, looking and listening for the vision*
> *and strength that would once again put America on the*
> *high road of world leadership. Instead, the world wit-*
> *nessed a vision turned inward, isolated, and sighted only*
> *toward domestic political advantage.*
>
> *America is not and must not become a second rate*
> *power, standing on the sidelines of world affairs. It de-*
> *serves more than promises devoid of recognition of world*
> *problems and global challenges. But last night in Atlantic*
> *City it got nothing more from Lyndon Johnson.*

> *The administration, with this final, fantastic refusal to even talk directly about the challenge of Communism, raises questions but gives no answers, raises doubts but gives no hopes, to a troubled, embattled, and divided world.*

I remember in 1964, also trying to get President Johnson to engage in conversations with me on what we were actually doing in Vietnam and what might happen regardless of which one of us were chosen President.

Of course, I was unsuccessful in every attempt, and I feel that as he reminisces about the problems he encountered during his last four years in office, Mr. Johnson will come to the conclusion that he should have accepted my offer. I believe he may realize now that if he had clearly told the American people why we were in Vietnam and why the war was being enlarged and at the same time declared his determination to win, his place in history would be entirely different.

Because of our determination to fight a limited war rather than a war aimed at victory, we entered into the longest war in American history and one which ultimately may become the costliest and which we might lose.

Now this brings us to the present-day isolationism which President Nixon has referred to as the "new isolationism" and others prefer to call a "neo-isolationism."

I first began to detect a growing desire in our country to isolate America once again some time in the early 1960's. And I became more aware of it as a definite phenomenon in the period following 1964, when I began my self-imposed four-year sabbatical leave from the Senate.

Most of this time I put in traveling around the country and talking to groups of our citizens, including a great many college gatherings. Of course, this embraced a period during which President Johnson was enlarging the scope of the Vietnam War, and the American people were beginning to ask questions concerning why we were in Vietnam and how many other areas we might be forced to become involved in militarily because of our worldwide commitments.

A great many eyebrows were raised and a great many questions asked every time I told my audiences that the United States had a total of 44 treaties which could involve us in military operations on behalf of fifteen nations if those nations were made the subject of an aggressive attack. Time and again in 1969 I raised the question of these foreign commitments during Senate debate on the military budget. It was ironic for me to listen to the very men who over the years had committed us to a firm policy of anti-isolationism, a firm policy of foreign alignments, a gigantic policy of foreign aid, all talking about reducing our defense expenditures to an absolute minimum.

Some of these suggestions would have cut America's expenditures in the military sphere so low that the problem of providing an adequate defense for our American homeland and its 204 million inhabitants would have been difficult to handle. But no thought whatsoever was given to the possibility that our foreign commitments might at any time in the future involve us in other Vietnam-type military operations. I argued time and again for a public airing of these foreign commitments so that the American people could judge for themselves what kind of commitments we had become involved in and how much military expenditure might be required to honor them.

The tendency among liberals in the Senate was to put the cart before the horse. They wanted to cut our defense budget so deeply that we would have trouble defending our own ramparts, let alone coming to the defense of a friendly neighbor to whom we were committed by treaty.

I explained it to the Senate during the debate on the military appropriations bill in these words:

> We are here debating a bill that eventually will authorize in the neighborhood of $77 or $78 billion for military purposes. And we are being bombarded from all sides with demands for retrenchment, economy and across-the-board reduction of expenditures for defense purposes.
>
> My point is that we must have an accurate picture of just what our total commitments might call for before we go in for any wholesale cutting back on our present level of defense expenditures. By this I do not mean that we should ease off in our efforts to cut back and eliminate as much waste and inefficiency as we possibly can in the area of military procurement. Instead, I am speaking of efforts

to eliminate or cut down on entire programs and systems which may be needed in the future.

There is a concerted effort within this body and in the intellectual and academic communities to pull back from our international commitments. President Nixon has referred to this as a form of neo-isolationism, and I believe that that is an accurate description. For if I understand correctly the opponents of the ABM and the critics of the Military-Industrial Complex, they would like to see this nation turn away from its foreign entanglements, go back on its foreign commitments, and forego the possibility of coming to the defense of any nations where freedom is threatened or where there is a threat of Communist aggression.

I believe there is no doubt that this desire for a resumption of isolationism stems in large part from a great yearning to be rid of the prolonged and irksome war in Vietnam. I yield to no man anywhere in my concern over the great cost to this country in lives and money that is being extracted in Southeast Asia. I can understand thoroughly the desire of the American people to rid themselves of this burden and the desire of public officials to find an easy way out of the dilemma. But I also know that if we cut and run in Vietnam and signify our intentions of avoiding any comparable conflicts in the future, we will—in the eyes of the world—be defaulting on our obligations as leader of the free world.

By the same token, I realize that we have on the domestic front many requirements for public expenditures. We need better housing, we need better hospitals, we need better schools, we need a vast variety of urban programs, and all of these cost money.

I realize, too, that it is popular to point at defense expenditures and regard them as wasteful in their very nature. And there can be no denying the fact that money spent on missile systems, naval vessels and military hardware of any kind is nonproductive in the accepted sense.

But it has a purpose to serve and that purpose is the defense of the American people and the cause of freedom. There is no way you can place a monetary or material *value on the type of yield which we obtain from military hardware. But I believe we must understand that in today's world we are required to make expenditures, and very heavy expenditures, in the name of freedom.*

It would be a marvelous thing if all the nations of the world were to decide once and for all that war and the implements of war and defense and the implements of defense are wasteful and unnecessary and that the money spent for these implements could be put to better uses for the good of humanity. Unfortunately, the nations of the world are not about to reach any such level of trust. And because of this, we must regard all recommendations for unrealistic reductions of military expenditures in the light of wishful and dangerous thinking. Just saying that a reduction in arms by the United States would lessen the chance of war does not make it true. But I do believe the chances for an outbreak of hostilities on the scale that the world knew in World War I and World War II are increasing rapidly with the expansion of Russian military might and our seeming interest in relinquishing our world leadership and its responsibilities.

And this has a direct bearing on the treaties which we now are a party to. I think there are a total of 43 such agreements and in at least fifteen of them we are committed to armed intervention if the other nations party to the treaties are attacked.

The connection appears obvious. The Russians, by expanding the reach of their military operations through the development of a large navy and air force, are enlarging the area of a possible world involvement. The Soviet Union, heretofore, has always been defensive in nature—content to confine its military defense to its own homeland. Thus the development of a powerful navy represents a significant departure from Russia's historic and traditional attitude.

The determined drive of the Soviet Union to become all-powerful in all areas of military endeavor—nuclear, naval, space and the conventional sphere—is bound to produce a new level of worldwide tension. We may as well acknowledge the fact that the Soviet Union shows every sign of making preparations on all fronts to move into any power vacuums which might be created through withdrawal of American influence, such as now is being urged for Southeast Asia, Germany and other areas. The theory is that the masters of the Kremlin believe that American "doves" will prevail and that this nation will retreat from its position of world leadership in order to devote a preponderance of its attention and its money to domestic problems. As right as this might seem, it would be wrong.

The Russians have already made their move in the Middle East. When the United States more or less declared a "hands-off" policy in that tense area where the world sea lanes cross and three continents touch, the Soviet Union moved in quickly to arm the Arab nations with the sinews of war. Our default of responsibility and the Soviet Union's aggressive intent have already caused one vicious all-out war between Israel and the Arab nations. Israel, of course, won the war of June, 1967, hands down and captured much of the Russian supply equipment. However, all of it has since been replaced and the Middle East remains one of the foremost tinderboxes of the world.

By the same token, the Soviets are obviously waiting for us to turn tail and withdraw from Vietnam so that its Communist counterparts can take over Vietnam and finally all of Southeast Asia. They also are waiting hopefully for us to withdraw from Berlin and other areas of western Europe.

It is obvious that the U.S.S.R. is reaching for a position which would enable it to exert undisputed world leadership.

The whole question of world power balance is now undergoing a very subtle but a very vital change as the Russians move into a position of nuclear parity with the United States.

President Nixon has told us that his purpose in the area of military strength is to make sure that we have a "sufficiency" of power to guarantee our national strategic interests. I believe that we do not now have a sufficiency in the area of missile defense. We certainly are far short of

*"parity" with the Soviet Union because we are only now
debating the deployment of an ABM system while the
Russians have been in the process of deploying their ABM
system for five years.*

*I believe that it is vital to our position in the world
that our defense against missile attack be strengthened
and that our military expenditures be kept equal to the
tasks that confront us today and may confront us in the
future in our role as leader of the free world.*

*And in conclusion I would suggest—particularly to
the members of the Senate Foreign Relations Committee
—that before they join in any concerted effort to cut our
military procurement below the level regarded as adequate by the Defense Department and the President that
they thoroughly examine the treaties to which we are a
party and whose provisions might require us to go to war
at some time in the future.*

*I believe that if we are to withdraw into a shell of
neo-isolationism, it is incumbent upon the Foreign Relations Committee to make recommendations which
would make our treaty commitments conform to a new
reduced stature in international affairs. If we are not to
have the arms sufficient to guarantee the provisions of
these treaties, we should not be bound by them, we should
not be a party to them.*

If nothing else, the first session of the 91st Congress, which
marked the beginning of the all-out attack on American military
expenditures and the defense budget, sparked increased interest in
the whole area of treaty commitments. The Senate Foreign Relations
Committee, for example, conducted closed hearings on the subject of
international commitments. As a result, the committee issued a report on national commitments which said that the traditional distinction between the treaties as an appropriate means of making
significant political commitments and the executive agreement has
substantially broken down. It added that sometimes a sense of binding commitment builds up from a series of executive declarations.

Through this means, plus repeated executive declarations concerning particular countries, there is sometimes created a situation
in which our honor sometimes becomes involved, the Democratic-

controlled Senate Committee contended. And Committee Chairman, Senator J. William Fulbright, described the process as "commitment by accretion" and cited the cases of Thailand, Spain and Vietnam as prime examples.

In this connection, Senator Fulbright, an arch internationalist during the most of his long career in the House and the Senate, sounded for all the world like the nation's number one neo-isolationist in an article he authored for *Look* magazine on December 2, 1969. Senator Fulbright, whose famous resolution of 1941 committed the United States to international cooperation in the post-war period, issued a warning which he entitled "The Wars in Your Future."

In this article, the Chairman of the Senate Foreign Relations Committee flatly declared that the United States is overextended in its foreign commitments, especially those involving military responsibility. He further complained that the United States had allowed its President to acquire almost dictatorial powers in the field of foreign policy.

"The United States now has security treaties—bilateral or multilateral—with 43 countries around the world. Every one of these defines conditions under which we would be expected to go to war."

Chairman Fulbright complained that "we tend to ignore the qualifications and limitations in the treaties and have interpreted our obligations as being absolute and unlimited."

He insisted nothing in our SEATO treaty, for instance, obligates us to be fighting in Vietnam. He quickly skips over the requirements in the SEATO treaty which would require us to consult immediately with our Asian allies anytime we judge South Vietnam to be gravely threatened. He further skips over the fact that in 1964 the Gulf of Tonkin Resolution was adopted upon recommendation of Senator Fulbright and his own Foreign Relations Committee.

Senator Fulbright, as the virtual epitome of the new isolationist breed, is very facile at overlooking or disregarding former statements as well as former commitments which he made. For example, because the Senator does not like the war in Vietnam nor what Presidents Johnson and Nixon did about it, he now complains that the national executive enjoys dictatorial powers in the field of foreign policy. Conveniently forgotten, of course, is the Fulbright attitude during the early 1960's when the late President John F. Kennedy was in the White House. At that time the Senator from Arkansas made some memorable speeches—one of which was delivered at Cornell in 1961

—complaining that the United States Constitution had become out-moded and was placing unnecessary restrictions on the Executive Department of the Government. In other words, like other liberals who launched their careers as red-hot internationalists and have now turned completely around, Senator Fulbright is for unlimited executive power when the executive uses that power to do what this former college president and Rhodes scholar feels should be done. On the other hand, he is bitterly opposed to executive power when it is utilized to further a policy with which he disagrees.

This kind of stance is nothing new to the Chairman of the Senate Foreign Relations Committee.. It may be recalled that in 1948 Senator Fulbright seriously suggested that President Harry S Truman resign because, according to Fulbright, he was out of step with the Congress on matters of foreign policy. One is tempted to suggest that the Senator might find it useful to apply the same principles to his present situation. Wouldn't it be just as proper to suggest that Mr. Fulbright resign as Chairman of the Senate Foreign Relations Committee inasmuch as he has long been out of step and out of sympathy with the Executive Branch on matters of foreign policy?

This suggestion is not as foolish as it may sound. Nor is it as foolish as Senator Fulbright's 1948 suggestion. But in my opinion it had considerable validity during the years when this nation had a Democratic President, and Senator Fulbright was issuing statements in his capacity as Chairman of the Foreign Relations Committee which went counter to the policies of his own party's administration.

My point is that Fulbright vastly confused and misled not only many people in this country but many officials and observers in foreign capitals.

Many governments did not possess the sophistication and the insight to understand that Fulbright in his repeated denunciations of the United States military and the war in Vietnam did not speak for the administration. The logical conclusion overseas was that the Chairman of the Senate Foreign Relations Committee spoke with great authority, and very possibly accurately forecast what a Democratic President and a Democratic-run State Department might expect to do.

Until now the internationalists turned isolationists have been spared the kind of acute embarrassment that their leftward-leaning turnabout could be expected to cause. In Senator Fulbright's case

—and this will be applied to many other liberal Democrats—the embarrassment may reach its high tide of red faces if and when the Senate votes on proposals to repeal the Gulf of Tonkin Resolution. As the ranks of the new isolationists begin to grow, it is more than just amusing sport to pick out for attention those individuals who played such an important role in guiding this nation into an all-out internationalist endeavor.

I want to emphasize that we cannot, merely because of the unpopularity of the war in Vietnam, suddenly change the entire force of our foreign policy. Our nation, through its military power and through its vast economic resources, has become the undisputed leader of the free world. This has given us enormous responsibility, both diplomatic and moral, which we cannot arbitrarily ignore beyond some future cutoff date. The kind of involvement this nation has accepted since World War II is so enormous that it must be studied very carefully from every possible viewpoint before any decision is made which might be regarded as a default on our leadership of the free world.

What I am saying is that America's role in the family of free nations is not one that can be shucked like a worn-out coat anytime Senator Fulbright and the Senate Foreign Relations Committee feel that it is time to withdraw. It must be remembered that America's role of "Rebuilder of Nations" and "Global Good Samaritan" was not assumed overnight. It had its inception some 23 years ago—on June 7, 1947. Strangely enough, the concept was contained in just 37 words spoken by Secretary of State George C. Marshall in an address at Harvard University. The former Chief of Staff was outlining the gravity of conditions in post-war Europe. He cited the vast loss of capital by banks, insurance companies and other financial institutions and businesses. He described how the industry of the whole western half of the continent was ailing, its machinery rusting, and its wrecked buildings waiting to be restored. He explained that food and fuel were in short supply and then, near the end of his grim tale of war's costly aftermath, he declared:

"The role of this country should consist of friendly aid in the drafting of a European program and of later support of such a program so far as it may be practical for us to do so."

Thus began America's heavy involvement in the international art of helping our sister nations. And the start was an auspicious one. Our foreign aid program for Europe, carried out under what came to be known as the Marshall Plan, was tremendously successful. It resulted in the rebirth of European commerce and industry and in the revitalization of the people residing in those war-torn areas.

There are many who believe that this early success has been the root of much of our subsequent foreign aid troubles. Too often we have tried to apply the techniques which proved so successful in war-ravaged Europe to other areas of the world, and of course, without the same instant and wholesale success.

Our trouble has been that we appear to forget the difference between an industrial society demolished by war, and an underdeveloped agrarian hunting society shaking off its static somnolence and emerging into the Nuclear Age.

Since that speech at Harvard, American largesse in international affairs has gone under many designations—the Marshall Plan, Mutual Aid, Foreign Aid, Foreign Economic Aid, Aid for International Development and, needless to say, it has cost the American taxpayers billions upon billions of dollars. As of June 30, 1969, we have spent approximately $182 billion for aid which encompassed everything from wine glasses and hair spray to food for the starving, machine guns for the soldiers, and, more recently, aid for population control. In all, five successive Presidents including President Nixon have declared foreign aid to be an essential component of our foreign policy. And ten successive Congresses have approved that concept.

Understand, I have never approved of our economic aid projects overseas. Many times I have felt that our heavy expenditures of foreign economic aid were doing nothing but creating future problems. Nevertheless, we made the expenditures—in the neighborhood of $200 billion—and we became deeply involved. We also became a counterforce in the world to a virulent and aggressive international Communism.

Should we now suddenly announce to the world that we have had enough, that we no longer regard ourselves as the force which can and should contain the spread of international Communism, the result could easily be chaos on a worldwide basis.

Any vacuums we happen to create in any strategic areas of the world will be filled quickly by either Soviet or Chinese Communist efforts. This is one factor which must be constantly borne in mind as the pressure, both public and private, for a return to a new brand of isolationism increases in this country.

We have, rightly or wrongly, taught many nations that we

could be depended upon under certain circumstances. In many instances we put this in writing. In other instances our actions bespoke such a continuing attitude on the part of our government. What we must be careful to understand now is that, having encouraged and promoted this process, we directly and deeply influenced the planning of many other nations and actually other regions of the world. This brings us not only to the hard reality of survival for some nations but also to the question of whether our honor and integrity is to be maintained in the family of free nations.

For example, serious questions are now being raised about our previous commitments. As David Lawrence, the nationally known columnist, put the question:

"Are the pledges by the President and the Senate in ratifying the Southeast Asia collective defense treaty and the North Atlantic Treaty going to be withdrawn?"

These are certainly valid questions which are occurring to peoples of Asia and Europe as they read the latest statements from the liberal leaders in the Congress. Some of them have seized on what they describe as President Nixon's "Guam declaration" as an instrument for pushing designs aimed at all kinds of withdrawal in our confrontations with Communism. For example, Senator Mike Mansfield, Democratic leader of the Senate, seized on the President's mild suggestion that Asian nations should manage their own internal defense problems so far as possible as justification for urging immediate reduction of the United States military and civilian presence throughout all of Southeast Asia. He is also suggesting that the Senate consider taking away from the President the broad military powers which he can exercise by reasons of actions previously taken by the Congress. Mansfield did not confine his attention to the Gulf of Tonkin Resolution but included also the Formosa Resolution, which was enacted to help protect Nationalist China from invasion.

In other words, Mansfield and other liberals are attempting to interpret the Guam statement by Mr. Nixon as a new doctrine meaning that the only way this country would ever become involved again would be when our own security was at stake and a nuclear showdown appeared to be in the offing.

Again, I am indebted to David Lawrence for the pungent way in which he describes what could happen if a Chief Executive of the United States suddenly adopted a new policy of isolationism in the conduct of our foreign affairs. As he put it:

"The moment a President of the United States is impelled to announce that our government wishes to back away from commitments made in the Southeast Asia Defense Treaty and the North Atlantic Treaty, the uncertainties which may be created could bring crisis after crisis and eventually plunge many nations including our own into another world war."

Unfortunately, the new isolationism in liberal ranks is getting its strongest push at a time when we are attempting to negotiate with the North Vietnamese to bring about a conclusion of the war in Southeast Asia. Any tendency to show our weariness with international affairs at a time like this is bound to play into the hands of the Communist negotiators on the other side of the table in Paris. We have yet to understand that negotiations, where the Communists are concerned, are much more of a tactic in foreign conflict than an attempt to find a reasonable ground for understanding.

In other words, in such talks our negotiators are striving to find a means for ending the bloodshed and suffering of the Vietnamese war; the Communists are playing a game designed to give them complete advantage. The sooner we accept the fact that the only language Communist negotiators understand is that dictated and backed up by superior strength the better off we will be. Entering into any kind of negotiations with the Communists, whether it be the Vietnam talks in Paris or the arms control negotiations in Vienna, is a mistake unless we go into these talks with a position of strength. An announced tendency to go back on our foreign commitments and withdraw into a nationalistic shell would seriously compromise our negotiating position vis-à-vis the Communists.

We are sailing on dangerous seas when the foreign policy of the United States is being placed in jeopardy by isolationists both inside and outside of the Congress.

The suggestions for repeal of treaties can be described as a direct frontal attack on our foreign policy. At least this has the merit of honesty. A more subtle attempt to bring about the same alterations in our stand as the free world's defender against Communism is being conducted on a completely different plane. This attack is being made in an attempt to reduce our capabilities to defend other free nations or to honor our military commitments abroad. It has taken the form of an all-out, no-holds-barred, open-end assault on the nation's military establishment, on its military leaders and its defense budget.

The determined and unrelenting efforts, both private and public, to convince the American people that the money we spend for defense is being squandered and should be channeled to other purposes is being pushed through every channel of communications. Some facets of this attack have a degree of validity and this unfortunately lends credence to the entire assault. For example, there is waste and inefficiency and duplication in our military procurement program which should be eliminated. But this does not mean that entire weapons systems and defense systems should be removed at the same time.

Too often, especially in Congress, we are inclined to confuse a good economist or an able efficiency expert with a military strategist. Let me illustrate. Senator William Proxmire of Wisconsin is Chairman of the Joint Congressional Subcommittee on Economy in Government. As such, he is almost unequalled as an investigator and a finder of waste and inefficiency and duplication in the government expenditures. But this does not make him an expert who should decide such questions as whether this nation needs a C-5A military cargo plane or an anti-ballistic missile defense system or a MIRV (multiple independently targeted reentry vehicle).

Much of what Senator Proxmire and his committee have reported can be useful in cutting down government costs and easing the load to our taxpayers. It is unfortunate that his findings lend themselves to overall charges aimed at something loosely called the Military-Industrial Complex. Unfortunately, too, the findings on waste and inefficiency, with which I do not quarrel, are being propagandized and used to credit broader charges which carry the inference that anything the Pentagon does or plans to do is wasteful and evil and a deliberate effort to deprive the underprivileged and the hungry ghetto-dwellers in our inner cities.

So adroit and so powerful has been the propaganda use made of a nation's discouragement and frustration over an unpopular war that public opinion at times threatens to endanger expenditures necessary for the defense of the American people. During the ABM debate in the first session of the 91st Congress, I tried repeatedly to cut through all the phony arguments that were raised by opponents to the administration's Safeguard program with one simple, unalterable sentence, to wit: "The safety of 204 million Americans is non-negotiable."

My point here is that if our military strength is reduced, the way some of the liberal groups are suggesting—by arbitary figures like 20 percent or $10 billion—we will have no alternative but to pull back on our foreign commitments. This is true because a treaty promise to come to another nation's defense in time of attack can carry no validity or credibility if the nation making such a pledge does not have the military forces necessary to the task.

When we seriously begin debating defense cuts which would endanger our own security, we are pretty well along the road to diverting our foreign policy from its recent course.

What we are faced with here is an effort to turn what we once proudly hailed as "The Arsenal of Democracy" into something akin to a "Fortress America."

From what I know of the American people, the conscience of the majority does not at the present time cry out for the type of neo-isolationism we see being promoted in the halls of Congress and the intellectual centers of our country. I believe the American people have become deeply disturbed and at least partially disenchanted with the whole idea of foreign adventures because of the war in Vietnam. But it must be remembered that there perhaps has never been a conflict so ideally suited to the task of heightening American frustration as this dirty little war in the jungles and rice paddies of Southeast Asia. There can be no doubt that the Americans are tired of the cost, both in lives and money, of the Vietnam undertaking. I believe, also, they are sick and tired of our inability or refusal to come out of it with a clear-cut victory over the forces of Communism.

But I believe the conscience of the majority is still deeply committed to the concept of honor in the dealings of the United States in the field of foreign affairs. It is perfectly clear from all sources, including opinion polls and other means of gauging the public temperament, that the American people have longed for a speedy end of this conflict for several years. Yet it is just as apparent that there is no compelling demand on the part of the American people that we heed the advice of the vocal, demonstrable minority that would like us to surrender and turn our backs on the South Vietnamese people as well as our national commitments in that and other parts of the world.

We are too deeply committed to the idea of living side by side with our foreign neighbors in an ever-shrinking world to pull back now into the false security of isolationism. The whole idea of rest-ing comfortably and prosperously and securely in the land mass between the Atlantic and Pacific Oceans has disappeared long since. Our involvement in World War II, our successful rebuilding of western Europe through the Marshall Plan, and our struggle to contain the spread of aggressive Communism through the Truman Doctrine and subsequent programs are embedded too deeply in the national psyche to be excised by an expensive and doubtful adventure in Vietnam.

I fully believe that the American people and their collective conscience are such that they want to continue sharing their blessings with the people of the world who are less fortunate. However, I believe they have long felt the need for a higher brand of responsibility in the devising and administering of programs of American help for overseas purposes.

I, myself, have long felt in accord with the vast majority of American taxpayers who doubted the effectiveness of outright money grants to other nations. Too often, these hard-earned American funds went into the pockets and the bank accounts of officials in the ruling cliques of the countries which benefited. The evidence is overwhelming that much of the $200 billion in American aid that has been sent overseas did not actually reach the underprivileged and the poor people which these funds were designed to help.

There was no way that a legislator such as myself could differentiate between the three forms of foreign aid—military, economic and technical. For strategic parliamentary purposes, one administration after another submitted their foreign aid requests to the Congress in a nonseparable package. I tried three times to get President Eisenhower to submit three separate foreign aid budgets, but I never succeeded. Consequently, if a member wished to follow the desires of the people and cut down on questionable monetary outlays to 90-odd foreign countries, he also would have to oppose measures to give technical help to these nations.

Many of us felt that technical aid was the important kind that could help underprivileged nations to help themselves. Under the technical aid approach, Americans actually became involved in showing less fortunate people throughout the world how to do things that would help them increase their standard of living. It was a form of exporting American "know-how" in various fields of endeavor such as agriculture, conservation, sewage treatment and so forth.

In my travels throughout the country during the early Sixties, I sensed this desire on the part of the American people to help our foreign friends in tangible, useful ways. I believe this feeling was what helped to make the Peace Corps an instant success with the average American. It made sense to send people who had been trained in this country to underdeveloped nations which desperately needed their skills so that their people could undertake the needed tasks on their own. Teach a man to use his hands in a way which will enrich him as our hands have enriched us, and he is forever a friend.

In summary, it can be said that the conscience of the majority on the subject of foreign policy is still one bound by honor and dedicated to the assistance of our less fortunate neighbors in the family of nations. It certainly does not countenance the abolition of our concern and the defaulting on our promises in the area of assisting less fortunate nations, both to resist totalitarian aggression and to improve the lot of their people.

It is undeniable that Americans are tired and irritated over the heavy drain placed on them by the war in Vietnam and by unsuccessful foreign economic programs in other areas of the world. But it would be a vast miscalculation to take this to mean that the conscience of America seriously desires a return to isolationism and a consequent heightening of the concept of the jungle law where only the fittest survive.

V

Money, Liberals and Defense

THE AMERICAN LIBERAL, PREOCCUPIED WITH THE MATERIAL SIDE OF man's nature, has developed a fixation over the expenditure of public money. For the past three and a half decades, money has become the answer to every problem the liberal has been able to observe on the domestic front. We have been told that whatever the crisis—unemployment, poverty, public health, education—spending at the Federal level will somehow work some kind of a magical cure. The amazing thing is that the American liberal persists in this argument even after long years of experimentation from the early 1930's on have proven that this is not the case.

By the same token, the liberal believes that when a problem arises that he is unhappy with, one way to attack it, one way to make it disappear, one way to erase it from the public concern is to starve it to death.

The rationale goes something like this: The Vietnam war is no good; the Vietnam war is supported by defense expenditures; ergo, the way to eliminate the Vietnam war and other wars is to reduce the amount of the defense appropriations.

In this oversimplification the American liberal confuses defense with war. The two are separable; however, there are many times when the conduct of a war like the one in Vietnam is the best defense that this nation can erect. We are today witnessing an amazing new development in the ranks of the American liberal. I say "new" because it is a development which finds the liberal in an unaccus-

tomed role. The American liberal in the Congress of the United
States is for a change becoming an apostle of Federal thrift. It is
true that this thrift, this determination to cut expenditures, is aimed
almost exclusively at defense-related activities. It is still unusual
enough to find American liberals in a political year recommending
a reduction in the level of Federal spending for any purpose to
make it highly noteworthy. It is, of course, very interesting to understand that this vast concern of the liberals, especially the Democratic liberals, has awaited the arrival of a Republican administration in the White House to find its full expression. What I mean
is that the overconcerned members of the United States Senate and
of the House who are arguing vigorously for a reduction in all types
of defense spending were not so concerned several years back when
this same defense spending was being planned by the regime of
former Defense Secretary Robert McNamara. For it was McNamara
and his "whiz kids," those computer boys who were so noted for
their so-called "cost effectiveness" methods, who gave us the bloated
defense budget which today is causing so much liberal breast-beating
and concern.

It is true that there are in the Department of Defense vast areas
where economies can be effected. There is no doubt about this. The
Republican administration and Defense Secretary Melvin Laird are
proving this day by day by finding new ways to economize and to
save the taxpayers' money and to give us the best possible dollar's
worth for the defense expenditures. However, I believe we make a
mistake when we assume that the liberal attack on the Defense Department and defense budget is limited merely to the liberals' concern for extravagance and for expenditures which might otherwise
go into domestic projects to relieve housing problems, the middle
cities problem, the ghetto problem, and so forth. I believe it is more
than that. I believe you must take a look at the entire broad approach
of our defense critics. I think you have to look at the attack on
something called the Military-Industrial Co nplex—the many-sided
attack by many, many groups—to accurately gauge what is going on
today.

It might be said that open season has been declared on all things
military. That's the way President Nixon put it in one of his more
memorable addresses on the subject of defense. I believe this is an
accurate assessment. I believe that what is going on today in the
name of economy, in the name of human rights, in the name of

domestic programs, is a dangerous attack on the defense establishment and on the military establishment and on the military men in our society.

I believe it is dangerous because it is too general, too broad, and too direct. In other words, what I am saying is that today in the assault on the defense budget we are seeing part of an overall strategy to bring about unilateral disarmament of this nation.

I say this with full understanding that I am speaking about people who have become convinced that the way to protect 204 million American people is to leave them unprotected.

Let me explain. There is a school of thought in this country which says that America, as one of the nation's leading nuclear powers, must assume the initiative, must lead the way, and be the first to start to cut down on its nuclear armaments and jettison the implements of defense which it has been amassing over the past 20 to 30 years. This belief is deeply and firmly held by many well-meaning and warm-hearted American people. We might call them pacifists. They sincerely want peace, but they mistakenly believe that peace is a one-way street. They mistakenly think that we Americans can, by our own actions, make sure that the world will become forever noble. This is patently not true—it never has been true. It goes contrary to all that we know about the nature of man.

In theatrical terms it might be said that we have been witnessing a left-wing extravaganza entitled, "The War on American Defense."

Unfortunately, we are not dealing with a Broadway production or a Hollywood presentation but with a definite line of attack on a basic concept of American freedom. That concept holds that freedom and liberty in today's world can best be insured and defended through the maintenance of military as well as economic and moral strength.

The attacks, from the very beginning, were anything but spontaneous. They were scripted and orchestrated by men highly skilled in the arts of Congressional relations, government relations, and—certainly not the least—public relations. The scenario began innocently enough with loud and prolonged objections to war. It rapidly moved from that generally approved attitude to specific objections to a single war—the conflict in Vietnam. From there the scenario began to encompass the military in very general but unmistakable terms designed to create the impression that all wars are the result of military men and military hardware. And from that line of argument, the scripting became conveniently blurred and the word "military" became intertwined with the word "defense."

Subtly, gradually, deliberately, the architects of this "war" on American defense moved all the way from an almost religiously conceived advocacy of peace in our times to a full-scale attack on the strategy, the methods, the men and the equipment required to defend 204 million American citizens from admittedly and openly hostile adventurism on the part of Communist nations such as Russia and Red China.

The attack on the military began in selected left-wing publications and cleverly played on the nation's weariness and discouragement over the failure of our efforts in Vietnam. The buildup from there was steady and concentrated to such an extent that soon general purpose publications were sending out teams of reporters and writers to analyze and judge something the left wing habitually described as a Military-Industrial Complex.

There is no way to overestimate the enormous attempt made to create a bogeyman out of the so-called MIC. Conveniently forgotten were such accurate World War II descriptions of America's defense machinery as the "Arsenal of Democracy" and the "Warehouse of Freedom." Any description that signified credit, or merely did not fit into the connotation of the MIC as something evil, was studiously shunned.

Instead, the poor old MIC rapidly became the major cause of inflation, the principal reason why slums and ghettos were not eradicated, the biggest cause of continued poverty in an affluent nation.

In line with these charges, careful attempts were made to cast reflections on the men most directly involved in providing the organization and the machinery for American defense. For example, a great furor was raised in the Senate and in the public press over charges that 2,000 former military officers had gone to work in defense-related industries after they retired from military service. It is sufficient here to say that the former military officer in this country has every right to seek employment in private industries which can best utilize his training and educational attainments. By the same token, it stands to reason that defense industries are obliged to seek the most competent and efficient and productive help they can obtain in carrying out the all-important task of contributing to the safety and security of American men, women and children.

There is nothing evil or suspect about large numbers of retired military men going to work at jobs that they have spent almost a lifetime understanding; nor is it strange or unusual that defense industries—like government itself—seek the best qualified personnel for the task at hand. Of course, the perpetrators of this blanket attack on all things military outwitted themselves on numerous occasions. On the one hand they credited the MIC with some great, ingenious conspiracy to hoodwink the American people, while on the other, they were charging that military men as a class are rather stupid.

In another phase of this concerted attack on American defense was the provision of forums which could be used as sounding boards for leveling any and all kinds of attack on American military.

In this respect good use was made of the Joint Economic Subcommittee on Government Expenditures headed by Senator William Proxmire of Wisconsin. I have on many occasions on the Senate floor complimented the Senator for the very fine job he did on ferreting out waste and inefficiency in the expenditure of our defense appropriations. However, I also made no secret of my belief that the job should have been done when the policies of waste and inefficiency were being cemented into our procurement system by Secretary McNamara and his misguided belief that "cost effectiveness" was totally applicable to a department engaged in planning for the protection of human beings. How Mr. McNamara or any of his "whiz kids" could effectively gauge the cost of one human life—to say nothing of thousands or millions of lives—was never explained during his regime, nor to my knowledge even considered. Cost effectiveness was an argument used by Secretary McNamara to kill off programs he didn't like. Significantly, it was not used to throw a multi-billion-dollar contract for the ill-fated TFX fighter plane to the highest bidder.

It is my feeling further that the effect of some of the reports put out by the Proxmire subcommittee as well as some of the statements made by its members contributed heavily to the effort to downgrade very substantially the entire concept of needed defense expenditures.

I believe it is time that questions relating fundamentally to the defense of this nation should be placed in their proper perspective. Let us take the Military-Industrial Complex and examine it closely. What it amounts to is that we have a big military establishment, and we have a big industrial plant which helps to supply that establishment. This apparently constitutes a "complex." If so, I certainly can find nothing to criticize but much to be thankful for in its existence. Ask yourselves, for example, why we have a large, expensive military establishment and why we have a large and capable defense industry. The answer is simply this: We have huge worldwide responsibilities. We face tremendous worldwide challenges. In short, we urgently require both a big defense establishment and a big industrial capacity. Both are essential to our safety and to the preservation of freedom in a world fraught with totalitarian aggression.

Merely because our huge responsibilities necessitate the existence of a Military-Industrial Complex does not automatically make the complex something we must fear or feel ashamed of. You might consider where we would be in any negotiations which might be entered into with the Soviet Union if we did not have a big military backed by a big industrial complex to support our arguments. You might wonder how we could possibly pretend to be interested in the freedom of smaller nations if the only Military-Industrial Complex in the world was possessed by Communist Russia or Communist China.

In many respects I am reminded of the problem which confronted our nation in the early days of World War II. The madman Hitler was running rampant. Freedom was being trampled throughout all of Europe. Suddenly the United States found itself forced to fill the role of the "Arsenal of Democracy." This nation had to start from scratch and finally out-produce the combined efforts of the Axis powers. And we had to do it quickly. The very existence of freedom in the world as we knew it in the early 1940's depended on it. And how did we perform this miracle? Well, I'll tell you that we performed it with the help of an industrial giant called an integrated steel industry. Although this industry and others like it performed miracles of production at a time when the chips were down all over the world, it still was the subject of long and harassing investigations after the war because of its "bigness."

Incredible as it seems, the very size of an industry which enabled us to defeat the Nazi and the Fascist armies and remain free became the reason for investigation by liberals in the Congress during the immediate post-war period.

We never seem to understand that size is not necessarily an evil.

When the Russian Sputnik went up, this nation was deeply concerned. And that concern had to do with our inability at that time to duplicate the Soviet feat. Now that we have the industrial capacity to equal the Russians in space or in matters related to defense, there seems to be a nationwide effort to make us feel guilty.

What would the critics of the Military-Industrial Complex have us do? Would they have us ignore the fact that progress occurs in the field of national defense as well as in the field of social sciences? Do they want us to turn back the clock, disband our military establishment and do away with our defense-related industrial capacity? Do these critics of what they term a Military-Industrial Complex really want us to default on our worldwide responsibilities, turn our backs on aggression and slavery and develop a national policy of selfish isolation?

Rather than deplore the existence of a Military-Industrial Complex, I say we should thank heavens for it. That complex gives us our protective shield. It is the bubble under which our nation thrives and prospers. It is the armor which is unfortunately required in a world divided.

For all those who rant and rave about the Military-Industrial Complex, I ask this question: What would you replace it with?

What's more, I believe it is fair to inquire whether the name presently applied is inclusive enough. Consider the large number of scientists who contributed all of the fundamental research necessary to develop and build nuclear weapons and other products of today's defense industries. Viewing this, shouldn't we call it the "Scientific-Military-Industrial Complex"? By the same token, don't forget the amount of research that has gone on in our colleges and universities in support of our defense-related projects. Maybe we should call it an "Educational-Scientific-Military-Industrial Complex." Then, of course, the vast financing that goes into this effort certainly makes the economic community an integral part of any such complex. Now we have a name that runs like this: "An Economic-Educational-Scientific-Military-Industrial Complex."

What we are talking about is an undertaking which grew up from necessity. It is the product of American initiative, incentive and genius responding to a huge global challenge. It is perhaps the most effective and efficient complex ever built to fill a worldwide function. Its ultimate aim is peace in our time regardless of the aggressive, militaristic image which the left wing is attempting to give it.

I don't find the employment of military officers by 100 of the largest companies in this nation alarming or menacing. Many of those officers were technically trained to provide special services, many of which are required by the companies involved. And I hasten to point out that these same companies employ other free Americans, some of them former Senators, some of them former Congressmen, some of them former civilian employees of the government. It is my contention that a retired military officer is a private citizen. He has a right to seek employment wherever he can. It is only natural that he should look to sources of employment which involve matters he was trained to work in. The fact that he once was an Army officer and the company he works for does business with the Army does not automatically insure an undesirable relationship from the public viewpoint. I would like to say that anyone who has evidence of wrongdoing, of deliberate and unlawful favoritism in the dealings which involve defense industries and former military officers should come forth and make the circumstances clear. I say that anyone who has evidence that a conspiracy exists between the Pentagon on one hand and former military officers on the other should say so and produce evidence to back it up. I say that anyone who charges that a "military elite" is at work trying to turn the United States into an aggressive nation should stop dealing in generalities and come forward with names, specific dates, meeting place locations, and all the rest of the kind of data it takes to back up such a charge.

So far I have yet to hear of any specific case of wrongdoing involving former military officers working for companies that do business with the Pentagon. In fact, I believe the record will show that the largest single cloud ever to hang over the so-called Military-Industrial Complex stemmed from decisions made by civilian officers in the Department of Defense. I am, of course, speaking about the incredible circumstances surrounding the awarding of the largest defense contract in the history of the world to a company whose bid had been rejected by nearly all the military specialists and evaluation boards in the Pentagon. The contract was the multi-billion-dollar TFX contract which former Defense Secretary Robert McNamara, former Navy Secretary Fred Korth, and former Undersecretary of Defense Roswell Gilpatrick jammed down the throats of the Navy and Air Force.

This was undoubtedly the costliest fumble in American history. It has never been properly dealt with, and I suggest to those who are sincerely interested in the dangers of a Military-Industrial Complex becoming too powerful in this nation that a full investigation be launched into all aspects of the TFX-F111 fiasco. I would recommend that the activities of all present and former military and civilian officials involved in the awarding of the TFX contract be examined.

This action should be taken despite the fact that the F-111 is now a very good plane. The Air Force, in cooperation with the manufacturers, has managed to eliminate most of the bugs which plagued this aircraft during the tenure of former Defense Secretary McNamara. Even so, circumstances surrounding the awarding of the initial TFX contract should be explored.

I want to be fully understood in this respect. If there is wrongdoing, whether of a conflict of interest nature or something else, in our defense establishment I want it investigated and stopped and the guilty parties punished. And this goes for wrongdoing by anyone concerned, whether he be a military man, a former military man, a defense industry executive, or a civilian officer of the government. I feel that this is our true concern. Maybe the hugeness of the system which we are now compelled to maintain does lend itself to improprieties. If so, let us concern ourselves with such improprieties and find means to deal with them legislatively. This is the constructive way to proceed. It does no good for us to gaze with awe on the tremendous increase in defense expenditures with which the McNamara era saddled us and then pretend that denunciation of a Military-Industrial Complex will somehow make it all right.

In the attacks on the military also you will find repeated reference to a speech once made by former President Eisenhower.

But I would remind you that when Dwight Eisenhower mentioned the possibility of unwarranted influence being acquired by such a complex, he had some other profound things to say. I want to quote one passage in particular. He said, and I quote, "We face a hostile ideology—global in scope, atheistic in character, ruthless in purpose and insidious in method. Unhappily the danger it poses promises to be of indefinite duration. To meet it successfully, there is call for, not so much the emotional and transitory sacrifices of crisis, but rather those which enable us to carry forward steadily, surely, and without complaint the burdens of a prolonged and complex struggle—with liberty the stake. Only thus shall we remain, despite every provocation, on our charted course toward permanent peace and human betterment. . . .

"A vital element in keeping the peace is our military establishment. Our arms must be mighty, ready for instant action, so that no potential aggressor may be tempted to risk his own destruction."

As I have pointed out, many of the problems that are being encountered in the area of national defense today stem not so much from a Military-Industrial Complex as they do from the mistakes and miscalculations of a "Civilian Complex" or perhaps I should say a "Civilian-Computer Complex." My reference here, of course, is to the Pentagon hierarchy of young civilians (often referred to as the "whiz kids") which was erected during the McNamara era in the questionable name of "cost effectiveness." And this complex was built in some measure to shut out the military voice in a large area of defense policy decision-making.

I suggest that the Military-Industrial Complex is not the all-powerful structure that our liberal friends would have us believe. Certainly nobody can deny that this combination took a drubbing at the hands of Mr. McNamara and his civilian cadres during the past eight years.

If the Military-Industrial Complex had been as strong and as cohesive as its critics would have us believe, it is entirely possible this nation and its taxpayers would not today be facing the need for rebuilding the defenses of freedom. I have already mentioned one example. The TFX decision which has proven to be such a costly fiasco was made by the civilian complex against the advice of experienced military men.

If the Military-Industrial Complex had been the irresistible giant its critics describe, we would certainly today be better equipped. We would undoubtedly have a nuclear-powered navy adequate to the challenge presented by Soviet naval might. We would certainly have in the air—and not just on a drawing board—a manned, carry-on bomber. We would never have encountered the kind of shortages which cropped up in every area of the military as a result of the demands from Vietnam. There would have been no shortage of military helicopters. There would have been no shortage of trained helicopter pilots. There would have been no need to use outdated and faulty equipment. No concern ever would have arisen over whether our supply of bombs was sufficient to the task in Southeast Asia.

I want to point out that a very strong case can be made for the need for a more powerful Military-Industrial Complex than we have had during the past eight years. At the very least, I wish to say that the employment practices of industries doing business with the Pentagon—practices which lead them to hire the most knowledgeable men to do their work—are no cause for shock. Nor are these practices dangerous to the American people.

I have great faith in the civilian leaders of our government and of our military services. I have no desire to see the voice of the military become all-powerful or even dominant in our national affairs. But I do believe that the military viewpoint must always be heard in the highest councils of our government in all matters directly affecting the protection and security of our nation.

Now I am one of the first to admit that even justified defense costs are becoming a heavy financial burden on the American taxpayer. And while I believe that we must take a hard look at every defense budget presented to the Congress, I do not feel that costs alone should be the ruling factor in any decision on Federal spending priorities. Where defense expenditures are involved, the overriding concern must always be the national interest and the security of the American people. I believe, with most other conservatives, that sound judgment and wise planning must be the implements used to reduce our military overhead. In this area I am very distrustful of arbitrary reduction figures and spending ceilings and pat-sounding mechanisms for coming to grips with the problems of defense costs.

For example, I am not about to come up with any easy-sounding solution such as the nationalization of defense industries doing more than 75 percent of their total business with the government. I have no desire, believe me, to extend the bureaucratic arm of the Federal Government, especially into the field of private enterprise. To understand how ridiculous nationalization would be, you might consider how long it would take us to receive delivery on a new plane if Lockheed or North American Aviation or Boeing or any of the other defense contractors were being operated with that marvelous bureaucratic efficiency with which our Post Office is run.

Critics of the military are always talking about the need for a dialogue on the important questions involved in the military budget and national economic priorities. I would like to see a dialogue too, but I must, in truth, say that from what I have read in the papers, the liberals seem interested only in providing sounding boards for those who want to criticize various facets of our military establishment or our foreign policy. And this does not make for a serious dialogue on where the defense of this nation should stand in any list of priorities.

For example, everytime that Secretary Laird tries to explain the necessity of a system like the ABM or MIRV, the hue and cry immediately is raised that he is attempting to frighten the American people. This is sheer demagoguery.

In stating the problems that face this nation on a worldwide basis from a militant, aggressive Communist nation like Soviet Russia, I do not believe the Secretary is engaging in a deliberate effort to frighten the American people. If the truth is frightening, so help me that's the way it's going to have to be. Because the American people have had enough of secrecy and distortion from the Pentagon, whether they be called justifiable lying in the name of national security, such as we used to hear from gentlemen like Assistant Defense Secretary Arthur Sylvester, or whether they are in the form of false information about low bids, efficiency performances, procurement practices, the American people have had enough from the Pentagon that sounds like cost effectiveness but which was really waste and inefficiency.

I am convinced that the American people want the truth about their government and about the challenges which face us as a nation. If the truth is frightening, if it gives us cause for concern, I am convinced that the American people will be able to cope. I don't want anyone in the present administration, particularly in the Defense Department, glossing over the true situation that confronts the American taxpayers and their collective security.

We are faced with a challenge, and let me say that it is not Secretary Laird nor President Nixon who is arranging the formidable military buildup in the Soviet Union. Nor do we know the facts of this buildup from their information alone. Many independent sources, including the British Institute for Strategic Studies, have also laid out the cold, hard facts of a Soviet armaments buildup.

The plain fact is the Soviet Union is building up all facets of its military capacity. Its nuclear capabilities are being extended. Its navy is being enlarged. All of its conventional arms are on the increase. The SS-9 missile is on an increased production schedule. They are spending a growing portion of their national income on military hardware.

These items are not related as a scare tactic; they are reported because they are facts. And I believe this nation has got to face these facts and the overall fact of a worldwide challenge to the United States in deciding about the disposition of military expenditures now and in the future.

I do *not* mean by this that there should be any condoning of or acquiescing in waste and inefficiency and extravagance in the military establishment. I believe that we must do everything in our power to eliminate waste and inefficiency and extravagance in the Pentagon and in all other departments of this sprawling, hard-to-manage Federal system.

President Nixon shares this view. In fact, in his speech at the United States Air Force Academy, he urged the graduates to be "in the vanguard of the movement" to eliminate waste and inefficiency and demand clear answers on procurement policy.

The new administration found out when it took over that the Defense Department over the preceding eight years had loaded the taxpayers of this country with billions of dollars that were unnecessarily spent.

But, I do believe that when the Congress begins to investigate and report on billions of dollars of the taxpayers' money lost in the Pentagon, it is, to some degree, reporting on its own delinquency.

We have to remember that no one forced the Congress to approve these funds. Those huge defense budgets over the past eight years were subject to Congressional inquiry. Nobody actually jammed them down our throats.

While I was not in Congress from 1964 to 1968, I have a pretty fair idea of what went on in the matter of defense expenditures prior to that time. And I want to say that it was no mystery to well informed and inquiring people that things were terribly wrong at the Pentagon and in its procurement procedures.

As a matter of fact, the TFX fighter bomber case alone was sufficient to point us in that direction. I say again, there was no mystery. Many stories were written about the investigative efforts of Senators McClellan, Jackson, Curtis and Mundt directed at cutting away some of the confusion and some of the misinformation that was being used to cover up a very, very bad piece of procurement by the Pentagon.

Now this was a big case. It involved billions of dollars. And it was a case where a multi-billion-dollar contract was awarded to the highest bidder for a plane over the advice of practically every expert in the military services affected.

As I say, there was no mystery about all this. Books were written on the subject. I have read a book called "The Pentagon" written by Washington correspondent Clark Mollenhoff in 1967 and another volume by the same author called "The Despoilers of Democracy." Both of these books told a frightening story of waste and inefficiency, extravagance and favoritism in the Department of Defense.

Now these were not generalities. Mr. Mollenhoff and reporters like him dealt with specific facts about the waste and inefficiency and squandering of the taxpayers' money in the Department of Defense. But I don't recall any outpouring of criticism aimed at the so-called Military-Industrial Complex. I don't recall any efforts to take a more than customary look at every facet of the defense budget. I don't recall either any strenuous attempt by any group in Congress to establish a system of priorities for this nation's critical needs.

Perhaps we failed in this respect because of the public relations ability of former Defense Secretary Robert McNamara.

As the *Washington Post,* in an article by Richard Harwood and Laurence Stern, observed on June 4:

"McNamara became a liberal hero despite the Bay of Pigs, the Dominican intervention and the war in Vietnam and despite the steadily rising costs of the military establishment (from $47 billion in 1961 to more than $80 billion today)."

I believe we must remember that it was McNamara, and not Laird, who presided over the Defense Department when all the waste and inefficiency and cost overruns were being piled up. He is the man I suspect who should have been called as a witness in the Proxmire hearings on waste and inefficiency in defense procurement. The Congress certainly ought to know what the man who decided the destinies of this huge undertaking for so long a period of time has to say about the mess that the incoming administration found when it took over the Pentagon.

In this connection, I twice urged Senator Proxmire to call Mr. McNamara as a witness in his hearings on waste in the Defense Department. Each time I was advised that the former Secretary's duties as President of the World Bank were so heavy that he could not find time to testify.

So much for past history. Now I believe it is time for Congress to direct its attention to how best it can come to grips with the current problem.

I am greatly concerned over the high cost of defense. It worries me greatly, but at the same time I recognize that the kind of emphasis which is continuously being placed on this problem could result in a dangerous lowering of our overall needed defense outlays.

I firmly believe in a system of priorities for the spending of Federal money. I have long advocated this and believe it should be as important a part of the process of spending in government as it is in the operation of a business or spending in our private lives. I believe such a system of priorities should not be confined only to broad subjects such as welfare, housing, urban problems and military spending and decisions as to which should come first, second, third or fourth. I believe it must be extended into every detail of these structures.

I believe there is no excuse for waste and inefficiency in any area of government, whether it is in the procedures and practices which have grown up in the Pentagon over the past eight years or in the expenditures for anti-poverty projects such as the Job Corps, or in expenditures for highways, schools and hospitals.

But the mere existence of waste and cost overruns and similar problems in military procurement must not be allowed to blind this country to the need for keeping its defenses strong. Nor should the inflated cost of military hardware become the overriding consideration in determining our level of defense expenditures.

Now on the question of inflated costs, it stands to reason that rising prices are not peculiar to defense projects alone. I say that this is an important factor which must be considered carefully.

We must recognize, for example, that testimony before the Senate Armed Services Committee indicates that perhaps as much as $500 million of the growing cost of the C-5A cargo plane is attributable to inflation. But at the same time, if the C-5A is considered essential to the defense of this nation, we must grit our teeth and accept the burden.

For if we permit rising costs to become the sole determining factor in deciding whether an essential program is to be developed, then we must automatically call into question such projects as the International Highway System, and programs for building new schools, new hospitals and additional housing. In this connection, the Department of Transportation reports that in less than eight years the cost of the Federal Interstate Highway System has increased by an estimated $15 billion and no extra miles are involved.

A study in Montgomery County, Maryland, shows that an elementary school which cost $347,772 in 1959 cost $666,200 to build in 1969. A high school in that same county which cost $2.3 million in 1959 is priced at $3.4 million today. The same skyrocketing price structure runs throughout all government as well as private costs. This is the price we are now paying for a period of uncontrolled public spending. And here, too, the Congress must assume its share of the blame.

But we still come back to the basic premise which led President Nixon to say that he has no choice in his defense decisions "but to come down on the side of security." In other words, regardless of inflation and other factors, the security of 204 million Americans is nonnegotiable.

Regardless of the emphasis placed on the need for economy, it is a mistake to believe that all critics of the Pentagon are motivated by a mere concern for the taxpayers. The most vocal of these critics want, not only authority over expenditures, but a voice in the actual decision-making processes of the nation's military establishment.

For example, Economist John Kenneth Galbraith, who has much more to say about the military considerations than his background warrants, is highly critical of the Pentagon's so-called "Blue Ribbon" panel on wasteful buying procedures. Because of his many public statements deploring defense expenditures, the panel understandably asked Professor Galbraith for his advice. It is entirely possible that members of the panel felt Mr. Galbraith had some interest in constructive suggestions for eliminating waste. In this they were mistaken, because the only advice the liberal professor had to offer to a conscientious group seeking ways and means of reducing unnecessary government expenditures was that it should disband.

Professor Galbraith's reasoning was no better than his advice. He explained it in a letter to Gilbert W. Fitzhugh, chairman of the panel, who is also chairman of the Metropolitan Life Insurance Company. This is what Galbraith had to say:

"You are studying the Pentagon subject only to the limitation that what it does, including what it buys, is outside of your charter. . . . You cannot afford to be associated with anything that is so patently and transparently and even hilariously a fraud. . . . I urge you . . . to get out of this one at once."

To this Mr. Fitzhugh replied:

"It is true that basic national policies are outside our jurisdiction but we feel there is a large area remaining as to how the Department of Defense can best implement the policies finally decided upon."

The blue ribbon panel had been created by President Nixon in June of 1969 during heated attacks from the liberal community on the Military-Industrial Complex, the Pentagon, and the military in general. But it did not satisfy Mr. Galbraith nor move him to join in an intelligent, reasonable discussion of defense expenditures. This was because the panel's instructions did not include considerations of basic national policy for priority within which the Defense Department carries out its assigned functions. As Galbraith put it in his letter to Fitzhugh, the President's commission couldn't consider whether money is being spent unnecessarily on nuclear aircraft carriers, the ABM, "the gold plating of that tank, or support to the indigent armies around the world."

In other words, Professor Galbraith's complaint was that the commission of wasteful procurement was not arbitrarily awarded the power of the Commander-in-Chief, the Joint Chiefs of Staff, and the heads of our various branches of service. He made it perfectly plain that policy, not waste, is the major concern of many leftists who criticize the Department of Defense. It is within the ranks of those critics who would like Congressional economizers to begin making vital decisions about strategic weapons that we find most of the genuine architects of unilateral disarmament.

Thus, it is always important to look carefully at the criticism made of our Defense Department in the name of economy and the saving of the taxpayers' dollars for ulterior motives. This is especially important when the screams for economy come from that part of the political spectrum—the liberals—which never in the past has concerned itself about extravagance in the expenditure of the taxpayers' money.

VI

The Legacy from Big Labor

A CARTOON PUBLISHED IN *Look* MAGAZINE ON DECEMBER 20, 1969, showed a couple in a metropolitan area preparing a shopping list. The wife standing by with pad and pencil has this to say to her husband: ". . . candles for power failure, plastic bag for Sanitation Department strike, canned goods for a grocery strike, and bottled water for a water main strike. Want to add anything to that list?"

The cartoon was meant to be hilarious, and this assumption could be made only because the residents of New York City and many other metropolitan communities have in recent years found themselves in the position of depending on modern, up-to-date services that all of a sudden ceased to exist for an extended period of time.

Most city dwellers could have added to that unusual shopping list. Many might have wanted to include the purchase of extra shoes for use during a bus strike or transit shutdown. Some would want to make sure they did not forget to purchase an out-of-town or underground newspaper to help them keep up with the day-to-day developments while the papers they ordinarily depended upon were on strike. Many additions could be made to such a list. And the situation has comic aspects only in retrospect.

Like most Americans possessed of a sense of humor, New Yorkers today can look back on the strike of the sanitation workers, when garbage was piling up on their front walks many feet deep, with a wry smile. But at the time of this crisis, when the sanitation union was deadlocked with the city administration and completely ignoring the health and the convenience of New York City residents, the situation was grim and almost desperate. It was at times like these that the American citizen began to question seriously a policy of permissiveness toward labor unions which had existed for so long a time that even the convenience and the well-being of the general public could not be allowed to interfere with what the union bosses' wanted.

In many areas and in many industries, arrogance and power of unreasonable leaders have been self-defeating. Many small businesses with a high employment potential have been forced to give up the attempt to exist in a free enterprise economy so heavily balanced by law toward the side of organized labor. In city after city, newspapers have gone out of business or merged with their competitors because of the impossibility of meeting the demands of several highly organized labor unions and trying to make a profit.

So far the loss of this existing employment pool and future potential reserve has had no restraining effect on the union leaders. They have been taught by long years of special privilege to expect special treatment. The liberal politicians have been guilty of providing extraordinary rights, privileges and immunities under the law for organized labor. They have also over the years zealously made sure that these privileges were not withdrawn. And many of them have been handsomely repaid and rewarded for their efforts through union political and financial support at the polls.

Union arrogance in this second year of the Nixon Administration calls out for the development of a new national labor policy. What is needed, and has been needed for many years, is a thorough reexamination of all the laws on the books regarding unions and a redrafting in code form of a body of law which will insure the American worker of his rights and freedoms in the working society and which will demand of the unions a degree of legal and financial responsibility equal to that which is now required of corporations.

It has been said many times that Lord Acton's rule (power corrupts; and absolute power corrupts absolutely) is especially applicable to the union problem. Long years of special consideration at the hands of politicians and lawmaking bodies alike brought on a degree of corruption so widespread in the union movement that it was necessary to enact the Landrum-Griffin bill of 1958. And while graft and corruption were the evils at which the Landrum-Griffin bill was aimed, it must also be recognized that graft and corruption

were merely the symptoms of the illness in the labor movement. The
cause of it is the tremendous concentration of economic and political
power in the hands of union leaders.

There is nothing new about this situation except that it has
now grown into such a troublesome national crisis that action on a
broad front is becoming imperative. I say there is nothing new in
the problem of overconcentration of power in the hands of the labor
unions because it has been pointed out many times in the past. I,
myself, made a big point of this unhealthy superstructure of power a
decade ago in my book "The Conscience of a Conservative." The
situation was not new then, but it has not changed. It is not new
now, but it is vastly more important in terms of the welfare of the
American people and the future of the American economy as a free
and viable entity.

In my earlier book I described the amassing of union power as
a development that "hurts the nation's economy by forcing on employers contract terms that encourage inefficiency, low production,
and high prices—all of which result in a lower standard of living
for the American people.

"It corrupts the nation's political life by exerting undue influence in the selection of public officials.

"It gravely compromises the freedom of millions of individual
workers who are able to register a dissent against the practices of
union leaders only at the risk of losing their jobs."

In the very beginning of my career as a United States Senator,
you might say I cut my teeth on the problem of overwhelming
union power. As a member of the Senate Labor Committee in the
days of the late Senator Robert A. Taft, I obtained a thorough and
invaluable training in the problems arising from the overbalancing
power and influence of the big union bosses. And I also learned
that there was an automatic price to be paid for criticizing the power
of big labor. I learned very early in my first Senate term that anyone
who had the temerity and the courage to challenge the authority of
the union bosses would be labeled as anti-labor and anti-union. No
matter how strong the incentive to freedom, no matter how strong
the desire to protect the rights of the individual worker, if lawmakers' statements or actions in any way reflect upon the union structure and the leadership hierarchy, they automatically become the
subject of intensive abuse. They also earn the financial and or-

ganizational opposition of the union bosses in any future political endeavors they might attempt.

In 1958, when I was seeking reelection to the United States Senate, I was not surprised to find my public criticism of labor leaders like the late Walter Reuther of the United Auto Workers and others had earned me the designation as "target for defeat." It was no surprise either to me or to my Republican constituency in Arizona when large amounts of union money and union manpower were funneled into Arizona in a frank attempt to silence Goldwater.

It did not work, I am happy to say, and more and more today I am gratified to find that union political power is no longer the omnipotent force that it once could claim to be. Today more and more American workers are thinking for themselves and voting their own minds and their own interests despite what the union leaders tell them. No longer is the flat endorsement of a union leader sufficient to guarantee election in industrial areas of the country. In some areas, indeed, union endorsement can be called a liability. In some areas, but not enough, I am sorry to say, the activities of organized labor's political arm—the Committee on Political Education (COPE)—were sufficient to guarantee renewed efforts on the part of the candidates they sought to defeat.

Now, it is very easy to convince thousands of people that anyone who opposes union power is automatically against the laborer and is engaged in grinding an ax for corporate management. But it has been my experience that the men in the Congress of the United States who have honestly attempted to come to grips with this grave problem are not against the working man, are not in league with employers and management and capital interests, but are sincere legislators worried about a dangerous lack of balance between our big economic forces—big business, big labor and big government.

Of course, I speak only for myself, but I do believe wholeheartedly in labor unions. I believe that unions serve an important purpose and, when kept within reasonable and proper bounds, accomplish a positive good for our nation. Unions have proven to be the instrument for achieving economic justice for the working man. In addition, they provide an alternative to collectivists' movements such as state socialism. But most of all they are an expression of freedom, and it should be thoroughly understood that my concern has nothing to do with those drives which periodically arise in this country to abolish unions and prohibit the right to strike. I have made it clear throughout my entire public life that I think the right to strike is the one that should be protected because it is an expression of freedom. By the same token, I am against compulsory arbitration because I believe that is a denial of freedom.

And I have long admitted my support for the movement which destroyed the monopoly held by management in the early days of this country. In other words, I believe that the laws to protect the working man's right to organize and bargain collectively were long overdue when they were finally written into the statute books of this country. The pendulum had too long been adverted to the side of management. It was time for an evening up; it was time for a swinging of the pendulum away from undue privilege and power for management in the direction of better-balanced power with unions and government. But as so often is the case, the pendulum became a popular swinging device, and do-gooders and liberals of all hues joined in pushing too far. Thus arose the enormous power and privilege and sanction and immunity under the law that the huge American unions enjoy today to the detriment of a great and growing and even more demanding society.

There is no suggestion here to abolish labor unions or to take away from them the gains which they have made and which they deserve; rather the urging here is to restore the balance and place the unions in their proper role in a free enterprise society.

The free operation of our labor unions is one of the ultimate expressions of freedom of association. The freedom to associate with other men or not to associate is a fundamental freedom of choice which should be enjoyed by all men. And in this context, I firmly believe that the element of compulsion, no matter where it enters into the labor picture, is destructive of freedom. It is for this reason that I oppose compulsory arbitration in the settlement of union contract disputes, and it is the strongest reason why I oppose compulsory unionism. I know that the phrase "right to work" has become misunderstood, misinterpreted and even stigmatized by big labor bosses who regard laws designed to protect this right as dangerous to their union power. However, I believe a man should have the right not to join a union and that this right should be as well protected under law as his right to join a union without interference. After all, this is a human right. I have never been able to understand why public officials who claim to be dedicated to the principle of civil rights and civil liberties are opposed to laws which would protect the right of a man to work without coercion or compulsion.

While I firmly believe that conditions which exist today in our economy require the development of a new national labor policy, I believe that a conscientious national administration can do much to correct what is wrong. The starting point, I believe, has to be with an honest enforcement of the labor laws we now have on our books in a fair and impartial manner designed to carry out the intent of the Congress which enacted them. The Republican Platform of 1968 expressed a strong belief that the protection of individual liberty is the cornerstone of sound labor policy. And while we have laws to insure the freedom of the individual in matters of labor relations, the fact is that the job is not getting done. The Republican Platform of 1968 adopted in Miami put it this way:

"Today the basic rights of some workers, guaranteed by law, are inadequately guarded against abuse. We will assure these rights through vigorous enforcement of present laws, including the Taft-Hartley Act and the Landrum-Griffin Act, and the addition of new protections where needed. We will be vigilant to prevent any administrative agency entrusted with labor law enforcement from defying the letter and the spirit of these laws."

The last sentence in that pledge was aimed unmistakably at the National Labor Relations Board which, under previous administrations, too often subordinated the rights of individual workers to the interests of labor unions. In decision after decision the NLRB has acted for all the world like an organization erected under law to defend union power. Actually, the intent of the National Labor Relations Act is designed for the protection of the worker. The so-called "Kennedy-Johnson Board" has not only repealed the Landrum-Griffin Act aimed at union leadership, corruption and abuses, but has distorted and disregarded the intent of Congress in the enactment of the Taft-Hartley Act. Thanks to the Kennedy-Johnson NLRB, most of the safeguards devised by the Congress for the protection of the individual have been rendered ineffective. The administration of labor law by the NLRB has been twisted in such a way as to protect unions and leave the individual open to exploitation.

For example, in 1963 a young married steelworker on the West Coast grew dissatisfied with the representation he received at the hands of his local steelworkers' union. Consequently, he drove 50 miles to an NLRB regional office to inquire if he had any rights under the law. He was assured by a government attorney that he had the right to seek replacement of the steelworkers' local with another union, and he returned to work and began circulating a petition to decertify the local steelworkers' union. The result was drastic and immediate. The leaders of the local union scheduled a meeting to put the young man on a trial on charges of "undermining the union." The workers' request for a secret ballot was denied, and with less than a third of the local membership present, the president called for a show of hands. Needless to say, the complaining steelworker was "convicted," fined $500, suspended from the union, and charged with the costs of his trial.

He filed charges with the NLRB, and while awaiting their decision, became the target of continued union harassment. Finally, the Board handed down its decision, but it gave the young man no help and no protection.

The agency, designated by law to defend the rights of individual members, held that the young man had the "right" to file the petition against the local. But it also held that the union's "disciplinary action" against him was permissible.

The message provided by the case (Richard Price vs. NLRB and United Steelworkers of America, AFL-CIO #154 NLRB 690) was unmistakable. It demonstrated that when the rights of the individual collide with the rights of the union there is no question as to who the winner will be under the Johnson-Kennedy NLRB. One might ask where the fairness lies in a system that requires a man to belong to a union to hold his job and then lets that union choose to discipline him when he exercises his rights under the law.

Many other examples could be cited to show that the entire thrust of the labor board's action under the Kennedy-Johnson Administration has been to strengthen the power of labor unions at the expense of the rights of the rank-and-file employees. There could be absolutely no question that the power of the labor unions has reached into the National Labor Relations Board. It stands to reason that organizations with as much political muscle as today's big labor unions enjoy will undoubtedly have a voice in the selection of the men who sit on the agency which is supposed to regulate and administer the labor law.

But it doesn't stop here. Even if the big unions did not get just about everything they wanted from the Kennedy-Johnson labor relations board, they have always got recourse to the courts. Even if a new majority dedicated to interpreting the law in accordance with Congressional intent and in a manner which would defend the rights of the individual were to take over the NLRB, the unions could count on the final words. For example, the present Board has frequently been reversed in the circuit courts but often has gone on to be sustained in the Supreme Court, where the bias on behalf of union labor is a matter of public record.

There also have been some recent stirrings in Congress which recognize a dire need for some kind of corrective action where the National Labor Relations Board is concerned. For example, a Senate Judiciary Subcommittee on Separation of Powers several months ago issued a stinging report of NLRB activities based on a two-year investigation in line with a policy of Congressional oversight of administrative agencies. Among other things, the Subcommittee majority report had this to say:

> *On the basis of its study, the Subcommittee has found that in choosing between conflicting values—in difficult cases and in some that are not so difficult—the National Labor Relations Board has of late unreasonably emphasized the establishment and maintenance of collective bargaining and strong unions to the exclusion of other important statutory purposes which often involve the rights of individual employees. Unions unable to persuade a majority of employees to opt for collective bargaining have been able to get the Board to impose it for them. And the Board has been able to do this by a freewheeling interpretation of the statute's more general provisions, by applying double standards and by ignoring plain legislative mandates.*
>
> *The Board has also, we find, in matters going beyond recognition and the establishment of bargaining, given interpretations to the statute which reflect an overemphasis on helping unions impose their will on employers and individual employees. The Board clearly believes that it knows what is best for employees and all too frequently subordinated individual rights to the interest of organized labor.*

So blatant did the Subcommittee find the NLRB's bias to be in favor of the unions, it actually raised the threshold question of whether the Board should be retained in its present form. It found that the Board is not an adequate vehicle for the carrying out of Congressional purpose. It pointed out that where the Board has discretion, it exercises it without a fair weighing of competing factors; and where the NLRB's discretion is limited, it goes out of its way to find any means to work its own will.

A large part of the Subcommittee's criticism was aimed at the exercise of power by the General Counsel of the NLRB. In fact, the report puts it this way:

"It is the Subcommittee's conclusion that the General Counsel's independence and unreviewable authority to issue complaints has been abused and that the lack of any check on that power has permitted it to be exercised arbitrarily and lawlessly."

Needless to say, the exercise of this power in recent years has greatly benefited the position of organized labor.

How does union labor get the power which gives it influence in government regulatory agencies, in the highest courts in the land, and in the Congress of the United States? Perhaps some statistical estimates from the last national election will be helpful. Neutral observers have estimated that between $60 million and $100 million was spent by labor in the national elections of 1968. It has further been estimated that COPE registered over 4.6 million new voters for those elections. From its headquarters in New York and regional headquarters throughout the country, COPE deluged the voters with a minimum of 115 million leaflets urging the election of labor candidates.

COPE itself is said to have reported to newsmen that some 24,000 union officials and volunteer squads used over 8,000 telephones in nearly 700 cities in the 1968 elections. At the very least, this would make in excess of 200 million calls that were made on behalf of candidates supported by the labor organizations. It is also worthy of note that labor availed itself of the newest, most sophisticated type of equipment in its political endeavors. Among these is said to be a huge vote-finding computer located in the headquarters of the Machinists Union.

These figures provide a fitting introduction for a discussion of what I think is one of the most serious problems demanding the attention of the Nixon Administration. My reference here is to the widespread use by unions of their members' dues money for political activities and for making cash contributions to political candidates which the unions have reason to believe will support their legislative and governmental aims.

This practice is downright inequitable because it involves money that is not freely given. The reason is that the dues are collected by the unions under compulsory union shop arrangements, with large numbers of workers having to pay dues to the unions against their will and with the knowledge that their money will be used to support candidates which the workers themselves may oppose. Regardless, the rank and file members have never had any voice in the decisions as to which candidates will be supported or opposed by the unions. Even elected officials at the local union level have no voice in these matters. Their function is to see to it that the dues money is collected and transmitted to COPE organizations.

In such an arrangement, freedom and the rights of the individual workers are completely ignored. By forcing a worker to support candidates and causes that he opposes, the union denies that worker his constitutionally protected freedom of association, freedom of speech, and freedom of political action. He also is deprived of property without due process of law.

The United States Supreme Court, in an action which I believe denies the very fundamental purpose for which the court was created, has refused to look into the constitutional aspects of compulsory union membership. However, not all of the members of the high court subscribe to this preferential attitude toward the unions. In one celebrated dissent (in the case of the Machinists Union vs. the Street, 367 U.S. 740) Justice Hugo Black had this to say:

> *There can be no doubt that the Federally sanctioned union shop contract here as it actually works takes a part of the earnings of some men and turns it over to others, who spend a substantial part of the funds so received in efforts to thwart the political, economic, and ideological hopes of those whose money has been forced from them under authority of law. This injects Federal compulsion into the political and ideological processes, a result which I have supposed everyone would agree the First Amendment was particularly intended to prevent.*

Doubtless, employers could make the same arguments in favor of compulsory contributions to an association of employers for use in political and economic programs calculated to help collective bargaining on their side. But the argument is equally unappealing whoever makes it. The stark fact is that this act of Congress is being used as a means to exact money from these employees to help get votes to win elections for their candidates and to support doctrines they are against. If this is Constitutional, the First Amendment is not the charter of political and religious liberty its sponsors believed it to be . . .

Indeed, nothing could be clearer. Up until now, the First Amendment and its guarantees of political liberty apparently do not apply to the "untouchables," i.e., the labor unions.

What's more, Federal statutes, written clearly and unmistakably in the law books, do not always apply where labor union activities in connection with their members' money are concerned. For in spending their members' money for political purposes, the unions are engaging in unlawful activity in direct violation of the Federal Corrupt Practices Act—an act which makes it a crime for any union to make any contribution or expenditure in connection with any election to Federal office, including President, Vice-President, Senator, or Representative. The act further provides for punishment by fine and imprisonment for any union official responsible for making or any candidate who receives any such contribution.

Although this criminal statute has been on the books since 1947, no serious effort has ever been made to enforce it; and as a result, the unions act as though it did not exist at all. I believe an administration committed to the vigorous enforcement of this law could perform a memorable service for individual freedom which would go a long way toward curbing a serious abuse of union power.

There are many other areas where unions are treated as something special and apart in our society in the administration of the law. For example, unions enjoy a tax exempt status under the Internal Revenue Code, and this alone should disqualify them from engaging in political activities. Section 501 (c) of the Internal Revenue Code lists various categories of exempt organizations among which are labor unions, fraternal clubs, religious, charitable and educational organizations, chambers of commerce, civic associations, etc. But of the more than two dozen groups listed, there is only one that can engage in political activities without being disqualified for tax exemption and that (you guessed it) is labor. A chamber of commerce group which spent any part of its funds for political purposes would quickly lose its exemption status. And the same would happen to a religious or educational organization, a social club, public welfare organization, or any of the others. Only one group enjoys the privilege: that special, politically powerful, influential group represented by the labor unions. This one group alone is permitted to engage in political action and still retain its tax exempt status.

Now why and how is such a situation allowed to exist? Is a labor organization more worthy than a church; or is it more important than a chamber of commerce; does it do better work than a public welfare organization? The answer, of course, is "no" all the way down the line.

One extremely interesting point pertains here. It is that there is nothing in the statutory language of the act which would authorize this special treatment for the unions, nor is there any legislative history to support it. It is purely and simply a position that has been followed by the Internal Revenue Service and one which was officially articulated for the first time under the Johnson Administration. In other words, this branch of the government says we will recognize the unions as tax exempt no matter how much of its money it spends for political purposes and notwithstanding the fact that the Federal Corrupt Practices Act makes such expenditures a Federal crime.

This almost incredible situation underscores indelibly the tremendous political influence wielded by organized labor under the previous administrations. It also underscores an area in which the Nixon Administration can take decisive action to correct an abusive power. It should be recognized that tax exemption is a privilege; and if unions are to continue to enjoy that privilege, they should be expected to abide by the same rules that pertain to other exempt organizations. There is no justification for carving out a special rule for unions, especially when this action, in effect, condones flagrant and persistent violations of a Federal criminal law.

Not only does a special rule for unions condone violations of the law, but it also causes distortions in the social and economic

life of the nation. For example, despite the strong liberal claims
of most of the union leaders, the unions themselves have been
guilty of practicing a type of racial discrimination which bears most
heavily upon the ability of America's minority to achieve an adequate standard of living.

This problem is not a new one, nor is it one with which I am
unfamiliar. During my membership on the Senate Labor and Public
Welfare Committee, I many times offered amendments to labor
relations bills which would deprive any union of benefits under the
Federal law if it should be found guilty of practicing discrimination against workers because of race, color or creed. These anti-
discrimination amendments were invariably erased from the bills
while they were still in committee. The erasures were performed,
of course, by the Democratic majority on that committee with the
help of some Republican liberals who argued that the inclusion of
such a provision would make the measure more difficult to pass on
the floor.

Through the years, then, the liberals who were talking the
loudest about civil rights were refusing to come to grips with a
problem of discrimination which not only affected the dignity of
American minority group workmen but also affected their ability to
obtain employment. This was a hard and fast pocketbook issue
where liberals who spoke so fluently and so often and so loudly
about the rights of the minority could have taken on a real job of
work to help these minority workers. The argument was always the
same. It ran something like this: If you write an anti-discrimination
provision into a labor-management bill, you will automatically insure the opposition of Southern members of the House and the
Senate. Therefore, the expedient approach would be to overlook
a provision aimed at the evils of job discrimination.

While I am not about to deny that this argument has some
basis in fact, I do not believe that of itself it was sufficient to war-
rant continued ignoring of the growing problem of union discrimination against black workers. This problem needed legislative
treatment many years ago, and it needs it today.

But I have noticed that some of our most outspoken liberals
are inclined to temper the vigor of their advocacy on issues that
might run counter to the desires of the large union leaders. Despite
all the glowing statements by Walter Reuther, George Meany and
other labor leaders, the fact remains that they have steadfastly over

the years refused to clean up their own house on the question of racial discrimination.

Much of the racial unrest in the North, especially in the metropolitan areas, has stemmed from the fact that many jobs were ruled out of bounds for black employees. The building trades in particular have offended in this regard through the use of artificial union barriers against the hiring of Negroes.

This situation is what led to the development of the administration's so-called "Philadelphia Plan." The plan involves the fixing of quotas for hiring of minority workers by government contractors. And regardless of what may ultimately be decided about the legality of permitting employers to set quotas of any kind on the basis of race or religion, the fact remains that the device was a direct result of restrictions used by the unions to prevent the hiring of black workers. As expected, George Meany has announced his opposition to the "Philadelphia Plan," and his action drew this very incisive comment from the National Republican Congressional Committee:

> *George Meany has revealed, by his opposition to the Administration's "Philadelphia Plan" designed to break down the artificial union barriers against hiring Negroes, that he is a captive of the past and is trying to continue the unions' old discriminatory apprentice practices into the present. Hobart Rowen, writing in the* Washington Post *(Jan. 18, 1970), notes that the unions require a four-year apprenticeship for carpenters. Yet most of them today only build forms for concrete work—a job that can easily be taught in 90 days. He notes the Air Force can "take a boy off the farm and train him to be a bomber and navigator in six months," but that the union requires five years to "train" a plumber. Rowen suggests that, to solve the employment and housing problems, the Federal Government may have to set up its own training programs on a realistic basis—aimed at turning out skilled workers, not bound by the 19th Century system employed by the unions. Meany's own salary has risen from $45,000 to $70,000 in four years—a 12 percent a year increase. Workers' wages in general went up 5.5 percent in 1967, 6.6 percent in 1968 and 8.2 percent in 1969.*

I believe there is great reason to hope that the problem of union discrimination against minority workers will eventually be overcome. However, I suspect that performance of this task may sorely strain some of the political ties (bonds fashioned out of financial and campaign support) now existing between the big union leaders and outstanding liberals in the House and the Senate.

But the economic consequences of an extended, years long period of government favoritism will be much more difficult to come to grips with. What we have allowed to happen can best be described as a distortion of the natural laws of supply and demand in a private free enterprise economy. We have done this by giving the unions too much power over the economic well-being of this nation by permitting them to control heavy cost factors in American industry. My reference here, of course, is to the great, seldom-mentioned factor in the whole picture of price inflation in the United States. That problem has to do with the inflationary aspects of higher and higher union wage hikes. It is the problem of wrestling with unions so powerful that they can demand and obtain from management wage increases which have no relation to increased productivity. It is the problem of union privilege distorting a nation's economy. It is the problem of unions becoming so powerful that they can force management and employers to disregard all the lessons of the past and all the historic applications of economic principles and grant wage increases far in excess of what is justified by the amount of labor performed.

And how did all this come about? There is no mystery. It has been an open secret in the Congress of the United States and the economic communities for many years. In looking over my records on labor union power, I came across a statement of my own which declared that "labor unions have attained their present size and strength, and hence their ability to defy the law as a result of a series of special benefits, rights, privileges, and immunities bestowed upon them by Federal law."

And that nine-year-old statement went on further to enumerate some of these privileges which are enjoyed by no other type of private organizations or institutions in our society. The enumeration was as follows:

1. Unions are immune from taxation.
2. Unions are practically immune under the anti-trust laws.

3. Unions are immune, in many situations, against the issuance of injunctions by Federal courts.

4. Unions can compel employees to join unions in order to hold their jobs.

5. Unions can use funds, which their members have been compelled to contribute in order to hold their jobs, to finance political programs and candidates which some of these members strongly oppose.

6. Unions have been given the absolute right to deny workers admission to union membership, and, in practical effect, are able to deny many workers access to jobs in general and to the higher-paying jobs in particular.

7. Unions have the exclusive right to act as collective bargaining agents even for those workers who either do not wish to join the union or who are excluded from membership in it, even arbitrarily.

8. Unions have the right, in some situations, to invade the privacy of workers, even against their will, thus depriving them of a legal right enjoyed by all other individuals in our society.

9. And finally, and of the greatest significance, the granting of these rights by Federal law has resulted in the exclusion of the states from many of the areas covered by these Federal laws, and the states may not lawfully act in these areas. This is known as the doctrine of Federal preemption.

But wage inflation is the big one for the 1970's. For we have moved from an inflation in which excess demand pulls up prices into an inflation in which big wage increases push up prices. The whopping wage increases of 1970 involved some 5 million workers in heavily organized American industry, including workers in the trucking, auto, rubber, meat packing, clothing and construction industries. Historically, wage increases are supposed to bear at least some comparison to an increased rate of worker productivity. However, favoritism and special privileges granted to the big unions in this country have effectively destroyed this historical ratio.

Since the late 1940's, wage costs in industry have risen more rapidly than efficiency. The result has been that employers have had no productivity cushion left after paying for wage increases. This means they have been unable to cut prices. Instead, they have had to raise prices steadily in order to obtain a margin for profit.

The disparity between increased productivity and increased

wages set something of a record in 1969. Government figures show that productivity increased approximately 3 percent during the year, but the union wage increases ran between 7 percent and 9 percent for the year.

In fact, the *Wall Street Journal* reported that wages during 1969 rose 8.2 percent as a median in union-negotiated contracts. The building trades got 11.9 percent boost.

We can see then that the wide and growing gap between annual wage rate increases and annual per man-hour output increases is the root cause of much price inflation. This is almost beyond argument, but it gets very little attention in the proper circles. I have been one of those who has been arguing for many years against the special privileges which we have granted the large labor unions through Federal law. I have, time and again, warned that we would someday reach a time of reckoning.

Now I believe that day of reckoning is at hand, and I don't believe that we are going to attack the root causes of this debilitating and discouraging price inflation until Congress develops some guts. Not until Congress takes action to cut down on the powers, the liberties, the immunities and the privileges of our large labor unions will we make the kind of progress which is needed.

And I can only cite to you the great power exercised by the union bosses in the Senate action in rejecting the nomination of Judge Clement Haynsworth for appointment to the Supreme Court as an example of their continuing influence. Many knowledgeable observers chalked up this administration defeat as a direct victory for union pressure.

But it also handed Senate liberals a sizable conflict of interest test which they flunked impressively.

Some of the most self-righteous of my colleagues who opted for absolute ethical purity in the case of the Haynsworth nomination neglected to apply the same standard to their own case in voting on an amendment to the tax reform bill last year.

The test of ethics came on an amendment to the bill sponsored by Senator Paul Fannin (R-Ariz.) which would have closed a major tax loophole by denying tax exemptions to labor unions that engaged in partisan political activities.

The amendment was offered in the same spirit that motivated liberal attempts to close loopholes that allow many organizations, such as the oil industry, foundations, even churches, to escape payment of their fair share of Federal income tax.

But the same people who argued that the law discriminated in favor of giants like the oil industry didn't carry their convictions to the point where they would apply to the giant labor unions and labor organizations.

Involved in the handling of the Fannin amendment was a direct and substantial conflict of interest for all Senators who depend on the labor unions for fat campaign contributions, not to mention help from union organizational muscles.

The National Right to Work Committee put the issue this way: "How, in good faith, can a United States Senator elected with money contributed from union officials (and collected mostly from compulsory union dues) vote fairly on a bill that would take away his source of re-election dollars?"

Applying what some people have come to describe as the "Haynsworth standard," it might have been expected that Senators with a substantial financial stake in the Fannin amendment might abstain from voting.

None of the liberals who devised the Haynsworth standard seemed to see any need for abstention—or any parallel in their actions on the labor amendment. Closing the tax loophole enjoyed by the big unions would at least have kept the Senate consistent with other votes on the tax reform bill. For example, it approved an amendment to halt the use of foundation money for political purposes.

Why are the labor unions given such heavy preference? There is nothing new in this approach. Many other tax exempt organizations have long been specifically prohibited from using their funds for political programs. It is a double standard in our present tax laws which permits union officials to extract money from millions of workers and spend the money on politics regardless of whether the workers object.

It wasn't hard to see what fate held in store for the Fannin amendment in the Democratic-controlled Senate. It was accurately forecast some months ago when the powerful Senate Finance Committee rejected a move to make the Fannin amendment part of the tax reform bill before it reached the Floor. The rejection came on a tie vote, with seven Republicans and Democrat Harry F. Byrd of Virginia supporting it.

The members voting to preserve labor's loopholes include such liberals as Senators Eugene McCarthy of Minnesota, J. William Fulbright of Arkansas, Russell Long of Louisiana, Albert Gore of Tennessee, Vance Hartke of Indiana, Abraham Ribicoff of Connecticut, and former Democratic National Chairman Fred Harris of Oklahoma.

Unfortunately, when it comes to closing a loophole or applying a standard of ethics in the Democrat-controlled Senate, it makes a large difference who is involved.

This being the case, I believe that the people most directly involved—call them "Forgotten Americans," "The Silent Majority," the "Unheard Consumers," or what you will—must be informed of the stakes involved in bringing this union power under some kind of reasonable management. We need, in short, an informed public. We need more and more spokesmen who know the root causes of inflation. It is the simple mathematical fact that a small percentage of increase in the huge sum paid to organized workers looms large in the price inflation. The public must be made to understand that liberal spokesmen who blame the entire inflation problem on increased corporate profits are playing the role of the demagogue.

I have a great confidence in the ability of the majority of the American people to reach the right conclusion once the facts are presented to them. Our current trouble is that we have not been diligent enough or determined enough to explain the economic facts of life in a fashion which can be readily understood.

Now I believe is the time to develop a public so well informed that it will overpower the influence of the union bosses in the halls of Congress. We now have an administration which is dedicated to sound fiscal policy. President Nixon has adequately proven his determination to cut down on unnecessary Federal spending and to strive to achieve the budget balance so necessary in the fight against inflation. It is time for unions and their leaders to display a degree of responsibility. And it is time for the Congress to make these powerful and integral segments of the national economy accountable for their actions.

PART

III

The Communications Media

CHAPTER

VII

The Press

No BOOK DEALING WITH PUBLIC AFFAIRS, POLITICAL ATTITUDES, AND the direction of our government can possibly be complete without giving attention to the nation's communications media. I am referring, of course, to those instruments through which our government, our politicians, our public officials and, indeed, all of our leaders and spokesmen, communicate with the great American public.

Time was when the only means of public expression was through direct contact with the people, then through the columns of the nation's newspapers. This, of course, was changed in the 1920's when a new dimension for communications and the transmitting of that substance known as "news" was added through the development of the radio as a household instrument. Since then, television receivers have given the vast majority of American people the visual access to many of the events which formerly were only read or heard about. It has been said that television has provided all Americans with a "window on the world."

In the era when newspapers had their heyday as the only means of transmitting developments of a general interest nature, a great deal was made of the concept of "freedom of the press." Newsmen still raise a great noise about this, but the concept has been enlarged to include all elements of the media. In the beginning, at least, the belief was that the majority of the nation's newspapers could attain a reasonable degree of objectivity and fairness in the presentation of the news. It is debatable whether the nation's press was even partially insulated from the wave of political, social, economic and even cultural partisanship which periodically swept the nation. But their freedom to be objective was jealously guarded.

Because of the advent of radio and television, however, the importance of the public information media has grown enormously. By the same token, its responsibility has grown even more. The media are now charged with keeping many more millions of people accurately informed than was the task once faced by the nation's newspapers and magazines. Instantaneous communications—now made possible via orbiting satellites from all corners of the globe—further underscore this responsibility.

Because of the enormous task which has grown up and because of its overwhelming importance, I believe it is nothing less than vital that in a book of this kind we examine very carefully the performance of the media and measure how well they are standing up to their new and enlarged and all-encompassing responsibility.

As a man who has spent most of his adult years in public life, most of them in the white-hot glare of political public attention, I claim a better than ordinary ability to make a judgment on press performance. There undoubtedly will be some who will contend that because of the treatment I received at the hands of the nation's press, radio and television in my campaign for the presidency in 1964 my viewpoint may be prejudiced in a critical direction.

It is fair to say that my experience in 1964 did not prejudice me in a noncritical direction. But I do deny that my intention here is either spiteful or vindictive. I fully recognize and acknowledge that no man can reach a completely objective conclusion about any series of events in which he played a major personal role. At the same time I insist that such a person is more capable than most others to realize how gravely important the responsibility facing the public information media really is. Such a person knows, from personal experience, how right or wrong the media have been in many given instances in reporting the true facts in a hotly contested situation.

Even allowing for an individual participant's personal bias, his experience in the overheated kitchen of a nationwide presidential campaign affords him a golden opportunity to see and to understand and to gauge such questions as (1) the degree of objectivity on the part of the press, radio and television newsmen, (2) the degree of error which innocently might enter into the media's reporting of a given event, (3) the degree of deliberate arranging of questions designed to bring about a preconceived news-type conclusion, (4) the degree of deliberate bias in the reporting of a situation, and even (5) the degree of opportunity presented by the mechanics of news gathering and reporting and publishing to those persons who would deliberately, with malice aforethought, attempt to portray the wrong conclusion and make it appear as a legitimate recital of news developments. Then there is the whole business of the recorded tape (visual and oral) which can be cut, spliced and altered in many mechanical ways to distort or change the thrust of news.

If the examples that I draw upon in this chapter are overwhelmingly on the side of showing bias and prejudice on the part of the media, it is because these are important and dangerous departures from what is supposed to be the normal function of the press, radio and television news people. I hope, herein, by concrete instances to illustrate the point that there is a sound basis in fact for the conservative claim of a built-in bias, a pro-liberal bias, if you please, which runs through much of the fabric of the public information media in this country.

I have listened to the many reasons given for this condition, and I believe the most reasonable and acceptable is the fact that a whole generation of newsmen grew up in the Depression and were spoon-fed by a bitterly partisan political regime known as the New Deal through many new devices of political and governmental propaganda technique. At the same time, there was a virtual blackout during this period of strong, penetrating arguments on behalf of the free enterprise system and constitutional government. A leading newsman in the Senate once actually told me that aside from myself he had never heard the conservative viewpoint strongly argued as a viable philosophy of government.

It may surprise many who read this book to understand that before Franklin D. Roosevelt no such thing as a presidential press conference ever existed. This was purely and simply a device cooked up by masters at the art of political propaganda, men like the late Charles Michaelson, who was the sloganeer master of the New Deal. The press conference was designed to provide Franklin D. Roose-

velt with a ready-made forum of his own choosing for the propaga-
tion of ideas which he wanted to sell to the American people in a
way that would bring pressure on the Congress.

In those days of the FDR press conferences, many of the questions were written by White House strategists and passed out to
favored reporters for presentation to a President who had all the
answers well in mind before the questions were asked. Reporters
have told me that it took a brave man to ask even a slightly embar-
rassing or touchy question at these press conferences. The technique
can best be described as "presidential ridicule." It worked this way.
When a reporter who was not one of the "ins" had the temerity to
ask a touchy question, President Roosevelt would tilt his cigarette
holder toward the ceiling, point jovially at the reporter, and tell
him to go over in the corner and put on his dunce cap. Once this
pronouncement was made, any further questioning by that particular
reporter was quickly drowned out by gales of laughter from his
journalistic colleagues. Many of the reporters who played this game
didn't really understand the technique that was being applied nor
why it was being used. Very simply, it was a clever device for avoiding a direct answer to a touchy question. By the same token, it
established the fact that reporters who trod on forbidden ground in
the presidential press conference ran a serious risk of being embar-
rassed and ridiculed. By careful planning in advance, FDR and his
advisors like his Press Secretary Stephen Early could make virtually
certain that the major news thrust of the day would be the answer
to a planted question. This was news management with a vengeance,
and it was as successful as it was skillful.

Other government officials soon adopted the press conference
technique. Before long it became routine for cabinet members,
bureau chiefs, governors and senators to hold press conferences
either on a regular schedule or when they had something of special
importance to them to announce or leak.

In these early days of the New Deal, too, the whole business
of news gathering was undergoing a revolution of sorts itself. Great
premium was placed on the gossip gatherers, especially those on
Broadway, in Hollywood, and in Washington. Perhaps the best
remembered of the Broadway gossip reporters was Walter Winchell.
The best known purveyor of government and political gossip was
undoubtedly the late Drew Pearson.

A skillful master of fact, rumor and half truths, Mr. Pearson exerted for many years a much heavier influence over the development of public policy and governmental affairs than he deserved. Like most reporters of gossip, Mr. Pearson held the distinction of having been described as a liar by many public officials, including several Presidents. Needless to say, Mr. Pearson pursued an extremely partisan, liberal approach to almost everything he reported.

Mr. Pearson's successor, Jack Anderson, is following in his late employer's footsteps. A specific example of this type of reporting will be cited at a later point in this chapter.

In the period of the early 1930's, of course, great changes were taking place in the government and the political life of the nation. They naturally stirred keen interest on the part of the public and made journalistic "scoops" and "exclusives" a much sought-after commodity. The New Deal, staffed by Democrats in command of the entire Federal Government for the first time since Woodrow Wilson, thoroughly understood the value of the secrets it possessed. It soon developed favorites among the reporters and these favorites became famous and extremely well paid because off their typewriters rolled the exclusive accounts of many new programs and new approaches which the Roosevelt government planned to take in the revamping of a nation's political and economic structure.

I go into some detail about this era in the life of American journalism to show that many of the people who were cub reporters in those days and now are the publishers and editors of today were taught very early the value of adopting a liberal approach to their work. In fact, with some, the liberal approach is really the only one they know. I am not saying here that the New Deal deliberately went out and bought reporters, but the effect of its news management was extremely persuasive. And I do say that many newsmen learned the hard way, from a devastating depression, that new answers were needed, that the liberals had answers to offer, and that a fine way to make friends and influence important people in the seats of power was to be pro-liberal in word, thought and deed. In fact, it was strictly a matter of good business for opportunists in the news-gathering profession to develop a prejudice toward liberal answers in those days. I must emphasize there were many newsmen who came by their convictions honestly and sincerely even though it led to the sacrifice of their objectivity.

Aiding and abetting what I like to refer to as almost the development of a journalistic frame of mind in this nation was the growing power and propaganda efforts of organized labor. The union bosses wielded enormous influence over the public information media just through the emotional presentation of their cause (i.e., to help the downtrodden, underpaid working man). But where the unions are concerned, the effort didn't stop at the art of persuasion. It became more direct through the thing that unions were doing best in the early 1930's—organizing.

It was in this period that the American Newspaper Guild gained its great power in the ranks of the nation's reporters. In those days, becoming a member of the newspaper guild almost automatically aligned a reporter with the overall objective of organized labor. It put him on the side of labor against the side of management, yet his job newswise often forced him to cover strikes and charged him with the responsibility to report accurately on the activities of both union and management officials. This, of course, was during the popular reign of a noted newspaper leftist and columnist named Heywood Broun. Mr. Broun, as President of the Guild and as a newspaper columnist, very often called the tune for a biased and slanted orchestration on the part of liberal members of the Fourth Estate. When he died, other "bell cow" columnists took over the unofficial but highly effective work of leading the pack.

I doubt if there was any official understanding, but over the years it could be observed that a thesis or argument which had its beginning in a column by some outstanding liberal writer such as Walter Lippmann or Marquis Childs was soon backed up and repeated in various forms by other writers and commentators. It almost seemed as though the pro-liberal members of the Fourth Estate read certain papers and certain writers each day to get the "morning line" to be followed.

Other facets of union pressure on a presentation of news were to be found in other kinds of union organization. For example, the truck drivers who distributed newspapers were unionized. The printers, without whom no newspaper can publish, were unionized. And in these days it was popular and accepted for some unions, including the Guild, to take public stands on national issues having nothing to do with their particular problems of employment, wages and working conditions. These actions, of course, placed the Guild on one side or the other of bitterly fought issues which all newsmen should have been free to report on objectively and without any affiliation strains at all. Another complicating factor which tended to influence this generation of newsmen was the Guild's affiliation with the CIO. The Congress of Industrial Organizations, at that juncture in our history, was bitterly partisan on behalf of the Democratic Party and liberal objectives all the way down the line. Not a few Guild units in the 1930's were infiltrated by United States Communists, some of whom were ousted in bitterly fought union meetings.

What I am endeavoring to show here is the fact that the proliberal bias which is thoroughly evident throughout the public media today had its beginning almost three decades ago and was fed by not only the conditions of the times but also by an atmosphere of great change in government concepts. It was further influenced by a general feeling that the instruments of capitalism, the large corporations, had failed the majority of American workers. In those days it was popular to sneer at the so-called "economic royalists" and the "Bourbons of big business." Many economic ills were laid at the feet of commercial monopoly and at the feet of the business community in general. And this was the favorite theme of the news propagandists of the New Deal. The pitting of the so-called "haves" against the so-called "have nots" became a political way of life for the New Deal Democrats. It was a propaganda vehicle which they drove to national election victories in 1932, 1936, 1940 and 1944. This, I believe, shows that the attitude which so many conservatives find objectionable in the treatment of news developments by the public media was the result of a series of conditions and events skillfully adapted by government bureaucrats. It was not, and I repeat, not, the result of a vast Moscow-inspired conspiracy, even though many of the results of this condition have aided and abetted the objectives of international Communism in this country and elsewhere throughout the world where its influence is felt.

Earlier I mentioned the tendency of the press to become influenced in favor of liberal causes during the early 1930's when the New Deal reigned unchallenged in this country. It should be noted that the propaganda experts of the Roosevelt Administration made much of the fact that a majority of the nation's newspapers at that time were owned and published by men strongly devoted to the Republican political persuasion. This was undoubtedly true, but this claim does not hold true today because as I mentioned earlier the men who now rule the editorial rooms and the newsdesk as well as the publishers' offices of most American newspapers are in sympathy with liberal Democratic politicians. Some publications which boast conservative ownership have publishers who pay slight attention to the editorial content of their publication so long as it makes a financial profit.

Let me give you a concrete example of what I am saying. This nation's great syndicates, the ones who sell and distribute political columns, are in the business of selling their product to American newspapers. Being good salesmen, they know what kind of package draws the most buyers. And if you will take a look at America's editorial pages today, you will find the majority of editorial columnists whose opinions are printed daily are heavily weighted on the side of the liberal approach to American government. And there is a very good reason. Many of these so-called molders of political opinion came right out of the ranks of the Democratic Party or of Democratic administrations or the offices of Democratic lawmakers. For example, the newest duo to enter the political columning business are Frank Mankiewicz and Tom Braden. Mr. Mankiewicz and Mr. Braden, in addition to having a newspaper column of political opinion, also have a television news show in Washington, D.C., "Seven Days." Many of the people reading this column and watching the "Seven Days" may believe that they are receiving an objective, unbiased observation and recounting of the news developments of the day.

Very few realize that Mr. Mankiewicz was unknown to the newspaper readers of this country and to the press generally until he turned up as press secretary to the late Senator Robert Kennedy. This background by its very nature makes of Mr. Mankiewicz a hard-fighting partisan for the Kennedy brand of liberal-Democratic politics. Mr. Braden's major claim to fame seems to be that he was a close friend of the Kennedy family during its time of importance in the nation's capital.

Also on the nation's editorial pages you will find the hard-bitten comments of columnist Carl Rowan. And to understand his built-in leanings to the Democratic side of the political spectrum, it is necessary to understand that Mr. Rowan first became prominent in the nation's capital as an appointee of the late President John F. Kennedy to an important post in the United States State Department.

Then we have Mr. Clayton Fritchie, whose opinions also are

prominently displayed on many editorial pages throughout the nation. If his columns appear to be fairly caustic toward the Republican Party, the Nixon Administration and conservatism, it is perfectly understandable. Mr. Fritchie has long been associated with the Democratic Party in various capacities, including that of a publicist for the Democratic National Committee and a close advisor to former Illinois Governor Adlai Stevenson during his presidential campaign.

In addition to columnists who actually served in big jobs for the Democrats, there is a smattering of newspaper columnists who came on the scene largely because of their close association and friendship with important elected officials. For example, Mr. Charles Bartlett, a long-time friend of the late President John F. Kennedy, did not attain the coveted status of syndication until Mr. Kennedy was inaugurated as the President of the United States. Then, we have the case of Mr. Leslie Carpenter, an extremely capable, long-time reporter for Texas newspapers. Without casting any reflection on Mr. Carpenter, whose abilities are considerable, the fact remains that his syndication on a nationwide basis did not occur until his old and personal friend, Lyndon Baines Johnson, became President of the United States and Mr. Carpenter's wife Liz became press secretary to the First Lady.

There is also a social factor involved in what I believe must honestly be called a deliberate effort to influence important journalistic commentators. It will be remembered that on the night of his inauguration as President of the United States, John Kennedy surprised everyone by making a surprise appearance at a party being given in the home of syndicated columnist Joseph Alsop. I want to make it clear that I am not implying here that Mr. Alsop is an easy person to influence in any direction. My observation of his work over the years convinced me that, like the rest of his generation of newsmen, he has an almost automatic sympathy for liberal causes but calls the shots the way he sees them when he thinks the liberals are wrong. For example, his publicly acknowledged friendship with the Kennedys does not in any way cause him to forego criticizing any member of that family when he thinks they are off base politically.

By the same token, you will find that social pages which carried guest lists at parties given by the Kennedys always contained an interesting sprinkling of influential newsmen and commentators.

One of the Kennedys' favorites in a social sense was Art Buchwald, the humorist political columnist, who can very often render a political action by a public official downright devastating through a very skillful use of humor and ridicule.

I detail these facts primarily to illustrate the many and varied forms of pressure which are daily exerted on the nation's commentators in favor of liberal objectives.

So much for the evolution of public-information media which have a responsibility to strive for truth and honesty and fairness in the plying of their trade but which lend much more enthusiasm if such striving can be beneficial to the left-wing sector of the American body politic.

Regardless of how it happened, the press, the radio and television stand indicted of the crime of failing in their great and growing responsibility to give the American people an honest picture of the news of the day. Perhaps it would help if the reader could understand just what the news of the day consists of. I like to think of it as a long string of objects moving across a stage, and at stated times during a 24-hour period a huge hand reaches down, grabs a fistful of these moving objects, and arranges them on a sheet of paper. The moving platform represents the life of the world, a very small part of which is periodically drawn up and presented in the form of news to give an indication of what transpired in the world's life during a specified period of time. At the very best, our news media can only handle and process a small portion of what transpires around the globe every 24 hours. But when they have their daily handful, they can pick and choose from those events in assembling a representative account for the American public. The media can select any kind of development they might want; and if the people doing the selecting have an almost unrecognized built-in bias, they will dictate the items to be selected automatically.

There are many ways to present a slanted or even an erroneous report of the news. One device is to quote a public figure out of context. Another is to put words in his mouth that he either did not say or that he said with a different meaning. Sometimes the gratuitous misspelling of a word can do the trick of carrying the wrong impression across the wires and into the world. And by the time it is corrected, the damage will have been done.

Just very recently I had an experience like this with the *Washington Post*. I made a speech to a Western States Regional Conference of the Republican Party in Honolulu. I spoke from a prepared text which was made available to the press, radio and television newsmen both in Washington and in Hawaii. In that speech I remarked that Vice-President Spiro Agnew might soon find himself being "boomed" for President if he continued to stress the sentiments of the overwhelming majority of the American people. It was a tongue-in-cheek remark designed primarily to drive home my belief that Vice-President Agnew was absolutely in tune with the American people in his criticism of this country's anti-war protesters. But in reporting this comment, the *Washington Post* used the word "groomed" in the place of the word which I used. Of course, there is no way of telling just where along the line this alteration occurred. The story in the *Post* was a United Press International account. Whether the UPI reporter in Hawaii misspelled the word or whether a teletype man somewhere along the line changed the word, or whether it was done in the composing room or the editorial offices of the *Washington Post,* we'll undoubtedly never know. But the fact remains that the *Post* managed to present the impression that somebody was getting ready to "groom" Mr. Agnew for the highest post in the land rather than just say he'd make a good candidate. In political circles there is a vast difference between being "groomed" for a post and being "boomed."

I might point out that this accidental or deliberate manipulation of words occurred after the Vice-President had criticized the anti-war protesters as "an effete corps of impudent snobs," but before he leveled his well-reasoned criticism of television network news and a monopolistic segment of the American press which publishes the *Washington Post* and *Newsweek* magazine in addition to operating television station WTOP in the nation's capital.

As I explained earlier, there are various ways and means to present in printed form a biased or self-serving point of view. I do not suggest that it is entirely possible for reporters and news commentators to be 100 percent objective in their recounting of the news developments on a day-to-day basis. Human nature, which gives us the sacred right of volition and freedom of choice for our thoughts and our attitudes, is just not geared to a completely impassive, nonemotional handling of the news. But I thoroughly agree with Vice-President Agnew and many other government officials and private experts that a reasonable degree of objectivity should certainly be a goal of the men who present the news of the world and of the nation and of the community for the millions of American readers, listeners and viewers. I state categorically that this has not been done in many large and important areas of the news media. I am a great believer in the device, practiced by most responsible American newspapers, of separating the news developments and the newspapers' editorial opinion. The first should be a flat, unembroidered account of the facts surrounding the item of news. It should be, so far as is humanly possible, free from the writer's or the commentator's personal interpretation or views. I am completely mindful of the fact that much latitude is required to insure the reader the fullest possible budget of details surrounding a newsworthy event. I am also fully aware of the very human tendency for reporters and commentators to color the events on the basis of their past experience or deeply held convictions. And I believe all men in public life recognize these limitations and are willing to make allowances for them. But as I have said before, it is the deliberate falsification of facts or deliberate twisting of words or deliberate misreading of intent that I believe is reprehensible. A reporter or commentator who accidentally lets his personal views or personal feelings influence his reporting of a news development is easy enough to understand and forgive. But when the reporter or commentator deliberately goes out of his way to arrange the facts and misinterpret developments to fit his own philosophical or ideological attitude, he should be called to account or disciplined.

And let me say that it is not possible to exonerate publishers and editors for the publication of erroneous facts merely because they appear on the editorial page and under the heading of opinion. For example, many harmful and damaging editorials have been written by biased writers who merely use a false basis or claim as a starting point. For example, an editorial writer can easily say, to give a fictitious example: "This newspaper finds itself in complete disagreement with Senator _____ who advocates the use of nuclear weapons in the war against the Communists in Vietnam."

This opening paragraph gives the reader to believe that the Senator in question has taken such a position and there is no doubt about it. The casual reader of that editorial would be inclined to accept the writer's assertion and assume that the position had escaped his notice when the Senator first assumed it. It doesn't occur to him to challenge the editorial writer's bland assertion of what the Senator has or has not recommended. More often he is inclined to accept the editorial's premise and go on to either agree or disagree with the newspaper's position.

This raises a question which I think is very important. Doesn't a responsible newspaper, which presumes to supply a given area with accurate news, have a duty to question the assertions published in their papers even when they appear under the name of a syndicated columnist who does not work directly for the newspaper in question? Let me cite a recent and ugly example of what I mean.

In the December 10, 1969, issue of the *Washington Post* there appeared a syndicated article by columnist Jack Anderson, the successor to the late Drew Pearson, which was carried under a four-column headline that read: "Sen. Goldwater Nettled by Navajos Aid." If you read no further than the headline of this article you have to believe that I was angry because some Navajo Indians received some help. In my own state I wouldn't have to defend such a silly assumption. Most of the Navajos who live in the United States are located in Arizona, and I have spent a lifetime concerning myself both privately and publicly with their welfare. But let's go on to the column itself. Its entire thrust is contained in the first paragraph, which read as follows: "Barry Goldwater, who makes heap big noise about his love for Indians, has become the Senate champion of the burcaucrat, ranchers, white traders and other Indian oppressors."

The entire column was devoted to my sponsorship of a bill to prevent lawyers from the Office of Economic Opportunity from setting up shop on the Navajo reservation to exploit complaints among some of the Indians. The writer of this smear—and that is exactly what it was—was not at all interested in discovering any of the facts behind this difficult problem affecting the Indians of my state. Strangely enough, he did not ask the Indians themselves. And, of course, he did not have interest enough to pick up the telephone and call my office and ask why my name was attached to that particular piece of legislation.

The reason for these omissions is plain enough. If Jack Anderson had asked the Navajo Tribal Council about this bill, he would have discovered that although my name is on it, it belongs to them. It was drafted at their direction to meet a situation which the Tribal Council—all fifteen members of it—realize was causing trouble and dissension in the tribe. That piece of legislation was introduced by me solely and purely at the request of the Tribal Council. This is a group of Navajos, incidentally, who are chosen democratically to serve as a governing body and spokesmen for the Navajos.

But Mr. Anderson's interest was not in the truth nor was it related to the facts. He was selling a newspaper column, and he realized that the more sensational he could make it, the better chance of following in the footsteps of his late employer and mentor, Drew Pearson. Anderson didn't want to risk spoiling his fabrication of the facts by talking to anyone who knew them intimately. In other words he didn't want to reduce the sensation quotient of his column for December 10, 1969. Of course, there is nothing new in this approach to a prominent conservative but the details. The Andersons and the liberal opportunists in the news media have long fattened on a special formula. It involves describing a pitiful situation, whether it be in relation to the American Indians, the American Negroes, the inhabitants of the city ghettos, or the Biafrans in far-off Nigeria, and then showing that their plight is either the fault of conservatives or is being continued because conservatives are blocking methods to help.

It is the old formula of the good guys against the bad guys. In Anderson's column and in Drew Pearson's before him, a good guy was always a leftist-leaning liberal with a publicly displayed bleeding heart who wanted to attack all of the nation's ills through the medium of the public treasury. The "bad guys" always were and always will be conservatives and Republicans and businessmen who would like to see the problems of this nation approached on the basis of responsibility and hard work.

But I return to my original premise—what responsibility does a newspaper have for publishing the writings of biased, prejudiced, professional liberals like columnist Anderson? I believe they have a responsibility to their readers on this score. When the *Washington Post* publishes Jack Anderson's column under a headline which they themselves wrote (the columnist never writes the headline that appears over his work in any newspaper), I believe they are adding to the evils which Vice-President Agnew has pointed to and which the public is beginning to want answered. When no effort is made by a metropolitan newspaper to confirm or disprove the kind of material submitted by the Jack Andersons, what is there to differentiate that newspaper from the scandalous, scurrilous underground press which is growing by leaps and bounds in this country?

I must say that the liberal righteousness of the *Washington Post,* which sits in judgment on political figures large and small, is very difficult to stomach under circumstances such as I have been outlining here and which were alluded to by Vice-President Agnew when he questioned the monopoly held by the *Washington Post* management through its ownership of the only morning paper in the nation's capital, *Newsweek* magazine, and TV and radio station WTOP in Washington.

If nothing else, the *Post* and newspapers which pattern themselves on the same liberal format are guilty of gross presumption which borders on the arrogant. Anderson's vicious charge, published by the *Washington Post* on December 10, 1969, read:

> *In Goldwater's native Arizona, the Navajos have been reduced to Biafra-level malnutrition by greedy white traders and water-sponging ranchers. The situation is so desperate that Sen. Gaylord Nelson (D-Wis.) has ordered his anti-poverty subcommittee to investigate.*
>
> *This column has now obtained documents collected by Nelson's investigators in preparation for upcoming hearings. The documents show criminal neglect of the Navajos so gross that it cries out for some bureaucrats' scalps.*
>
> *The Bureau of Indian Affairs licenses all white traders on the reservation. Although charged by law to protect Indians from raw deals, the bureau has let the white traders become virtual dictators. They act as postmasters, welfare check agents, food stamp dispensers, pawnbrokers and, of course, general storekeepers.*
>
> *Lately, a valiant little band of Poverty Corps lawyers, invited by Navajos, has moved into the bleak reservation to aid the poorest of its 125,000 people. They have documented for Sen. Nelson how the traders and other whites have terrorized and impoverished the Indians.*
>
> *Sen. Goldwater carried the traders' case against the Poverty Corps lawyers to the Senate Floor. He charged that the attorneys were causing dissension in the tribe and demanded that their $1.1 million anti-poverty grant be restricted.*

In appraising this particular example of what I think is irresponsible and phony journalism on the part of both the columnist and the newspaper, let me point out that the column appeared while Congress was still in session and Washington was characteristically attuned to political awareness.

But, when the Indians themselves (the Navajos for whom Mr. Anderson bled so copiously) set the record straight in a letter to the *Washington Post,* it appeared under a small head which read, "The Navajos on OEO and Senator Goldwater," whereas the original column carried the offensive headline, "Sen. Goldwater Nettled by Navajos Aid," in type several sizes larger than that used over the clarification signed by Mr. Raymond Nakai, Chairman of the Navajo Tribal Council. No effort was made to correct the impression that I was irked by attempts to help the Indians in my state. What's more, the *Washington Post,* in characteristic disregard for any brand of fairness toward a political conservative, chose to run the Indians' defense of me on, of all days, December 25, 1969. Any newspaper reporter, editor or publisher will explain that if there is one day out of 365 when their publication will be read by the least number of people, it will be on Christmas Day, when America's newspaper readers are involved in the religious celebration of Christ's birth and the celebration of the most joyous day in the year for their children.

Needless to say, this did not surprise me one bit. In fact, it was entirely predictable that this bastion of liberal journalism would use every trick in the book to hide the fact that a story which fit right into their ideological life pattern was shown to be without foundation and in such a flagrant manner that they were forced to print an explanation.

It would be much easier to accept this kind of slanted, unfair treatment of political news affecting public figures if it were not for the *Post's* great pretensions of righteousness and its general assumption that its readers are all too stupid to understand that they are being tricked merely to further a publisher's biased and prejudiced point of view.

It is often claimed that conservatives are too sensitive to inequities in the treatment of their public positions and public actions by the journalistic media. In this account of media sins you will find no shadow area of complaint. I am being careful to confine my observations to examples of the most flagrant kind which I was involved in personally and concerning which I had intimate, detailed information.

Mr. Nakai's communication to the *Washington Post* contained this particular passage, "Senator Goldwater, far from being the oppressor of the American Indian, understands the real concern of our people and is one of the very few in our halls of Congress who has the courage to speak out concerning this unwarranted action by the OEO.

"Whatever attack Mr. Anderson may choose to make on Senator Goldwater, you should know that the American Indian holds him in high esteem. The Navajo people, in particular, have a sincere affection in their hearts for him. They know that his office door is always open to the most humble of them, and that he will not give mere 'lip service' but will do his utmost to solve his problem."

It is difficult to credit Mr. Anderson's article with any element of truth when the people he says I am oppressing speak in these terms. However, I do not want the reader to believe that I am resorting to any of the tricks that newsmen such as Mr. Anderson excel in, such as quoting out of context. I am including the entire text of Mr. Nakai's letter as it appeared in the *Washington Post*. My purpose is simple enough. Given the contents of the two communications, the headlines that were used to present each, and the days on which they appeared in print, I wish to let the reader make his own judgment as to whether this is responsible journalism or whether it is as spiteful and petty and unfair as I believe it to be.

Mr. Nakai's letter read as follows:

The Navajos on the OEO and Sen. Goldwater

The article of Jack Anderson which appeared in the Washington Post *on Dec. 10 does not present fairly the controversy between the Navajo Tribe and the legal aid service of the Office of Economic Opportunity (DNA, Inc.) which operates without approval of the Navajo government on the reservation.*

Had Mr. Anderson cared enough he might easily have learned from almost any of our people that the real crux of the problem is the sovereignty of the Navajo Tribe which the Navajo people affectionately refer to as the "rainbow."

It will be recalled that the United States government solemnly entered into a treaty with the Navajo Tribe in 1868 setting aside for the exclusive use of the Navajo people a certain area of land. The United States, in return for certain promises on the part of the Navajo, promised that the land should remain forever the home of the Navajo, and that the Navajo people should have the right even to determine who "shall ever be permitted to pass over, settle upon, or reside in, the territory described in this article."

Not reflected in Mr. Anderson's article is the fact that the Office of Economic Opportunity saw fit recently to fund DNA, Inc. directly against an express resolution of the Navajo Tribal Council that such funds be funded through the Tribal Council and in turn through the Office of Navajo Economic Opportunity. It should be noted that of the 196 such legal aid programs throughout the United States only three are funded directly.

The Navajo people resent this bitterly and can but conclude that the United States again has chosen to disregard the sovereignty of the Navajo nation and has forced a controversial legal aid program down its throat.

Senator Goldwater, far from being the oppressor of the American Indian, understands the real concern of our people, and is one of the very few in our halls of Congress who has the courage to speak out concerning this unwarranted action by the OEO.

Whatever attack Mr. Anderson may choose to make on Senator Goldwater, you should know that the American Indian holds him in high esteem. The Navajo people, in particular, have a sincere affection in their hearts for him. They know that his office door is always open to the most humble of them, and that he will not give mere "lip service" but will do his utmost to solve his problem.

I do not wish to imply that Senator Goldwater is the only champion of the American Indian. There are others, of course. But should they choose to speak out for the welfare of the American Indian, I am sure your ill-informed correspondents would castigate them as severely as they did Senator Goldwater.

> *Every administration for the past 20 years has piously declared that the American Indian should be allowed to make his own decisions through his legally constituted government. Mr. Nixon has forthrightly declared this to be the cornerstone of his administration in its relations with the American Indian. How unfortunate it is that the lines of communications between the White House and Mr. Rumsfeld's office have broken down.*
>
> *The American Indian looks sadly at the passing of the buffalo from the American scene, for he is increasingly aware that his demise is just as certain and that those who wring their hands and shed false tears for the "poor and wretched Indians" seek only an invitation to their funeral.*
>
> *Our sovereignty is precious to us. Without the protection of our treaty we will soon lose our identity to the hordes of white men now hungrily poised at our borders. Surely our cause is worth championing. If the press chooses to applaud those who seek to destroy our sovereignty, where can we turn?*
>
> *Raymond Nakai*
> *Chairman, Navajo Tribal Council*
> *Window Rock, Ariz.*

Down through the history of our country, freedom of the press has always been one of our cherished pillars of democracy. It has been jealously guarded by politicians and public figures, as well as editors, publishers and reporters themselves.

In the question of politics, this freedom has been maintained in the history of this country with an especial vehemence. It has become downright slanderous and libelous in many instances. However, this has always been regarded as one of the prices we must pay in this democracy for this basic freedom. Like all freedoms, freedom of the press is often abused, not by the majority of the press, but by some special groups in the press who are very hearty partisans and who have a feeling of righteousness, which, although it might be misplaced, is none the less sincere.

Strong statements about politicians and political candidates are nothing new to American history. For example, Thomas Paine, that great sloganeer of the Revolutionary period, once was quoted as saying of George Washington: "Treacherous in private friendship and a hypocrite in public life. The world will be puzzled to decide whether you are an apostate or an imposter, whether you have abandoned good principles or whether you ever had any."

By the same token, it can be found that the newspaper entitled *The New England Courant* once warned that if Jefferson was elected, the constitution would be destroyed. Many Senators at one time compared President Andrew Jackson to Nero and Julius Caesar and suggested that only a Brutus could save the nation from the tyrant. You will find that the editor of the *Newark Evening Journal* once called Lincoln "a perjured traitor who had betrayed his country and caused the butchery of hundreds of thousands of the people of the United States."

The campaign of 1964, in which I had the honor to represent my own political party as the Republican nominee for President, you will find was no exception from the old rule. In fact, it has become a matter of published record that that campaign perhaps set new heights in the whole area of campaign denunciations. In a book entitled "Hysteria 1964," Mr. Lionel Lokos reported on his research into the press treatment of my candidacy, and he had this to say about it: "In a period of ten months, Barry Goldwater was accused of:

"Being another Adolf Hitler.
"Fomenting a racial holocaust.
"Advocating a nuclear policy that would destroy half the world.
"Seeking to destroy social security.
"Being a lunatic.
"Wrecking the Republican Party.
"Trying to subvert labor unions.
"Paving the way for totalitarian government."

Now there can be no doubt that my candidacy in 1964 attracted some of the most uneven political commentary of modern times. I do not blame the press as a whole. I believe that many elements of the press honestly strove to be objective and even-handed and fair in the treatment of that campaign. I believe that the amount of character assassination and of outright personal abuse which was heaped upon me was a symptom of the fact that this nation now has a press with a built-in bias which is strongly weighted to the left-hand side of the political spectrum.

I cite my own experience because it is an experience which I know best. I can cite chapter and verse in this regard to show what I believe is an unhealthy condition which exists today in the press treatment of political news. I do not believe that the press is entirely fair. I do not condemn all branches of the press or all parts of the communications media. I do say this, that perhaps never before in the history of this country has the press been any more heavily weighted on the side of one particular approach to the solution of political problems than it is today on the side of what passes under the title of "liberalism." In other words, a conservative candidate, such as I was in 1964, has an additional burden to carry. The bare fact that a person is conservative is almost prima facie evidence of inadequacy to many sections of the press.

Even to this day appointments being made in Washington by the Nixon Administration are questioned on the sole grounds that a man's political judgment was not good. In one editorial attacking an appointee of President Nixon, the question was raised that the man's judgment was unsound, at least in matters political, because he had been wrong enough and irresponsible enough to support the presidential candidacy of Barry Goldwater. Now this takes in a vast part of the population of the United States. It will be remembered that 27 million Americans cast their ballots for my candidacy in 1964, and among those 27 million were some of the finest brains, some of the most intelligent people, some of the best minds that this nation or this world has ever known. And I say that for any newspaper to raise the fact of my candidacy being supported as grounds for questioning a man's judgment is proof in itself of a completely overbalanced prejudice against anyone who stands for conservative principles.

Now I have tried to trace earlier the development of this built-in bias, this built-in prejudice against conservatives. In my generation the relationship between conservatism and something that is evil or wrong has become particularly synonymous. I believe the cause of this is the fact that conservatism, the capitalistic system, the free-enterprise system, the business community, and people generally aligned with the feeling or a belief in a *laissez-faire* type of government and a belief in the proved traditions of the past are regarded as "square." I believe that anyone associated with such a political approach became almost evil in the minds of many Americans because it was this branch of the political system which was blamed primarily for the great depression.

Throughout my career in public life I have never been subject to an especially favorable overall treatment from the press. However, going into the campaign of 1964, I really found little to complain about other than the built-in bias which I have already alluded to in this chapter. However, I wasn't prepared, nor do I think my campaign team was prepared, for the vehemence and the type of denunciation which would be leveled at me once I announced my active campaign for the Republican nomination for President. If I had any illusions, they were put to rest very early in the New Hampshire presidential preferential campaign primary. For there I found what a newspaper deliberately out to knife a political candidate can and will do in these days of so-called sophistication and press freedom and alleged responsibility on the part of the public information media.

The incident occurred in Concord, New Hampshire. There I had delivered a speech on January 7, in which I included my recommendations for enlarging social security, for increasing benefits, for amending the existing law on social security to bring many more millions of people under its provisions and to increase the amount of monetary benefits they received from this system. To my complete amazement, when I got back to my motel that evening, I read in the local newspaper (the *Concord Daily Monitor*) a headline which said, "Goldwater Sets Goals: End Social Security, Hit Castro." The story was a top head on page one. I think the headline ran three or four columns, and it left no doubt in anyone's mind that I was for wiping social security off the books entirely.

But the story was something else. That story, written by a reporter for that newspaper, was perfectly honest and accurate and right. There was not one word out of place. The man who covered that speech and wrote that story held fast to the finest and the highest traditions of honest and fair political reporting because he told it like it was. He told exactly what I had said and what I had recommended. The headline writer, perhaps he was the editor, I don't know, but whoever wrote the headline for that story had to be motivated by a desire to destroy. He had to have a reason which was entirely political in nature to put that kind of a headline on that kind of story. It was totally unfair; it was totally untrue; it was totally inaccurate. However, a member of my campaign staff contacted somebody of that newspaper, I believe it was the editor, and asked him how anyone could interpret that story the way that headline interpreted it for the consumption of the reading public.

He was given this bizarre, this strange formula for deciding on how a headline should be written.

The argument went something like this: Senator Goldwater proposed changes in the existing social security law. To this there is no argument; I did suggest changes. They were changes that would have improved and expanded the social security coverage in this country. But the editor's argument was that to change a law, the man proposing those changes would abolish that law as it now exists. In other words, if my amendments had been adopted, the Social Security Act as it existed before those amendments were voted upon would no longer be the law of the land. It would be the law of the land as amended. The editor's argument was that when anyone proposes a change or amendment to a law, he automatically proposes abolishing the law as it existed before the change.

Now I submit this is the strangest and the most ridiculous type of reasoning I had ever heard seriously advanced for a patently political attempt to misguide and mislead the readers of a newspaper about views of a political candidate. I say that happened early in the campaign. I wasn't a novice to the whole business of the slanted news story or the slanted headline when I went to New Hampshire. However, I must say that that particular example directed at a candidate for the nomination of his party for President of the United States literally astounded me. I couldn't believe it. To this day I think it will stand for all times as a record for unfairness on the part of the press toward a political candidate.

As the campaign progressed, it really got to be too much for some members of the press who knew what was going on. For example, early in the campaign John S. Knight, the highly respected publisher of the *Detroit Free Press* and other newspapers, wrote this in an editorial, and I quote:

"Barry Goldwater is not my candidate, and I have done nothing to promote his Presidential aspirations, but I do think the Arizona Senator is getting shabby treatment from most of the news media."

Publisher Knight said that he could find "only a few newspapers that were not savagely cutting down Senator Goldwater day after day." As for the editorial cartoonists, he said they portrayed Goldwater "as belonging to the Neanderthal age, or as a relic of the 19th Century." Then the respected publisher concluded: "Some editors are disturbed because Barry Goldwater is teeing off on the newspapers and other new media for failing to present the news of his candidacy fairly and objectively. I can't say that I blame him. He has not had a fair shake."

Overall, for those who like statistics, *Editor and Publisher* magazine was able to report in the middle of October in that campaign year of 1964 that 300 daily newspapers had endorsed Lyndon Johnson while 272 daily newspapers had endorsed Senator Goldwater. But I submit that that 272 contained a lot of papers which are not regarded as among the leading public opinion molders of the nation, for the pro-Johnson newspapers had three times the circulation of the pro-Goldwater newspapers.

So much for that old New Deal claim that the United States of America has a one-party press and that that party is the Republican Party. If that argument was ever demolished, my candidacy and my campaign saw it demolished completely. And the open attacks were only one phase of the campaign. Actually, that's what I have to call it, the campaign of the liberal newspapers against my candidacy.

These papers exercising freedom of the press also exercised their freedom to refuse to print news stories about some of my speeches. They exercised the freedom to bury on the back pages any kind of a news story that might possibly benefit Senator Goldwater. As the political columnist Ruth Montgomery once expressed it: "Goldwater's occasional gaffes have been played up out of all proportions. Attacks against him are headlined while praises are buried in the last line. The public has the right to know the good as well as the bad. Slanting the news in an attempt to defeat a candidate for elective office is no prettier than the sham one-party elections held behind the Iron Curtain."

In the space I have here it is not possible for me to give any precise rundown on the press treatment of my candidacy in 1964. What I have attempted to do here is to cite some examples which show unmistakably that when the press insists that it is objective and fair, this is plainly not the case. I am not sure that a complete system of objectivity and unprejudiced and unbiased reporting will ever exist in any nation in the world; however, I am sure that a better balance can be obtained than the one that existed in this country in 1964, and exists in this country today.

That is why I feel that Vice-President Agnew performed a very great and needed public service when he drew attention to some of the bias and some of the overbalanced treatment of news by the press and the other elements of the communications media and when he asked for a searching examination by the press itself of its own attitudes and its own performance. You would have thought from the reactions that Mr. Agnew had stood up and announced that the press forthwith would be bludgeoned into submission so that every single objective of the Nixon Administration and of conservative Republicans would be adopted without criticism. That is patently not the case. One of the finest examples of unfair, biased, misleading reporting in this country has been the way the Agnew statements relative to the press and television have been presented editorially to the readers of this country.

Much space has been given to almost anyone who will blast Ted Agnew for what he had to say about the news media. For example, one Congressman accused Agnew of a "creeping socialistic scheme against the free enterprise broadcast industry." That is patently ridiculous and anyone who knows Agnew knows it is. Yet the American press saw fit to give this great prominence. Others charged that Agnew was proposing censorship, that he wanted to place the government in a position of authority which would be unquestioned, that he wanted to import to this country totalitarian methods as they are practiced behind the Iron Curtain, and so on and so on.

All of these things followed a very, very well-reasoned, thoughtful and long-needed dissertation on the press and its treatment of the news by a man in public life, but as I have already pointed out, the words or the views of a conservative politician on this score are suspect. In my case I presume they are especially suspect because of the treatment my candidacy received in 1964.

Therefore, I can think of no better way to present the matter of the Vice-President's question, the Vice-President's concern, than the way it was presented in the *Washington Post* of all places by columnists Richard Harwood and Laurence Stern. Nobody can suspect these men or this publication of being unduly biased or prejudiced on the side of Vice-President Agnew. Yet on November 19, 1969, these two gentlemen wrote a column which pointed out that Agnew's blast at the TV news industry brought cries of foul throughout the entire land. It also pointed out that such cries often happen when a public figure of any kind attacks the media, probably because, say Harwood and Stern, "there is a theory in the industry that people shouldn't bite back at their dog." Mr. Harwood and Mr. Stern very astutely conclude that the issue of media performance is not going to evaporate simply because publishers and network presidents wrap themselves in the First Amendment and sneer at Spiro Agnew. For the facts are that the media are as blemished as any other institution in this society and that there is a growing public concern over their performance.

What these gentlemen are saying is that despite all disclaimers and despite the holier-than-thou righteousness in which some newspaper columnists, reporters and publishers wrap themselves, they are not above public criticism. And these two columnists very, very astutely prove that.

> *One of the reasons for all this agitation is that people have come to recognize that the selection and presentation of information and news is a very unscientific enterprise. Except for a few platitudes about objectivity, responsibi'ity, and news that's fit to print, there are no accepted or enforceable standards in this business.*
>
> *News is that what the media says it is, and the definition varies from day to day and place to place. It was "news" in the "Washington Post" and the "New York Times" last week when three doves in the Senate announced support for the anti-war demonstrations on November 15. It was not "news" at all in the "Times" the following day when 359 Congressional hawks and doves endorsed the President's negotiating posture on the war.*
>
> *In some part of the country last week people were told that Washington was braced for war against the howling mobs in the city. Elsewhere they read about love and singing and picnics on the public lawns.*
>
> *There is no conspiracy in any of this despite Spiro Agnew's dark suspicion. But there is much room for criticism, debate and discussion, and that debate and discussion need not be limited, should not be limited to the dreary convention halls of the broadcasters and the editors.*

I say this is one of the clearest presentations of the actual facts. There is only one part of this thing that I would disagree with. I found in the Vice-President's remarks, and I might say I read all of his speeches on this subject, no dark suspicions about conspiracies or anything else. I did find a clean, hard-hitting, questioning attitude which says that merely because these people are necessary and important to politicians and public figures there is no reason why they may be placed above criticism, above being called to account even as they themselves criticize and call to account anyone who is elected to public office. And, of course, part of the big problem that arises in this particular episode regarding the press is the source of the criticism. Mr. Agnew's critique was very, very incisive and it was extremely well done; however, from the standpoint of pure criticism, it was indeed pallid compared to that of some other politicians. For example, here's what President Franklin Roosevelt had to say about the press in 1941:

"The American people are beginning to realize that the things they have read and heard both from the agitators of the legislative variety and the agitators of the newspaper owner variety have been pure bunk—b u n k—; that these agitators are appealing to the ignorance, the prejudice, and the fears of Americans and are acting in an unAmerican way."

And here's what Adlai Stevenson had to say in 1942:

"The failure of the commercial press, with few exceptions, to honestly report the news and be fair in their editorial columns has served to retard the war effort. Generally their campaigns for special interest have created confusion in the minds of the American people and in several instances have bordered on acts of treason."

And more recently, here's what Vice-President Hubert Humphrey had to say in 1968:

"I am convinced that just as the media can tell the facts to the people, they can also exaggerate and inflame the situation."

But none of these criticisms of the press by public figures ever got much attention, but we must remember that all of them were certified liberals. Thus their sharpshooting aroused little concern. On the other hand, Mr. Agnew is aligned with a Republican administration and is suspected of being a conservative. Thus he has been singled out for the full treatment.

It is astounding the way the press, radio and television misinterpreted the Vice-President's remarks. He has been accused of trying to intimidate the press; he has been accused of trying to censor the press; he has been accused of almost everything in the book. And just to put the cherry on the cake, that very important, prestigious International Press Institute which operates out of Zurich, Switzerland, unleashed an attack on the Vice-President and said that his speeches criticizing the American news media constituted the most serious threat to freedom of information in the Western world last year. In an annual review of press freedom around the world, the Institute called attention to Mr. Agnew's attack on the news selection and presentation on television and in the press and tried to read into the Vice-President's remarks an attitude or a policy on behalf of the White House itself.

But those who accuse Mr. Agnew of intimidation would do well to realize what effect their own attacks on his request for an examination of news treatment has had on others who might feel inclined to criticize the press. If there is any intimidation involved, I believe the shoe is on the other foot. In other words, if you put all the criticisms of Mr. Agnew end to end, you would have an astounding indictment of a public servant by editorialists and newspapers and commentators on radio and television. He is accused of trying to censor the press; he is accused of trying to drive critics of the administration off the air and out of print; he is accused of trying to put down the intellectuals, of dividing the nation, you name it and he's been charged with it merely because, and this is very important, a Vice-President of the United States had the temerity to criticize the American press.

If anyone who had a legitimate beef against the newspapers or the radio and television industries for their treatment of news concerning an issue in which he was interested was assured that any voicing of that criticism would bring about the kind of attack that has been unleashed on Mr. Agnew, he would perhaps think many times before ever opening his mouth. In other words, I believe that in their very reaction, their intemperate and untruthful reaction, to a request for a sober analysis of their own action, the press, radio and TV news industries of this country are, in effect, trying to blackmail the Vice-President into not pushing his criticism any further.

I cannot understand why an industry as large and as important as the communications industry is so thin-skinned and sensitive. I believe it is because of something called the arrogance of power. They are so powerful and have been treated so long to the fawning, overweening solicitude of public officials and candidates for public office, that they cannot understand, nor can they actually believe, that someone in public life would have the temerity to criticize them, unless it was a defeated candidate.

Many times I have been asked why ı did not make a speech similar to Ted Agnew's about radio and television and newspapers. Believe me, I could have made such a speech long ago. However, how would it have sounded coming from a defeated candidate for President? All the media would have to say to such criticism or such a speech is "sour grapes." No, the vital thing about Mr. Agnew's call for an examination of news treatment was the fact that he is not a defeated candidate. He is not a Nixon who had just been voted down for Governor of California. He is not a Goldwater who has been defeated for President of the United States. No, he is a live and very active holder of the office of Vice-President of the United States.

What's more, I believe the media are very much aware of the fact that this criticism, this unexpected criticism, I might say, struck a very responsive chord with the American people. It must have been a shock to the network officials, who were unctuous and so horrified and so righteous in their reaction to Mr. Agnew's original statement, to find their switchboards flooded with calls saying "hurrah" for the Vice-President. It certainly hasn't helped the newspaper publishers' frame of mind to read the overwhelming number of letters to the editor saying "hurrah" for the Vice-President. In other words, Mr. Agnew is riding a wave of public indignation.

Apparently, the American public is not quite as stupid as many people thought it to be. In other words, many commentators and many news manipulators, I believe, have labored under the misapprehensions that their sly little slanting of the news and digs at certain types of politicians and public officials were being accepted whole-hog by the listening, viewing and reading public. Such, apparently, is not the case. Because Mr. Agnew, who has been made the subject of every kind of a sick, sad and ridiculous liberal joke on television, in hotel lobbies, on radio, in the newspapers, still is the first Vice-President in the history of this country ever to place within the first three men named as the person that the American public most admired in a public opinion poll.

Mr. Agnew's own mail and the telegraphic and telephonic response to his speeches must have been highly gratifying to him. The figures that I have heard, and I believe are correct, show clearly that the public, the vast American silent majority, if you will, believes that he has a good case and believes that it should be pushed further.

I believe it is time for the communications media and the public information media of this country to reexamine their attitudes. I believe it's time for them to face up to the fact that they do have a liberal bias running through most of their operations. I believe it's time that they sought to do something perhaps about a better balance of attitude in the presentation of the news. I do not say, and I don't think Mr. Agnew said, nor do I think that anyone ever asked that the networks, the newspapers and the radio stations go out and deliberately hire political conservatives to balance or to equalize the high liberal content of the attitudes on their staffs.

However, I do think it is important for the media to be aware that the American public is aware and that the American public does not entirely approve of this one-sided attitude. I believe that Mr. Agnew's comments, despite all the criticism, despite all the ridicule, despite all the misinterpretation that has been heaped on his remarks, have had a very salutary effect. I believe that we are getting a fairer examination of the news; I believe we are getting better presentation of the news; and I think that we are getting a better shake all around because of the Vice-President's criticism.

As a matter of fact, the TV networks, when they present a public affairs show, almost look self-conscious; they almost look as though they knew that Mr. Agnew's criticism was correct, and they are almost acting like little boys caught with their hands in the cookie jar.

VIII

The Networks and the News

IN ANY BOOK TOUCHING ON THE NEWS MEDIA AND THEIR RELATION TO politics and government, room has to be made for focusing attention on a great new dimension—the powerful and oftentimes irresponsible major television networks.

As a candidate for President in 1964, I believe on this subject I can speak with even more authority than Vice-President Spiro Agnew. I yield to no other American politician for the dubious distinction of being a political candidate whose image was totally distorted by the television news medium. I know this phase of the media delinquency. Anyone who has had my experience, who has stood in front of the cameras as often as I have, and whose words have been reported on the evening news as often as mine have can attest to the fact that Vice-President Agnew's criticism of networks was anything but perfect—it didn't go nearly far enough.

What I am saying here is that Mr. Agnew has stirred up a hornet's nest over a situation which was a national disgrace. He raised thoughtful and penetrating questions about a medium whose influence over American lives has grown almost imperceptibly to the point where it now has become one of the most powerful instruments for the formulation of public policy ever devised. Every night —in fact, three times a day at a minimum—millions of American viewers are exhorted and influenced by a small, poorly chosen group of news commentators. In fact, these millions of Americans are to a very large extent captive audiences. Some of them get their news locally, but most of them are subjected to the outpourings of three major networks which share one thing in common—a liberal-leaning bias in political and governmental affairs.

Many times I have stopped to wonder why all Americans in public life, or all Americans aspiring to public life, should be required to pass muster with a group of individuals whose only assignment and whose only job is to record and recite the news. Nobody has endowed Mr. Huntley, Mr. Brinkley, Mr. Reynolds or any of the other network TV commentators with special powers. My feeling has long been that Mr. Brinkley's opinion is about as important as that held by the boy who brings you your evening newspaper. Mr. Reynolds, who gives you his opinion on ABC every night, was not chosen by heaven, was not elected by the people, he was not even anointed by his fellow peers to be the beginning and end of all political wisdom and morality. Even that elder statesman, Eric Severeid, is no better qualified than many other men who have spent 20 or 30 years in the news business. Yet all of these men not only announce the news, but they weigh it, judge it and punctuate it— sometimes with sneers and open ridicule. The viewer has no recourse but to sit and take it.

But every once in a while a viewer of some eminence, like the Vice-President of the United States, arrogates to himself the temerity to criticize the TV news medium. Vice-President Agnew's speeches on this subject are classics. They were long, long overdue. They would have been made long before this, and by myself, had it not been for the fact that as a defeated candidate for President my criticism would have sounded like sour grapes. But this should not in any way subtract from the fact that now that the ice is broken, now that a debate is ensuing, now that the objectivity and fairness of the TV news medium has become an open question, I have a considerable contribution to make. And I wish to emphasize again that in this field I hold special qualifications. I have been there. I have seen the whites of Severeid's eyes just before CBS handed me a blindfold, offered me a consoling cigarette, and issued the order for my political execution.

I would caution the reader in appraising these comments to allow for a little healthy bias of my own. I believe I almost deserve it after the treatment I received at the hands of a lot of righteous, holier-than-thou commentators who insisted on sitting in judgment on every move and every comment I made in the political arena for a two-year period in 1963 and 1964.

One of the major revelations of Vice-President Agnew's campaign for truth in packaging for the news media is the reaction that followed his first two speeches. After the initial statements from the presidents of NBC, CBS and ABC, the networks participated in a virtual orgy of duologue discussions on nationwide television. I use the word duologue advisedly, and I do not want it confused with the word very popular with the network commentators which is spelled d-i-a-l-o-g-u-e. A duologue is where two people get together and voice their own opinions but don't listen to each other. A dialogue, on the other hand, is an exchange of views—a healthy process of verbal give-and-take used for an honest attempt to reach constructive conclusions between two different points of view.

The self-conscious way the networks have responded to the Agnew attack virtually proves Mr. Agnew's point. The reaction from the general public, which overwhelmingly endorsed the Vice-President's complaints, further drove home the validity of the critique. But let us concern ourselves here with the network officials and commentators themselves. For the first time ever, they were suddenly confronted with the kind of problem which they themselves hand out every night in the week to hundreds of men in public life. In other words, they were criticized. What a calamity. The righteous, the upstanding, the TV pure-in-heart, the "Dudley Do-Rights" of the networks, those men who believe themselves to be "stalwart, true with eyes of blue" all of a sudden became something less than a sacred institution and a medium commanded by mere mortals. For the first time in the history of television, the networks were confronted with a crisis. And in the few hours immediately following Agnew's hard-hitting criticism, they separated the men from the boys on the nation's visual airways. Let it here be recorded that in this crisis Mr. Goodman of NBC, Mr. Goldenson of ABC, and Mr. Stanton of CBS promptly stood up in front of the U.S. public and were measured for short pants. The commanders of the critics showed a fascinated nation that they could not take it. The bosses of those who dish it out to 60 million Americans 365 days out of the year yelled like a bunch of naughty children who had been subjected to their first spanking.

Their reaction was entirely lacking in intelligence on the one hand and appreciation for another point of view on the other hand. Their course was plain enough for anyone to see. They should have admitted very readily that they had made many mistakes and that their news operations were long overdue for a critical examination.

They should have realized that every viewer with any awareness of, or appreciation for, public events can point personally to examples of lack of fairness on the part of the networks. If they had been really smart, they would have borrowed a leaf out of the book of the nation's large motion-picture producers back in the late 1920's when that entertainment medium came under heavy public criticism for the content of the product they were peddling to the American people. The moviemakers saw the handwriting on the wall and opted for self-censorship. The result was the establishment in Hollywood of the famous "Hays Office," which passed on movies for their contents and taste. In other words, the industry adopted a policy of policing itself; and instead of increased criticism, it got high marks from the general public for recognizing and accepting a responsibility which the industry growth had given.

But in the case of the networks, we are supposed to believe that the Vice-President of the United States is an irresponsible, spiteful and unprincipled politician who is out to dragoon and intimidate the major elements of one of the most powerful industries on earth. The fact that Mr. Agnew had the courage to call the shots the way he saw them, or in the parlance of the day, the courage to "tell it like it is," made him an instant enemy of an industry and a monopoly which, while still very young in terms of years, should be able to prove the fact that it had grown beyond the stage of adolescence. The fact that it did not has already been alluded to in my earlier comments about Messrs. Goodman, Goldenson and Stanton donning knickers for their public outcries.

The more you study the charges of "intimidation," "coercion" and "censorship" which have been hurled in the direction of TV's major critic, the more you come to realize how really irresponsible and lacking in maturity and poise is this new industry. In effect, the network officials and commentators made an immediate false assumption that the American public either (1) is stupid or (2) doesn't understand what it heard. For a TV network to present a half hour of Mr. Agnew's calm, well-reasoned, thoughtful and penetrating analysis and then label it as an attempt to intimidate a multi-billion-dollar industry is ridiculous on its face. If the network wanted to try and push this viewpoint, they should have begun by denying nationwide exposure to the Vice-President. It puts the networks in the place of a retailer who shows his customers a shining product and tells them that it's as dull as dishwater.

Of course, today a great deal of confusion exists over exactly what Vice-President Agnew had to say about the networks and how they cover the news. And with every passing day this is being further compounded by people with a special interest in confusing the whole issue of network responsibility with the news of the day. For this reason, I feel it might be important here to quote some parts of the Vice-President's very notable speech at Des Moines, Iowa, on November 13, 1969.

A week ago, President Nixon delivered the most important address of his Administration, one of the most important of our decade. His subject was Vietnam. His hope was to rally the American people to see the conflict through to a lasting and just peace in the Pacific. For 32 minutes, he reasoned with a nation that has suffered almost a third of a million casualties in the longest war in its history.

When the President completed his address—an address that he spent weeks in preparing—his words and policies were subjected to instant analysis and querulous criticism. The audience of 70 million Americans . . . was inherited by a small band of network commentators and self-appointed analysts, the majority of whom expressed, in one way or another, their hostility to what he had to say. . . .

Every American has a right to disagree with the President of the United States, and to express publicly that disagreement. But the President of the United States has a right to communicate directly with the people who elected him, and the people of this country have the right to make up their own minds and form their own opinions about a presidential address without having the President's words and thoughts characterized through the prejudices of hostile critics before they can even be digested. . . .

At least 40 million Americans each night, it is estimated, watch the network news. . . .

How is this network news determined? A small group of men, numbering perhaps no more than a dozen, . . . decide what 40 to 50 million Americans will learn of the day's events in the nation and the world.

*We cannot measure this power and influence by tra-
ditional democratic standards, for these men can create
national issues overnight. . . .*

*The views of this fraternity do not represent the
views of America. That is why such a great gulf existed
between how the nation received the President's address—
and how the networks reviewed it. . . .*

*A narrow and distorted picture of America often
emerges from the televised news. A single dramatic piece
of the mosaic becomes, in the minds of millions, the whole
picture.*

*The American who relies upon television for his
news might conclude that the majority of American students are embittered radicals, that the majority of black
Americans feel no regard for their country, that violence
and lawlessness are the rule, rather than the exception, on
the American campus. We know none of these conclusions
is true. . . .*

*Tonight, I have raised questions. I have made no at-
tempt to suggest answers. These answers must come from
the media men. They are challenged to turn their critical
powers on themselves. . . . And the people of America
are challenged, too—challenged to press for responsible
news presentation. The people can let the networks know
that they want their news straight and objective. . . .*

*We would never trust such power over public opinion
in the hands of an elected government; it is time we questioned it in the hands of a small and unelected elite. The
great networks have dominated America's airwaves for
decades; the people are entitled to a full accounting of
their stewardship.*

And the replies of the network presidents at the time would
serve a useful purpose here, because I believe they show how in-
applicable most of their remarks are to what the Vice-President had
to say. First, Julian Goodman, president of NBC:

"Vice-President Agnew's attack on television news is an appeal
to prejudice. More importantly, Mr. Agnew uses the influence of his
high office to criticize the way a government-licensed news medium
covers the activities of government itself. . . . Evidently, he would

prefer a different kind of television reporting—one that would be subservient to whatever political group happens to be in authority at the time."

Frank Stanton, president of CBS:

"No American institution, including television-network news organizations, should be immune to public criticism. . . . We do not believe, however, that this unprecedented attempt by the Vice-President of the United States to intimidate a news medium which depends for its existence upon government licenses represents legitimate criticism. . . . Whatever their [newsmen's] deficiencies, however, they are minor compared to those of a press which would be subservient to the executive power of government."

Leonard Goldenson, president of ABC:

"In our judgment, the performance of ABC news had always been and will continue to be fair and objective. In the final analysis, it is always the public who decides on the reliability of any individual or organization. We will continue to report the news accurately and fully, confident in the ultimate judgment of the American public."

It strikes me that the reaction of the TV network presidents was completely uncalled for and totally unresponsive. It is interesting, too, that the Vice-President's criticism of network bias struck a responsive chord among many, many people who called, telegraphed or wrote to express their agreement. There is nothing to suggest, however, that the tonal gradations of that responsive chord have penetrated deeply into the hushed chambers where TV network policy is made. It has been suggested that perhaps the executives of America's television networks suffer from tonal deafness and have developed what amounts to a dangerous inability to see faults in their own operations and to regard as a frontal challenge to freedom of speech every single word of criticism ever aimed in their direction.

I suggested earlier that it is possible that the television industry actually suffers from a delusion, a belief that it is beyond criticism. It certainly has always felt that it was beyond any kind of serious attack from anyone bearing conservative credentials.

Now I know this personally. I have had experience with network news that goes back a long, long way. Let me give you an example of what I think is complete network bias and irresponsibility. I know the details of it because it happened to me. It was some time in 1963 that a young man named Lee Coney, local representative of the Columbia Broadcasting System, came to me and asked if he could make an appointment for several officials of his network on a matter of extreme importance. I agreed to the appointment and shortly thereafter received in my office in Washington Mr. Fred Friendly, at that time in charge of all CBS news; Mr. Eric Severeid, who was a CBS commentator and general analyst of news events, and Mr. Coney. Several members of my staff sat in on that meeting, and they could testify to the fact that I was asked to cooperate for a period of six weeks in an endeavor to obtain televised information for a documentary which was to be entitled "The Conservative Revival."

The CBS men asked if it would be possible for their camera crews to follow me around for this period of time and televise all of my activities, especially those which had to do with addressing public audiences. At the time, I had a very heavy schedule, and I was not always speaking from textual material. Thus, it was something of a burden to realize that I had, at all times, the famous CBS eye recording everything I did and said in public. Now this may not seem like much of a mental hazard. But for a public official, it is more than just routine to have this kind of concentrated television attention directed at all of your endeavors.

However, I was a genuine conservative and much of my time was devoted to promoting conservative principles of this country. I saw no reason why I should not cooperate and to the fullest extent with any effort by a major network to come to grips with what I believed was a new American phenomenon, a conservative political revolution. The CBS team also got me to promise that at the end of this period of observation I would submit to two and a half hours of televised questioning by Mr. Eric Severeid for use in the documentary.

You can easily see that the plan outlined to me was quite extensive, required a lot of work on my part, and also presaged a rather important documentary presentation to the American people. I faithfully kept all of my commitments. I subjected myself to televised coverage of all of my activities for a longer period than I like to think about. And then in a room in the United States Capitol, I sat for two and a half hours one afternoon and was questioned by Mr. Severeid on every conceivable public position that I had ever taken or might take. As I recall that session, and it was televised, the first question started out by establishing the fact that my formal education did not include a college diploma. If my memory serves, Mr. Severeid asked me if I felt any way limited in my public role, even if it should involve seeking higher political office, by the fact that my formal education did not include a college degree.

From there on the questions got tough. At one point in the question, my press secretary spoke to one of the producers and asked, "Doesn't Severeid have any nice questions to ask the Senator?" To this, he got the reply, "This is the kind of questioning that makes for a good show."

And here I believe we get right to the core of one of the big problems in TV presentation of the news. The producer was talking about theater; my press secretary was talking about politics. In other words, mean questioning, tough questioning, antagonistic questioning, of any public figure, especially a member of the United States Senate who had been mentioned as a possible presidential candidate, would be calculated to have a much more enthusiastic viewing audience than questioning which had to do with seeking to find out why there was a conservative upsurge in this country.

This did not seem to be the major motivating force behind the questioning which took place that afternoon. It was more like a concentrated and lengthy badgering of a conservative politician by a liberal expert. In all events, I put up with it in all good faith. Some time passed before one of the underlings at CBS contacted my press secretary to say that there was a program being shown that night which would include some of the material from the Severeid questioning. That little presentation turned out to be a special called "Thunder on the Right." In it, CBS televised all the crackpot kooks of the radical right it could find, and then switched to Severeid's questioning of me. He isolated a question involving the John Birch Society in which I refused to read them out of the human race, and very, very skillfully tied me in with every crackpot on the Far Right. Much time was given to the Minutemen organization. Much time was given to radical speakers who were showing their bigotry and racial prejudice. And then the switch to Goldwater. In other words, CBS managed to take all the kooks they could possibly lay their cameras on and in one short session, wrap them all around the neck of a conservative presidential possibility and leave them there. Needless to say, I was upset. I summoned Mr. Coney to my office the next morning and told him that I had never seen such a dirty, irresponsible, degrading attempt to assassinate an

American political figure as CBS put on the night before. I told him that he had come into my office with his friends, Mr. Friendly and Mr. Severeid, and completely and thoroughly misrepresented the CBS network's intentions. I not only did that, but I wrote Dr. Frank Stanton, president of CBS, outlined exactly what had taken place and told him that I felt that this was a typical example of total and complete irresponsibility and bias and prejudice on the part of CBS. As a result of my complaints, CBS finally televised a half-hour, carefully edited version of those two and a half hours of questions with Mr. Severeid and presented it without fanfare and without advertising—not as a "conservative revival," but as a conversation with Goldwater, or something to that effect. In other words, these CBS officials had come to me, a member of the United States Senate, and represented themselves as responsible people interested in doing a special television documentary report on a subject in which I was deeply interested. They obtained from me all the cooperation that I could possibly give them, even though I knew of their liberal bias, and even though I knew that Mr. Friendly and Mr. Severeid did not share any of my political beliefs. I felt they were responsible news executives and businessmen. I was wrong. I have never experienced more shabby treatment at the hands of anyone in politics than I did from that particular team of CBS newsmen.

Now I recount this because I believe, and I am certain this is true, that at the time CBS could not have cared less. They had made use of a conservative who might possibly prove dangerous some time. They had done everything they possibly could to sink him politically on a nationwide basis. And they never, for one minute, suspected that the "conservative revival" which they had used to con me into cooperating was an actual fact, was a fact that would later come to fruition, would not only bring about the presidential nomination of the man they had victimized, but would also elect in 1968, a Vice-President who knew fully and exactly what their deficiencies were and would not be afraid to stand up and call his shots. In other words, I believe that the CBS officials, had they thought there was a chance that Goldwater would ever become President or even a candidate for President, would never have sanctioned this kind of operation. But they did not believe that. They had no belief in a conservative resurgence, and they played fast and loose with a Senator from a small, Far Western state to serve their own partisan purpose.

Now I want to make it clear that this was an operation by CBS nationally; and I want to say here that I am not condemning, because of this act, the entire network nor every station affiliated with CBS. In my home city of Phoenix, I get nothing but fine, honorable cooperation from the CBS outlet there. And in most other areas of the country, I have had fair and courteous treatment.

Only at the national level do the networks show their bias. And I might emphasize here that networks do not need to be licensed. There is a great deal of confusion on this particular score. To hear the network executives complaining about Mr. Agnew, you would think that they, as networks, were subject to regulation and to licensing by the Federal Communications Commission. This is not the case. Individual stations are subject to regulation; networks of stations are not. So it ill-behooves any network to complain that speeches by a government official threaten them with intimidation by a government.

Now to carry this CBS thing a little further, I think I may have surprised Dr. Stanton and his minions by not standing still for their type of operation. I accepted it for what it was and acted accordingly. I very often in my travels and in my speeches after that excluded, where it was possible, CBS newsmen from coverage. I didn't ask anyone's permission. I just made it very plain that I didn't like the way they handled public officials; I didn't like the way they handled politicians; I didn't like the way they handled the news and I was not going to assist them in any fashion. This attitude of mine continued and eventually became a matter for almost nationwide interest. And it continued until a good friend of mine named Walter Cronkite, a CBS news commentator, made a special effort. He came to Washington and spent an hour with me in my office. He outlined all of his views and said that he felt that a network as large as CBS should have at least one contact with a prominent Republican Senator who had been mentioned as a possible presidential nominee of his political party.

As a result of this conversation, I became the first public official interviewed by Mr. Cronkite when his program was extended from a 15-minute segment to a half-hour segment each evening. I might say this, that all my relations with Mr. Cronkite and with many other CBS newsmen, Harry Reasoner, for one, have been completely amicable. They do not agree with all my political beliefs. I do not share all their views of public events, but we do not try to double-cross each other. We have an honest respect for each other's opinions, and this is the way I think it should be.

However, my friendship with Mr. Cronkite was sorely tried in the immediate aftermath of President Kennedy's assassination. During the confusion of constant television reporting of the events surrounding that tragic event, Mr. Cronkite commented that of the many notables who had expressed their shock and grief, the name of Barry Goldwater was missing. The Arizona Senator, he reported, was en route to a political rally in Muncie, Indiana, and had not been heard from. The fact of the matter was that my telegram of condolence had been sent to the White House long before Mr. Cronkite's comment, and my trip to Muncie was not designed for political purposes. I was accompanying my wife on the sad journey to her mother's funeral.

No sooner had Mr. Cronkite made his remarks than the CBS switchboard began receiving calls of protest from friends of mine, including Arizona Governor Paul Fannin, who knew the true state of affairs. Some time later the mistake was corrected; and in a letter to me, Mr. Cronkite explained that he had been handed the information about me on "a little piece of paper" which was handed up to him by someone on his news desk. He readily admitted the error and said he hoped that I was not only a forbearing but a forgiving man.

I don't want to appear churlish or unduly sensitive to such mistakes. I believe they can happen, especially in the kind of confusion that is bound to prevail in all newsrooms at the time of a presidential assassination. Because of this, I was willing to accept Mr. Cronkite's apology in good faith. However, no politician who had been subjected to the kind of treatment that I had received at the hands of CBS previously could help but wonder about that "little piece of paper" and who was responsible for writing it and handing it to a man who was talking to a badly shaken nation of millions of politically sensitive people. Any conscientious editor who wanted to take the trouble to check the wire service news could have easily established the true facts about my activities and my whereabouts. In fact, the trip to Muncie had received unusual attention earlier in the day from political reporters, because I had been forced to cancel a meeting in my office with Governor William Scranton of Pennsylvania. Mr. Scranton had made the appointment to talk with me about delegates to the Republican National Convention from his state. The projected meeting was regarded as "hot" political news prior to its cancellation.

Now, lest this appear to be too heavily weighted on the critical side, let me explain that all of my experiences with all newsmen, or even with all CBS newsmen, were not unhappy ones. Quite the contrary. Most of my relations with the press were congenial and fair. I did not ask for, nor expect, any special treatment or consideration from any segment of the communications media. All I wanted was fair treatment, not only from CBS, but from all newsmen covering my activities. I had had sufficient exposure to be able to appraise the treatment I received long before I became a presidential candidate. I had, of course, been covered as a member of the Senate from Arizona, as chairman of the Senate Republican Campaign Committee for a number of years, and as a spokesman for a large segment of the Republican Party, the conservative wing.

It is important, I believe, for the casual reader to understand that the men covering political campaigns are assigned primarily to work as reporters, not as judges. The ones assigned to me during my presidential campaign filed reports to their newspapers and went on the air over television and radio several times a day. Their job was to record, if you will, what happened and report it fairly to the American people. Where this was done, I had no objection. Even when I made mistakes, when I blundered, when I made ill-considered remarks and they were recorded and reported, I had no objection. I had no objection at all to the truth. My objections were reserved completely for dishonest or slanted coverage, for misquotation and misrepresentation of my remarks, for special parceling-out coverage. By this I mean, coverage which was performed by the deliberate selection of particular items in a day's events to show the candidate or the subject in the worst possible light. I also resented being judged by newsmen who were not elected or chosen to pass as critics on everything and anything that a politician had to say but who every day constituted themselves as "experts par excellence" and whose word was final. This was just plain nauseous to informed politicians and public officials who listen to newscasts knowing full well how poorly informed are the newsmen doing the reporting on particular situations.

Now let me bring things up to a real climax, or to two climaxes, where CBS is concerned. During the Republican Presidential Nominating Convention in San Francisco, in 1964, a special CBS program was televised, I believe the date was July 12, from somewhere in Germany. CBS newsman Daniel Schorr took it upon himself to put on a news report which did its best to portray the idea that I was trying to forge links with far rightist neo-Fascist groups in Germany. As correspondent Schorr reported:

"It is now clear that Senator Goldwater's interview with *Der Spiegel* (sometimes called Germany's equivalent of *Time* magazine) with its hard line appealing to right-wing elements in Germany was only the start of a move to link up with his opposite numbers in Germany."

Schorr dealt heavily in false facts which neither he nor CBS newsmen in this country made any attempt to check with my office. He said I had accepted an invitation to speak at an Evangelical Academy near Munich and tried to imply that this school was a gathering place for neo-Nazis. The fact is, I had neither received nor accepted any such invitation to speak in Germany. I had never heard of the academy in question, although I later discovered that Chancellor Adenauer, among other respectable public officials, had spoken there.

Mr. Schorr's broadcast, including his innuendos and his outright declarations that "it is now clear," was false.

All by itself, Schorr's TV report, coming at a time when the Republican National Convention was in progress, was bad enough; however, *The New York Times,* in a special unchecked dispatch from correspondent Arthur J. Olsen, promptly headlined "Senator in Touch with Bonn Right." If there ever was any truth in the belief that *The New York Times* is meticulous about checking all the news "that's fit to print," Olsen's report was a distinct departure from policy.

Without any apparent effort to check Schorr's information, Olsen enlarged on the CBS line with completely false details. He said I had been "in 'frequent and friendly' correspondence for some time" with the Sudeten leader Hans Christoph Seebohm, who had recently figured in a dispute over "militant" statements, and "other conservative West German politicians." Olsen further contended that I had given an interview to the *Zeitung und Soldaten Zeitung,* an extreme rightist weekly.

There was only one thing wrong with Olsen's story. It was 100 percent false. I had never corresponded with anyone named Seebohm. I had never heard of his name nor of the controversy over

militant statements. I have never corresponded with any West German politician, conservative or otherwise, and I had never granted
an interview to the *Zeitung und Soldaten Zeitung* newspaper.

Needless to say, the CBS program from Germany in the midst
of the Republican Convention was picked up and carried far and
wide by other segments of the news media. And then later, when I
had been asked about it and branded the whole thing a lie, *The
New York Times* had this to say about it on July 13, and I quote:

"Senator Goldwater has decided not to take a post-convention
vacation in Germany. One reason was a Columbia Broadcasting
System news report yesterday that asserted Mr. Goldwater's trip
signaled a link between the right wing of the United States and that
of Bavaria. . . ."

Now this charge by the CBS which was widely picked up by
the newspapers was also used by my opponents at the convention.
For example, Governor Scranton, who was publishing a daily tabloid
of news for convention delegates, reproduced almost every bit of
these charges even though they were known, by people right in
Governor Scranton's campaign camp, to have no basis in fact whatsoever. Five days later, *The New York Times* carried this so-called
"clarifying statement" broadcast by CBS news correspondent Daniel
Schorr:

"In speaking the other day of a move by Senator Goldwater to
link up these forces, I did not mean to suggest conscious effort on
his part, of which there is no proof here, but rather a process of
gravitation which is visible here."

Of course, the "clarifying statement" was never seen by most
people. And this deliberate smear in the midst of a political convention was allowed to stand for all important purposes. I suggest
that the timing, the motivations, the presentation and the material
used all add up to deliberate bias based upon deliberate falsehood.
I know of no other way to characterize that particular program from
Germany and by that time in 1964 I had concluded that there was
no way for a Republican candidate named Goldwater to do business
with CBS without being distorted and presented in a completely
false and unfavorable light. Therefore, I decided that CBS would
not be any part of my campaign plans.

Thus it was on the night I was nominated as the Republican
candidate for President of the United States in San Francisco, I
agreed to appear before the television cameras and make a statement

regarding my selection. This scheduled appearance before the TV
cameras and microphones the night of the action which nominated
me as presidential candidate was arranged in response to a request
by the networks to present something live from the newly selected
Republican candidate prior to the time when I went before the convention to make my acceptance address. In other words, in my acquiescing to this plan, I was not only presenting an image to the
entire voting population of the United States, which was of no mean
consideration, but I was also providing the networks with a service.

And I concluded that that service did not necessarily have to
include CBS. I decided that a network irresponsible enough and
biased enough to deliberately present a program like the Daniel
Schorr program from Europe in the midst of a nominating convention was not responsible enough to be considered. And make no
mistake about it, that program was designed to make Barry Goldwater look exactly like a politician with neo-Nazi leanings. I had
no illusions about this, and the people who saw the program
had no illusions about it. I found it absolutely astounding that a
major network would permit such a thing to go out over their
stations without absolute assurance that every word and innuendo
was correct. Apparently no effort, at least none I was aware of nor
my staff was aware of, was ever made to check the Daniel Schorr
program.

Therefore, on the night of my nomination, with the entire
country waiting, I gave my press representatives orders to have the
cameras set up on the fifteenth floor of the Mark Hopkins Hotel. I
said that I would appear before the cameras and the microphones
but only if CBS was not included in the plans. I was absolutely
sincere in issuing that directive, and it is impossible to describe the
kind of scurrying and pressuring and telephoning that went on prior
to the time set for my appearance before the microphones.

It just so happened that about five to ten minutes before the
scheduled appearance word reached me to the effect that the network officials might try to blame their local CBS correspondent
and that Robert Pierpoint, the man who had traveled with me
many weary miles during my campaign for the nomination, was
to be held responsible. And this was the only reason—and I repeat—this was the only reason that CBS was included in one of
the most important television appearances of my entire political
career. And it was easily the most important political telecast of that

particular month. Needless to say, I was amused at some of the argument used in that last-minute scramble to get CBS included in a television presentation that was going to easily carry every major station in the country. And they went along these lines: "After all, you can't exclude a major network." "After all, CBS is an important part of the communications media." "After all, CBS is one of the three largest TV networks." And my reply in each instance was "Yes, but after all, CBS has shown itself very, very clearly to be irresponsible in the presentation of political news. It has been irresponsible in the presentation of political news regarding my candidacy. I see no reason to include it in another episode of television history."

As I say, the decision was reversed merely because I was afraid that some innocent bystander, a young man who had to my knowledge and to my way of thinking done a fairly good job to be objective for a very biased team of news television commentators, would be hurt. It was only my belief that this young man might be held accountable that in any way influenced me to alter my decision. In all events, CBS like ABC and NBC finally was admitted to the television studio room and was able to televise my remarks, my appearance with my wife Peggy, and my replies to questions put to me by TV commentators at that particular time in my career.

I recount these things to illustrate to the reader that I am not dealing in generalities nor do I think Spiro Agnew is dealing in generalities when he says that the TV networks need to reexamine their handling and presentation of the news. I know what was done to me by the Daniel Schorr broadcast. I know that nothing in the way of correcting that was accomplished by the statement that was televised by CBS five days after the fact and which had a lot of gobbledy-gook words from Mr. Daniel Schorr about something called "a process of gravitation." Another point I wonder at is what chance there would have been to obtain even a clarification five days later from CBS if the subject of their report from Germany had not by that time conclusively sewed up the Republican nomination for President. I am fearful to speculate on this because I have a feeling that the people who were then in charge of CBS news had not the slightest interest in being fair or objective in any way. I have every reason to believe they were motivated only by partisan self-interest. I have no reason to believe that their objective was to inform the American people or to present a clear, unbiased report on a presidential candidate. I think their consideration was for public image of CBS, for their ratings, and for their own particular political preference. This is the only conclusion I can reach about a network that would go on the air in the midst of a national political convention with a program apparently designed to influence the rejection of a particular candidate. I repeat, I'm not dealing in generalities, nor in suspicions, nor in any of the other allegations or types of allegations that go with charges that the networks slant the news, present biased news, present prejudiced news. I am talking about deliberate falsehood and deliberate efforts at political tampering by a major network and by the reporters for a major network. I am not speaking from hearsay. I am speaking from bitter personal experience.

And while I am speaking of the 1964 campaign, I might mention that it was another network television broadcast which served to launch one of the really major falsehoods of the entire campaign. This happened on May 24, 1964, on American Broadcasting Company's "Issues and Answers" program. But I want to make it very emphatically clear that neither the network nor the program participants were guilty of any kind of bias or distortion or misrepresentation of the facts. All these things came later in news stories based on that interview, which perhaps will go down in presidential campaign history as the "defoliation issue."

It came about while I was being interviewed by ABC's correspondent Howard K. Smith, who asked for some suggestions on how the war in Vietnam might successfully be prosecuted. I mentioned bombing bridges, roads and other routes by which the Communists moved troops and supplies into South Vietnam. Then I added, and these were my exact words:

"There have been several suggestions made. I don't think we would use any of them. But defoliation of the forests by low-yield atomic weapons could well be done. When you remove the foliage, you remove the cover.

"The major supply lines, though, I think would have to be interdicted where they leave Red China, which is the Red River Valley above North Vietnam and there, according to my studies of geography, it would be a difficult task to destroy those basic routes."

That interview occurred on Sunday. By Monday morning, the newspapers had me suggesting the use of nuclear bombs in Vietnam. Even one of the usually reliable wire services moved such a story based on the ABC interview. When its editors got a look at the transcript of the show, however, the Associated Press quickly put out a correction. The fact that the correction never caught up with the original incorrect account is still evident to this very day. Not many weeks ago, a friend of mine called to tell me that he had heard once again a TV news commentator state flatly that Goldwater had suggested the use of nuclear bombs to defoliate the jungles of Vietnam.

This incident, among many others, shows how important it is for news correspondents, especially those whose reports are carried to millions of readers and viewers, to be absolutely sure of their facts before they give them glib public expression. Because it is a political fact of life that a "clarified" TV report (such as was belatedly put out by CBS in the Daniel Schorr incident) or a newspaper correction never catches up with the original allegation. And this is particularly true when the first news account is of an especially sensational nature. And, of course, it is always true that media people—especially newspaper editors—will give big black headlines to a sensational story and very small, carefully hidden display to a later correction.

The *San Francisco Examiner*'s handling of the defoliation interview was as irresponsible and as prejudiced as anything I have ever seen. Its front page headline on May 25, 1964, screamed:

GOLDWATER'S PLAN TO USE VIET A-BOMB

The subhead presumed to be a quote of mine. It read:

"I'd risk a war"

The headline inside the paper where the sensation-mongering tale was continued from page one carried this neat little example of editorial misrepresentation:

BARRY'S PLAN: USE A BOMB

The above account might be entitled "The Anatomy of a Political Lie," because it is fairly typical of how newsmen with a built-in bias will jump to place the worst possible construction on the statements of a candidate with whom they disagree. The whole treatment given to that interview by liberal newspapers throughout the country, I believe, was an accurate measurement of how extremely uninterested some liberal journalists were in 1964 to get at anything resembling the truth.

This defoliation incident was misinterpreted so far and so wide that I feel it is important to explain it in my own words even at the risk of being unfair to Mr. Howard K. Smith. I have known Mr. Smith for a long time. I know that when he began his news career he was almost unreasonably liberal. It will be remembered that he figured in the famous ABC-TV show that presented a requiem for the political career of Richard M. Nixon after his defeat for Governor and included on his panel none other than the notorious Alger Hiss, whom Mr. Nixon had investigated during his House career and prior to Hiss's conviction for perjuring himself in a celebrated Communist spy trial 20 years ago.

But Mr. Smith represents something special to me these days. The best way to describe it is that I believe he can be called an "honest liberal with an open mind." There is no other way to account for his widely publicized conclusion, following Vice-President Agnew's criticism, that there "is a network news bias" in favor of liberal causes. Not only did ABC's Smith say that he agreed with much of what Mr. Agnew said, but he actually claimed credit for saying it before the Vice-President did. In an interview in the magazine *TV Guide* published February 28, 1970, Mr. Smith described himself as being "left of center." But he added: "Our liberal friends today have become dogmatic. They have a set of automatic reactions. They react the way political cartoonists do—with oversimplification. Oversimplify. Be sure you please your fellows, because that's what's 'good.' They're conventional, they're conformists. They're pleasing Walter Lippmann, they're pleasing the Washington Post, they're pleasing the editors of the New York Times, and they're pleasing one another."

Touché. No conservative could have described the knee-jerk liberals of the communications industry any better or with more accuracy. In fact, he gives special mention to the TV news media's attitude on conservatives. He put it this way in that *TV Guide* interview:

"If Agnew says something, it's bad, regardless of what he says. If Ronald Reagan says something, it's bad, regardless of what he says. Well, I'm unwilling to condemn an idea because a particular man said it. Most of my colleagues do just that."

I am almost inclined to say "thank heavens" for at least one honest liberal in the news media. In my travels I have actually overheard newsmen say to each other, "That wasn't a bad idea, I wish it wasn't Goldwater who had said it."

What I am getting at here, what Vice-President Agnew has been working on, and what the American people are beginning to understand is that, politically, where much of the TV medium is concerned, the crime is of an ideological hue. In the oversimplification which Mr. Smith speaks about, it adds up to a belief that conservatives are "devils," but they are devils who should not be given their due at the hands of the media. The consideration becomes, not what is said, but who said it.

This is a disgraceful situation to exist in a large, vital segment of the American economy like the television industry. It has been getting away with murder—political murder, that is—for much too long a time. Mr. Agnew was absolutely correct in calling the industry to account, and I for one am not going to stand by and let the whole thing get obscured under false charges of threats to the freedom of the press. It was for this reason that I challenged a statement made on March 11 by Mr. Julian Goodman, president of the National Broadcasting Company. Addressing a Sigma Delta Chi Foundation lecture at the University of Texas in Austin, Mr. Goodman asserted that "Not since 1798—when newsmen were sentenced to prison under the Sedition Act for statements displeasing to the government—has American journalism been under greater attack." Mr. Goodman saw what he calls a "clear and growing danger to freedom of information" in almost every action and statement made by government officials since President Nixon took office. He literally issued orders to the government with this ringing declaration:

"The government must stand back from the press. The use of subpoenas on the news media—especially for off the record or similar unpublished material—should be abandoned by both Federal and state officials as a matter of constitutional self-restraint."

Mr. Goodman's intemperate and irresponsible declaration struck me as interesting. If such a great danger existed to freedom of the press from statements by Mr. Agnew, one wonders why Mr. Goodman waited until he was asked to lecture to the Sigma Delta Chi four months after the Vice-President's criticism of television news treatment to raise this vital question. Being an important policy maker in television, one would have expected Mr. Goodman to be fighting such a threat on a daily or at least a weekly basis if he felt it were so dire.

In all events, in talking to a Young Republican Leadership Training School in Washington on March 12, I called attention to Mr. Goodman's sensational charge and remarked:

For a responsible industry executive to expect the American people who watch a steady stream of criticism aimed at the Republican administration on TV newscasts everyday to believe a great threat exists to the freedom of the press is downright ludicrous.

Mr. Goodman coupled his irresponsible charge with a call on Federal and state officials to abandon serving subpoenas on the news media.

I think it's time to ask just who these TV news people think they are. If one of their employees has information or material that would be useful to a grand jury or a district attorney in legal proceedings, why shouldn't he be asked to produce the items requested? Are we to take Mr. Goodman's word for the fact that the news media is above the law? That's not my understanding of freedom of the press. I strongly believe in freedom of the press, but I also believe that it carries with it a very heavy responsibility for members of the press to be civic-minded and helpful to law enforcement agencies.

The treatment my remarks received on Mr. Goodman's major news telecast—the Huntley-Brinkley Report—that day was typical. Mr. Brinkley quoted from my speech saying that Barry Goldwater had noted that "liberal comments about the Nixon Administration have taken on an edge of desperation and hysteria since the Vice-President began to give voice to some of the pet peeves of the Silent Majority." Mr. Brinkley then assured his nationwide audience that the Senator had given no examples or explanations of what he meant. Neatly ignored was the following sentence in the prepared text of my speech which read, "For example, only this week Mr. Julian Goodman, president of NBC, became the author of one of the most dishonest and ridiculous statements of the new decade. In a speech at the University of Texas in Austin, he characterized recent criticism of the news media as the greatest threat to freedom of the press since the Sedition Act of 1798 when newsmen were jailed for making statements which were displeasing to the government."

While Mr. Brinkley carefully left his viewing audience with the impression that I had made a wild, unsubstantiated charge, he smiled smugly and went on to say that he couldn't help but observe that

TV officials seldom receive complaints from politicians whom the medium had praised.

This, of course, was designed to be cute, but upon examination it makes one really appreciate Mr. Brinkley for being a "master of the obvious" in some respects.

It is interesting to ponder what NBC viewers who heard Mr. Brinkley thought the next morning when the news report on the NBC "Today" show carried a film clip of my criticism and reported on a letter which Mr. Goodman wrote to me in response to my published remarks to the Young Republicans. I can only say that one newspaper, the *Arizona Daily Star,* in its March 13, 1970, issue, carried an account of Mr. Goodman's letter to me with a subhead which accurately summed it up. It said, "Goodman Denies He's Ridiculous." Actually, what the NBC president said was that he was sorry to find me in sharp disagreement with him, but he had no intention of entering into a debate. He made two points which I want to record verbatim in an exercise of courtesy which I am glad to extend to the NBC president, but which his employee, Mr. Brinkley, refused to accord me. Mr. Goodman's two points are as follows:

"First, my reference to the Sedition Act was as follows: 'Not since 1798—when newsmen were sentenced to prison under the Sedition Act for statements displeasing to the Government—has American journalism been under greater attack.' That is my own judgment, based on more than 20 years in journalism and my knowledge of the history of the profession. I believe it was a fair statement, and not a ridiculous one, as you chose to characterize it.

"The other, is that I felt I made clear in my Austin speech that I was referring to subpoenas that compromise news sources or prejudice further news access. I base this view on the Constitutional guarantee of press freedom, and I suggested that Constitutional self-restraint should discourage Government from 'the broad use of subpoena powers.' I did not and do not suggest that the news media should be above the law. On the contrary, I have been emphasizing the Constitutional protection of press freedom, which is such a basic part of the law. In taking this position, the press is defending the nation's basic law, and those who are in opposition are in fact undermining it."

PART

IV

The Shape of the Future

IX

Tomorrow's Leaders

AMERICA'S FUTURE IS BRIGHT INDEED IF ALL WE HAVE TO WORRY ABOUT is the quality of the upcoming national leadership.

It is my firm conviction, based on years of observation, that today's youth—tomorrow's leaders—are exceptional. Contrary to some opinion, tomorrow's leaders, I believe, bring a higher degree of intelligence, training and judgment to the problems of democracy than any generation which preceded them. Make no mistake about it—this is a new breed. It is a new breed of Americans which is finding a new dedication to the concept of individual freedom.

My conclusions are founded on first-hand observation and study. I doubt if there is another politician in America who has more consistently visited our colleges and universities and our high schools than have I during the last decade.

Nobody on my staff has kept an exact count, but I believe it is safe to estimate that my visits to the campuses of this country and my talks with college groups have averaged around 100 per year over the past ten or twelve years. Except in very rare cases, these appearances and discussions have all included question periods which afforded me an unrestrained experience of give-and-take with America's college youth on all the burning issues of the day, as well as many that had an importance confined to the age group involved.

When I say this is an exceptionally well-trained, evenly balanced generation of Americans, I say it in full knowledge that a great many people are inclined to equate the entire generation with the radicals and the kooks and the extremists and the out-and-out screwballs who have gained so much attention in the public press, on the television screens, and on the radio.

With all other law-abiding Americans, I certainly deplore the far-out activities and tactics of many of our young people today. I am, of course, referring to the hippies, the heppies, the yippies, the Weathermen, the SDS, and what have you, who insist on chaos, confusion and disruption as a way of life. My reference is to that element which will seize upon any alleged grievance, whether justified or not, to demonstrate and protest and find an outlet for the newest verbal obscenities which they have picked up. I am saying that there is an element in our society which is inclined to mount a protest for the sake of the action, that is, for the sake of the protest itself. What is desired is action of a disruptive nature regardless of the cause. This is why today you can find sincere advocates of peace and honest critics of the Vietnam war mingling with protesters and demonstrators among which are those who object to a certain course of study, to a certain type of campus lighting fixture, or to the way the Dean of Men buttons his coat.

Part of my point here is to convince the reader, if possible, that the responsible young people of today, those most likely to assume the positions of leadership in our government, in our society, in our business corporations, and in all of our important institutions, are not on display. They constitute not only the silent majority but an unseen majority of young Americans who are busy pursuing courses of study which will fit them for the enormous challenges which must face us in the future.

As a matter of fact, these responsible young Americans are so undemonstrative in their conscientious approach to important questions that they actually constitute a mystery for liberal reporters who have become accustomed to riots, demonstrations and attitudes printed on a placard. For example, Mary McGrory, a columnist for the *Washington Evening Star,* has publicly confessed her inability to understand. In describing a Young Republican Leadership Training School in Washington on March 12, 1970, Miss McGrory complained as follows in her column:

"It is a mystery why young Republicans are the way they are. They do not resemble Democrats of the same age. They love the police and hate the press. They are all-out for the Establishment and would not be found dead storming a dean's office or marching in a peace parade.

"Some people have the theory that Republicans are born old, or at least conservative. Whatever the reason, when young, or at least under 35, they are all for law and order and organization. They talk about freedom, never civil liberties."

It doesn't seem to have occurred to Miss McGrory that more than just a few young Americans are living up to their responsibilities as citizens. Her view has apparently become so restricted that she is unable to understand that not just young Republicans but a vast majority of young Americans are all for law and order and organization. These are the foundation stones of an ordered society devoted to justice. It may seem mysterious to the Mary McGrorys of the press that some young people today are in favor of the police, are in favor of authority, and are against storming a dean's office and against destroying both peace and property which do not belong to them. But to the silent majority, it is not mysterious; it is common sense. It is the way of responsible young people in a free society.

Another part of my original point is to show that the very restlessness which today leads some of our young people to courses of action which, by our standards, can only be called reprehensible and unsocial—even illegal—may in the future be a force for good and betterment of the human condition. The activities of today's youth —especially those designed to shock and anger their elders—may easily spring from the kind of adolescent ferment which will lead to fresh ideas and new approaches to the problems that confront this nation.

We used to say when I was in college that no young man was worth his salt who didn't flirt with Communism or some other radical departure from the status quo at the age of 17 and think his way through it by the time he was 18. Who are we to say today that our bearded young protesters and demonstrators are not merely going through a phase in the process of growing up? Is it not possible that at least some of the kids who are hauled in and prosecuted today for stealing automobile hubcaps in America's ghettos are comparable to those barefoot kids of Mark Twain's era who caught an occasional fanny full of rock salt from an irate farmer whose watermelons or roasting ears they had stolen?

I believe there is a very serious aspect to the current youthful trend toward lawlessness and the use of drugs. However, I hasten to suggest that it does no good to see only the dark side of the question. Nor does it do any good to merely deplore and complain without making an effort to search out the causes for such kinds of youthful behavior and try to find proper methods for remedying the situation.

We hear a lot of talk today about the so-called "generation gap," and I have heard some especially righteous adults claim that the problem should rather be called a "veneration gap." So much for slogans. I believe there is today a condition in our society which can be called a generation gap but which has been grossly over-simplified on one hand and entirely misread or misinterpreted on the other. Too often the generation gap is taken to mean a gap existing between today's parents and their children. I suggest this divergence of interest, attitudes and concerns may possibly fit into such a category but only by an accident of time. My belief is that the generation gap today exists between young people who never knew at first hand either the problems of worldwide depression or worldwide war and older people whose entire early lives were conditioned by one or both of these transcendental concerns.

I have heard people claim that today's youth have their priorities confused, that they do not have the proper regard for the correct pursuits in today's society. Most often such appraisals come from men and women whose entire youths were colored by a concern for obtaining the necessities of life or protection from global annihilation.

The oldsters who grew up in the Thirties actually knew what a warping effect on the human spirit can be wrought by genuine concern for sufficient food to eat, clothes to wear, and shelter to live under. They saw it at firsthand when the Great Depression idled millions of employable Americans and wiped out their entire store of savings or other financial assets. They experienced the shock of having men trained in the professions forced into menial labor or even panhandling to obtain the elements of subsistence.

To today's child of American affluence, it is almost impossible to realize the trauma that really and honestly existed in the early 1930's when songs appeared with titles like "Brother, Can You Spare a Dime?" There was pathos and understanding attached to the opening words of that refrain, which went: "Once I built a railroad; I made it run; Brother, can you spare a dime?"

Children of the Depression were born in an era which had an excess of fear in the national atmosphere. They were the generation whose members listened to commencement speakers talk about them becoming the nation's leaders but who never really believed it. Some of us thought vaguely about promises that we would "inherit the future," but nobody really considered such claims anything more than flowery commencement-night rhetoric which had no application to the world outside. In other words, here was a generation saddled with such an overwhelming concern for how it was to feed and clothe and house itself that it had little time to spend debating about or protesting over the great social issues of the day. Its members had plenty to complain about where their elders were concerned. They could look about them and see very little promise but plenty of economic chaos and discouragement. It did them no good to charge their elders with the crime of "lousing up" their handling of civilization. They had to speak quickly to beat their elders' own lamentations and expressions of self-criticism.

Everyone agreed things were in a mess, and scapegoats were actively sought in the body politic and in the economic structure of the nation. But it seems to me that we seldom heard the entire older generation held to account for the unhappy circumstances which prevailed. If there was a priority for youth in the 1930's, heading the list was the problem of getting a job and holding it. By the same token, if there were any overriding priorities for the youth coming to bat in the 1940's, heading the list was the problem of how to stay alive through World War II and adjust to the domestic upheavals which were bound to be part of its aftermath.

Another big factor confining the activities of these earlier generations was a very basic one—lack of money. It isn't generally understood today how easy the national affluence makes it for today's disgruntled youngster to move about the country joining his own selected form of protest in whatever section of the country he might choose.

It accounts, also, for much of the campus unrest. So many people today have the kind of money it takes to put their children in college that this nation's institutions of higher education are greatly overburdened. Schools and colleges and universities, which once numbered their students in the hundreds, today have enrollments which in some instances outnumber whole communities.

When you get campuses which accommodate 10,000, 20,000 or 30,000 students, you naturally get a high degree of confusion. You also get a heavy quotient of students who are in school for reasons only casually related to the search for education. In earlier generations a higher percentage of people in the colleges and universities carried with them the determination to obtain as much learning as their meager funds would permit. Many times the raising of tuition costs themselves caused so much effort and scrimping on the part of parents and children alike that the students by whom it was expended felt a special reason for making good.

Today things are vastly different than they were when my generation was going to school, and there is no doubt that we are seeing today a high percentage of student protest and rebellion. But I wish to be emphatic here, as I have been in my talks on campuses, on television and on radio in various parts of this country, when I state that this generation of American youth does not worry me. In fact, I think it is the best generation I have encountered in my lifetime.

You have to keep in mind that we have some 2,500 campuses in this country, and we have student problems of varying degree on perhaps 200 of them. The serious problems are confined to 20 or 25 institutions involving less than a fraction of one percent of the students. Here is a situation where I believe statistics serve a valuable purpose. They put the whole problem in a perspective that is impossible for the readers of many of today's newspapers and the viewers of many of today's TV news reports to obtain. Regardless of how inconsequential by comparison the student unrest happens to be, I believe it is a problem which raises valid questions about the youth of this nation which should be pursued.

I have that happy faculty of being able to remember my own youth. And among the things I remember are some rebellious thoughts which today occupy the minds of many students and young people. Foremost, of course, was that age-old affliction of the late teens and early twenties which finds its outlet in a youth's refusal to accept the established order without question. That might not be the best way to put it, but I believe it says a lot about the perpetual questioning of authority—whether it is in the home, the high school, the university, the armed services or on the streets—which goes on today in the minds of many of our young people. Perhaps it is the way that that questioning, that challenging of a status quo handed them by their elders, finds its expression that is important. I believe the majority of our responsible young people today go about the whole thing in a logical, almost scientific manner. They study carefully the existing system and institutions, define their opposition to or questioning of this system and these institutions, and begin exploring ways and means for making them better.

By the same token, there is an unthinking fringe-type of youthful rebel who feels that he must identify anything with which he disagrees or questions and confront it directly in the hope of destroying it. If you study carefully the campus riots and many of the youthful revolts throughout the country, you will find that many of the grievances expressed are vague and the solutions offered are quite often nonexistent. There is also an emotional factor moving among these groups which prevents older citizens or even level-headed youth from convincing the protesters that it is useless, even dangerous, to destroy systems and institutions without having substitute mechanisms to move into their place.

What I am saying is that there is plenty of room for youthful disagreement, even rebellion against the established order, but that it is absolutely essential that such opposition be positive and structured to improve rather than destroy. Any parent or older citizen who today thinks he can deny the whole idea of youthful questioning and probing and opposing merely by insisting that he himself has been around the barn and knows absolutely what is right and what isn't needs his head examined. To begin with, I don't know anyone wise enough to make such a claim; and even if there were, I am sure that his insistence would come under challenge from newer human beings coming up in our civilization.

It stands to reason that today's youth, having been born and raised in conditions totally different from those existing for earlier generations, should have different ideas, should believe that what their elders have handed them is a less than perfect society—call it even an "Establishment," if you will.

It is my feeling that a great deal of the blame which today is being laid at the feet of teenagers and college students belongs at a higher level in the age structure of our society. I believe the delinquency comes in where young adults, assuming their first positions of importance in today's world, show a total lack of responsibility equal to their jobs. One group in particular comes to mind. It is the group of young college and university faculty members. In this age group, in the upper twenties and early thirties, are individuals who have contributed heavily to the disorder and disruption that could, if allowed to go unchecked, someday destroy the entire system of higher education. In school after school, we learn from the news accounts that youthful faculty members not only have given aid and comfort to student revolts but too often have been found to be the architects and planners of these uprisings.

Here I believe is a youthful delinquency which is chargeable. It is my feeling that a young man old enough, and trained sufficiently to become a teacher of men, should also be mature enough to understand the need for order in a society of justice for the majority. If we can't look to the instructors of our college-age groups to understand the proper place of authority in academic life as well as in civic life, then I believe we are headed for serious trouble. There is nothing deep or devious about an attitude on the part of older Americans which points out that without a structure of authority in the home, school and community, we must revert to a society where only the fittest survive—to a civic jungle so chaotic that the services of a dictator or a Cosa Nostra king would actually be welcome. Down through history people have insisted on some order in their lives even if the source of that order should ultimately prove to be tyrannical and evil.

But let's return to America's youth and its honest and healthy questioning of the system which for three and a half decades has bragged of its liberal humanitarianism only to confront today's graduates with a bigger, more complex bundle of domestic problems than any previous generation has ever known. I have two sons. A few years ago I remember asking both of them when it was in their lives that they began to suspect that the Old Man had some sense. My elder son, a Congressman now and even then a politician among the young adults of his acquaintance, said, "Oh, I guess it was around the time I reached 21 years of age." But my younger son, who has a disconcerting habit of candor, shot back, "I'm still not sure."

Like most other young people of their age, they are not about to accept and embrace the established order as being the beginning and end of all social answers merely because their father or other elders claim this to be true. Sometimes, when I am dead certain that my contention is correct—even when I base it on that old conservative premise of proven lessons of the past—I begin to get hot under the collar when my contention is questioned in my own family. It isn't nearly as difficult when I think back and remember my attitudes toward the problems of the 1920's as my father tried to explain and rationalize for me with the reasoning of his generation. And while I later came to understand that he was right in many instances, I must confess that I did insist upon and enjoy that period of argumentation with him and with other older men of that period.

Basically, I wanted to know, "Isn't there a better way to do it?" And I believe that the responsible young people of today who question our social attitudes as well as our governmental procedures and our economic maxims are seeking the answer to a similar question.

And who—at least who among those that today identify themselves as working conservatives—can deny today's youth the right to ask, "Isn't there a better way?"

In this I feel a kinship with America's young people. I have been asking that same question year in and year out about the mess which has been handed to me and my children and my grandchildren by the phony approaches and policies of leftist liberals. Who wouldn't ask, "Isn't there a better way?" when one looks at the total mess which the liberals have made out of America's welfare system, its housing problem, its health standards—to say nothing of the problem of environment and pollution. Can we honestly say that today's youth have no right to question a fiscal policy which runs up a national debt so astronomical that even the interest payments are a major item to be allowed for in the budget? Can we honestly deny them the right to question why after three and a half decades of paternalistic liberalism we have a serious racial discrimination problem on our hands? Can we possibly say they have no right to ask if there isn't a better way to control inflation, to handle crime in the streets?

But no matter how much merit may exist in the questioning which surrounds the failure of American liberalism, it will never be sufficient to justify the wholesale disregard for authority and for law and order. When I consider the alleged problem of America's youth, I have a feeling that some of it goes deeper today than may have been the case with earlier generations. I think this may best be expressed by a deficiency of trust. Where it began is anybody's guess, but I always have had a feeling that prohibition and the advent of the motor car had the effect of making cross-eyed crooks out of many American fathers. I am thinking of the family heads who would come home and brag about having gotten a bottle of Scotch or some other kind of liquor "right off the boat" and in violation of the Volstead Act. Then, of course, there is the impression that may have been made on young minds by fathers who bragged around the family dinner table of having exceeded the speed limit or parked illegally without falling afoul of the traffic policeman. I am sure other children were exposed to some parental explanations over how their Old Man succeeded in outwitting the Internal Revenue Bureau on some minor, dollar-saving avoidance of the Federal Income Tax law.

Now I may be making a big thing out of something that actually might be described as American table manners, but the whole idea of playing fast and loose with laws with which you or a majority of American people may disagree does not add up to a good example to set for younger children. Some of this casual attitude of "ha-ha-I-broke-the-law-and-got-away-with-it" on the part of parents was bound to rub off on some younger people. Some, especially those with an underdeveloped ability to learn and a faulty sense of individual responsibility, might well and quite easily adopt the attitude that, "Well, if the Old Man can cheat the government and break the law, I can do it too." In other words, parents sometimes unknowingly present children with almost an automatic license to break the law. From my observations, a large part of the increase in youthful crime in this generation is traceable to parental neglect or just parental stupidity.

I sometimes think that too much of the blame for today's juvenile delinquency and youthful unrest is attributed to broken homes and to contentious situations where parents fight and argue and ultimately separate. While I do not in any way want to create the impression that I believe broken homes are not a major cause of youthful disorientation and confusion which leads to unlawful behavior, I want to suggest that some of the trouble lies with homes which are not broken but where the parents are too busy with outside activities.

A friend illustrated this to me one time in a rather interesting way. He asked me to take a piece of paper and a pencil and to write down the names of all the committees to which I belong and to which I felt obligated to devote some of my time. You can imagine the length of that list considering my interests in politics, civic affairs, veterans affairs, amateur radio, the church and so forth. It gave me a quick glance at how many small but persistent and acknowledgeable demands are made upon my time.

Fortunately, my list was made after all of my children had grown up and moved. But consider the average, responsible, civic-minded person with an interest in politics, social activities and hobbies. When you do, you begin to get an idea how little time some people actually have to devote to their families and to their children. It is utterly amazing the number of committees and subcommittees upon which some people serve—none of which can receive their full attention, but all of which take time away from their families and the business of instilling in their children the proper values of life. Some people devote so much of their time to the welfare of others that they overlook the demands which require their attention under their very noses in their very own homes.

It strikes me that the whole concept of leaders, be they parents or government officials, setting an example for our younger Americans has much more validity than it is accorded in liberal circles. I believe it is possible for a national administration, by its actions, to set the tone for an entire nation's conduct. How much, of course, is entirely debatable, but the need for high moral standards in persons holding important government positions cannot be denied.

Another aspect of the youthful unrest, especially on college campuses, is one with which I am sure my older friends may easily take issue. I might even be judged guilty of a brand of heresy, but it is my considered opinion that the young people of today understand freedom much better than some of their elders who have forgotten the fundamental aspects. Too many fathers and mothers have come to accept a species of government control and regimentation because it has been a gradual process with which they grew up and which has become almost a way of life with them. These older people, I believe, realize way down deep that some of their highly vaunted freedom has slipped away, but they are afraid to complain. I believe there are many adults, many of them in my age group, who fear not for their freedom but for their affluence. Take, for example, some of the farmers in my state. Over a cocktail or in a friendly street-corner conversation, they will tell you how sick and tired they are of farm regimentation and agricultural programs dictated by Washington. But these are the same farmers who will go out and vote time and time again to renew subsidy programs which benefit them personally.

We hear much today about the young person who says "I want to do my thing." It is my feeling that the elder all too often assumes that every youngster's "thing" is to demonstrate, fight with the police, dress up like hippies, and prove generally disruptive to the status quo. It doesn't occur to enough of us that the young person who "wants to do his thing" is merely using the vernacular of the day to express the same desire which we had when we were kids of his age. I believe most of America's young people—those leaders of tomorrow upon which our entire destiny depends—are insisting upon the right to "do their thing" and do it in the right manner. I believe their insistence—and again I am speaking here of the great numbers of responsible youth—ends at that line where the doing of their thing runs into the rights of others, prohibits or interferes with the ability of other human beings to do their thing. The problem arises, of course, when the kooks and extremists and radicals and misfits of the Far Left begin insisting that they have a right to do their thing in the name of freedom no matter who it injures or how much damage it might cause. If the fringe groups would once learn that individual freedom is the most noble and rewarding of all government experiments, they would begin to catch a glimmer of the great truth of civilization: that individual freedom carries with it individual responsibility to respect the freedom of others. Unless their freedom is thus restricted, it becomes freedom for them alone and tyranny for other people.

The real tragedy enters into this equation when the troublemakers move in and use the natural tendency of young people to desire freedom of action and freedom to "do their thing" as a vehicle to destroy society. When any group, whether it be the Black Panthers or some other professional troublemakers, begin to believe that they have a right to do anything to achieve the performance of "their thing," they depart from rational society. They forfeit any claim on rational consideration. Unfortunately, many of them do not understand this and go on demanding rights that their actions have actually forfeited for them.

Regardless of how the radicals perform, I do think that there does exist a gap of sorts in the understanding of freedom between young people and their elders. But I would caution my peers on one important point: don't try to kid today's young people. They can see through a phony argument as though it were glass. And believe me, any politician who has spent any considerable time in Q and A sessions on American campuses understands this thoroughly. If you don't plan to level with these young people and tell them the truth as you see it, you might as well forget the endeavor. Not only will they spot a phony argument, but they will penalize you immediately by making you the subject of ridicule.

In my appearances on America's campuses, I always try to "tell it like it is," and by that I mean tell it the way I think it is. For example, I have no hesitancy in admitting that I believe that students in today's colleges and universities have a perfect right to protest against inadequate lighting, poor air conditioning, lousy food and similar things. But I also have no hesitancy in disagreeing 100 percent with any undergraduate student who believes he has a right to tell the Board of Regents or the university president what he should or should not be allowed to say, how he should be taught, when he should study, and what research projects the university has the right to conduct. These may be questions for debate, but certainly not for action on the part of students. I have absolutely no use for people, whether they are students or faculty, who take over administrative offices in our colleges and universities, burn up valuable papers, and destroy property for the mere sake of causing disruption and possibly gaining the attention of the communications media, preferably the TV cameras.

But I have to say this, too. While I have no use for people who violate the law to express their views and to make their point in campus debates, I have even less use for the cowardly attitude of some college presidents who allow this to happen and who follow a weak-kneed, mealy-mouthed attitude of conciliation toward the perpetrators of unlawful campus activities. Across the length and breadth of this land where we have seen courage shown on the college campuses, and I think the campuses of Arizona schools qualify here, we have little or no trouble, but neither are the students denied the right to express themselves.

There can be no doubt that while student dissent must be understood, our colleges and universities—both large and small—must be operated for the benefit of the great majority of responsible, conscientious students. Too often, public attention is captured by a few hundred or even a thousand members of a university's student body cavorting in support of some demand or petition or issue of protest, and it is forgotten that many, many times their numbers are busily trying to obtain an education. The worth of educating our young people should be placed high above the antics of a few radicals— even in situations where those radicals might have a justifiable complaint in the scale of human values. The education of 20,000 students can never be weighed against the protest of a few hundred. And I believe that university presidents, most often for the sake of their personal popularity with liberal academic groups and publications, who forget this important consideration are certainly not worthy of the positions they hold and should not be placed above the contempt of their fellowmen. It doesn't seem to occur to our liberal "bleeding hearts" that when a few hundred screaming Vietnam peaceniks run and shout over our college campuses they are detracting from the much more worthwhile endeavor of many thousands of students who are trying to learn what they need to know to become productive members of our society and leaders in our nation in the years ahead.

I must say we live in strange times indeed when a college president who displays the courage to stand up for law and order and obedience on the campus where he is the chief administrator is so unusual that he becomes a figure of national prominence. This happened, of course, in California to a college president who did nothing more than perform the duties and the job for which he was employed in a reasonably efficient manner. His heroism stemmed from the fact that he was willing to take his stand with the so-called "squares" on his campus and his community who happen to believe that the precious right of dissent does not extend to disruption and inconvenience. In doing this, of course, he incurred the enmity of the Far Left segments of the intellectual community.

Now without in any way condoning the riotous and the oftentimes unlawful actions of protesting students, I am one of those who believes that there are some measures that could be taken to lower the temperature gauge on America's campuses. It strikes me that many of my generation who deplore all the antics of young Americans and assume the righteous position that protesting students cannot possibly have any legitimate grievances are asking for more trouble. This kind of shortsightedness can make a bad situation very much worse. In fact, I believe adults who close their minds in this fashion are comparable to the youthful radicals who urge their followers to distrust everyone who is over the age of 30 years. I think both attitudes add up to an eloquent plea for abject stupidity and a total lack of understanding.

It so happens that long ago I was able to identify some of the sources of student dissatisfaction with what they like to refer to as "the Establishment." Of course, the reference here when I say "Establishment" is to instruments of authority, such as the Federal Government. One of these sources of irritation, of course, is the government's denial of the right to vote to American citizens below the age of 21. This has always struck me as arbitrary and unfair.

And, if my reaction can be described in those terms, I am sure the attitude of thinking young Americans who are actually penalized by this restriction are far stronger and more emphatic.

Consider for yourself. At the age of 18, an American citizen can be made to stand trial before the law as an adult thoroughly responsible for his actions. At the age of 18, every male American citizen in sound health is liable for drafting into the military services. At the age of 18, every American citizen whose gross annual earnings exceed $600 is required to pay a Federal income tax.

But at the age of 18, no American citizen is allowed to vote. He can be imprisoned by his country; he can be compelled to risk his life and perhaps lose it for his country; he can be forced to contribute a portion of his earnings to his country; but he is not permitted any voice in the affairs of his country. We talk a lot about democracy and about how people who disagree with government policies should work through our political system to change that. If this is the case, what are we to tell an 18- or a 19- or a 20-year-old man who has been convicted under a law he feels is unjust as to how he can go about changing it? He can't even vote for people who sit on the lawmaking bodies of his community, state and nation.

What do we tell a man in this age bracket to do about a draft law he does not believe in? Can we honestly suggest that he become politically active and try to change that law in the best lawful, democratic fashion, and then hastily add that he can't vote for candidates who might share his disagreement?

And when it comes to the payment of Federal income taxes by persons who do not enjoy the precious right of franchise, are we not back where we started in 1776? Are we not indulging in that crime that was so heinous that our colonial forefathers went to war over it—"taxation without representation"? By whom, we might ask, is the 18-, 19- and 20-year-old American represented in the Congress of the United States which drafts our tax laws and devises ways for expending money collected from these youthful Americans? Can we honestly tell them that they are represented by their parents? In today's context, and allowing credibility for the so-called "generation gap," this can be a highly perilous procedure. Most of the 18-, 19- and 20-year-old people I know do not want to be represented by proxy, especially by proxy exercised by parents with whom they often bitterly disagree.

Needless to say, in this matter I am on the side of youth. I have

long favored lowering the voting age for American citizens from 21
to 18 years of age. I am, and always have been, against all forms of
discrimination whether it be on racial or some other ground, and
my feeling is that the 21-year-old voting requirement is rank discrimination against some 12 million Americans in the 18-to-21-year
age group. This is why I vigorously supported legislation in 1970
to pave the way for 18-year-olds to vote in all elections—national,
state and local.

Another source of irritation among the youth of this nation
which I believe should be removed as quickly as possible is the
present law requiring military conscription of young able-bodied
American males. In this I have always felt that the only proper and
lasting method would be elimination of the draft and the creation
of an all-volunteer armed force. I have long felt that young Americans who have been subjected to a permanent and mandatory military system since 1948 have a legitimate cause for complaint. Over
the years, too many promising young Americans have had their lives
disrupted, complicated and confused by a military draft system
which to them made very little sense. In this I am proud of the fact
that I was among the first public officials in this country to urge
measures to provide this nation with a professional, all-volunteer
military force to defend our people and our strategic national interest. And it was at my insistence that the Republican National
Platform of 1964 pledged to reevaluate the nation's armed forces
manpower procurement programs "with the goal of replacing in-
voluntary inductions as soon as possible by an efficient voluntary
system, offering real career incentives."

Above and beyond everything else, this is a moral matter. The
fundamental right of man is the right to life. The use of force
against that right—as in the draft law—is clearly wrong. It would be
wrong to assume that free men have to be forced to fight for their
country. In essence, this is the message that came through loud and
clear in the latest study of the subject.

The value of the recent Gates Commission Report on conscription lies in the fact that it investigated thoroughly the major
arguments against a professional, all-volunteer army and disposed of
them completely. It emphasized that the difference between an all-
volunteer force and a mixed force of conscripts and volunteers, such
as exists today, is limited to that minority who would not serve
unless conscripted and who would not volunteer in the absence of

conscription. It stands to reason that this minority does not constitute the most effective element in our military system. The commission also pointed out:

> *An all-volunteer force will attract men who are not
> now conscripted and who do not now volunteer but who
> will do so when military service imposes less of a financial
> penalty than it currently does.*
>
> *Contrary to much dramatic argument, the reality is
> that an all-volunteer force will be manned largely by the
> same kind of individuals as today's armed forces. The men
> who serve will be quite similar in patriotism, political atti-
> tudes, effectiveness, and susceptibility to civilian control.
> The draft does not guarantee the quality of our armed
> forces, and neither will voluntarism. There are no simple
> solutions or short cuts in dealing with the complex prob-
> lem that must always concern us as free people.*

As I say, today's youth is not without some justification for its
grievances. I have mentioned here only two that are of particular
interest to me in a legislative way, but I want to return now to my
original thesis that we are today training an exceptional brand of
young Americans for leadership of the nation in the years to come.

One of the things that strikes me most forcibly about this generation of young people is that most of them, particularly the responsible element, understand what we are attempting to do and
are actually training and planning to take over positions of leadership and responsibility. I see this especially in my own field of
politics. In my generation, men who went into politics did so rather
haphazardly—almost by accident, in many respects—but very few of
them took up the profession as a deliberate career. My own entrance
into politics was something of an unforeseen accident. Until the late
1940's most of my adult life had been spent as a merchant. I had
observed a long-time family tradition and followed my father and
my grandfather into the business of shopkeeping. And I was perfectly content to continue on for the remainder of my life as an
official of the Goldwater Stores, which were beginning to make a
credible mark in the fastest-growing state of the union. I became a
member of the Phoenix City Council in the late 1940's largely as
a result of my outspoken concern about a number of problems

having to do with the development and progress of the city of Phoenix. Not long afterwards, it began to look as though the traditional Democratic sentiment in Arizona was beginning to shift in the direction of Republicanism, and I was prevailed upon to serve as a campaign manager for Howard Pyle, who was to become the first Republican governor of our state in 22 years. That gave me my first taste of statewide politics, and it followed naturally that I should become a candidate for the United States Senate in 1952. Although Republicans had been making sizable gains in Arizona, I must say that my bid for the Senate in 1952 looked like the nearest thing to a hopeless case the state's politicians had ever seen when we first started hitting the campaign trail. My opponent was a well-known and respected Arizona Democrat named Ernest McFarland, who had served in the Senate long enough to hold the powerful position of Majority Leader.

I recount this personal history for one important reason—to show that there was a whole series of accidents of timing and change which attended the development of my political career.

This is not the case with the young people coming up in the Republican Party today. The ones who you can look to as future leaders are not leaving anything to chance. They are taking advantage of every given opportunity to further their training and their advancement in the field of public service. Take a look at the young men who have served in recent years as chairmen of the Young Republicans National Federation. Two of them are serving in the Congress of the United States—Rep. Donald E. "Buz" Lukens and Rep. John M. Ashbrook—and most of the others are actively engaged in public service or politics. One important YR strategist, young William Timmons, is now serving as Chief of Congressional Liaison for the Nixon Administration.

I know of another young man who is still in law school. He is taking his law at Georgetown University so that he will have a front-row seat from which to observe happenings in the nation's capital. His plans are very specific. He intends to return to his home town after graduation and begin laying the groundwork for a later campaign for a seat in Congress. He understands that this will take some years inasmuch as the incumbent Republican is not yet ready to step aside, although he is a close friend who understands what the young law student has in mind.

Of course, there are many things that can go wrong with this well-laid-out plan of action. However, I believe it is a sign of the times that young men are taking the trouble to seek out the role they want to play in the leadership of this nation and actively map out concrete stratagems for stepping into those roles. Not long ago a young Republican member of the House of Representatives startled his elders by giving voice to the fact that someday he hoped to be in a position to run for his party's nomination to the presidency. Even ten years ago such a public acknowledgment on the part of a brand-new House member would have been considered so presumptuous and so out of order that it might well have brought about his early retirement from all politics. In the light of today's political climate, perhaps as many people took this Congressman seriously as laughed him off.

Thus it is that as we enter the decade of the Seventies we find a new breed of young Americans coming along to replace those who are moving toward retirement. It is a fresh, imaginative and courageous breed—one that I feel is entirely worthy of its heritage and one which we can thank God exists. The challenges of the future are such as to require exceptional men and outstanding leaders. And let us never forget that when the world has been in trouble, youth has always saved the day.

X

Saving the Earth

THE TITLE OF THIS CHAPTER, "SAVING THE EARTH," SOUNDS LIKE A dramatic and all-encompassing kind of project. I use it deliberately because the problems confronting mankind in the blue-green planet upon which our moon-walking astronauts looked back add up to just that—a dramatic and all-encompassing task.

Our job, in the simplest kind of terms, is to prevent that lush orb known as Earth—once described as the prettiest jewel in the universe—from turning into a bleak and barren, dirty brown planet.

It is difficult to visualize what will be left of the Earth if our present rates of population and pollution expansion are maintained.

In this instance, when the discussion involves population, pollution and ecology; when the debate involves what might happen to our environment—in the air, on the land and in the water, it is possible to credit the most exaggerated claims of the most hysterical alarmists.

There can be no doubt about it. We are in trouble on this Earth in our continuing efforts to survive. We have greatly lengthened the longevity of human beings and made it easier to raise large families without at the same time coming to grips with the problem of population control.

In the underdeveloped countries, they use a term called "death control" to describe the growing success of these nations in counteracting disease which heretofore claimed a large percentage of their populations before they even grew to maturity. The problem in these countries and elsewhere is that death control—encompassing all known means to eradicate health hazards and the causes of death —has not been matched by comparable measures of birth control. Consequently, we are spawning too many people for the space available and for the means which are available to provide additional millions of individuals with the necessities of life.

Statisticians tell us that by the year 2000 the population of the world will exceed six billion people. That is more than double the present total of human beings on the blue-green planet. By that time, too, the population of the United States will be close to 350 million, compared with 204 million today.

The problem presented by these figures is as obvious as it is frightening. Provision must necessarily be made to greatly increase our food supply, but plans also are required to assure adequate shelter and the implements of living for a greatly expanded population. And quite obviously, birth control programs, not only in this country but worldwide, hold the key to whether population increases will outstrip food and other material supplies—especially in the underdeveloped nations of the world.

In the face of such a population expansion, the world will find itself running out of all kinds of necessary supplies—not excluding pure air and land.

Mr. Roger Revelle, director of Harvard University Center for Population Studies, estimates that in the year 2000 there will be two Americans for every foot of coastline in the country. If present population rates continue, only a very small fraction of this coastline would be available for public recreation. Mr. Revelle believes the problem of adequate recreational space is so vital that it may be necessary for the government or private contractors to build artificial offshore "islands" for ocean bathing in the 21st century. By the same token, the nation is rapidly running out of inland park facilities at a time when a combination of affluence and leisure has greatly increased the number of people seeking to visit playgrounds, parks, zoos, golf courses, etc. For the future it will be necessary to set aside more land for parks, and we may also have to develop patterns for rationing visits.

These are only a few of the problems which arise from the growing population crush. They will grow in variety and numbers as our citizenry expands.

By the same token, our technological progress in almost every field of endeavor is presenting us with problems of pollution. Much of it is strictly a matter of waste, whether it be in solid, liquid or gaseous state.

Of course, it is impossible to do justice to a subject this enormous in the space allowed here. However, in any attempt to appraise past effort in the light of present problems and future challenges, the overall complexion of this situation has to be acknowledged.

I want to hasten to say that I am full of optimism for the future—which means I believe man's ingenuity and know-how will be more than equal to the task of saving the blue-green planet. At the same time, I hasten to say I don't think our problem will be solved through the medium of advertising ballyhoo. I think this is one that will take greater effort and more persistent endeavor than the displaying of bumper stickers which order people to "Pounce on Pollution" or radio programs which punctuate their broadcasts with "Stop Pollution" phrases. In other words, I believe that this battle has got to be more than the "fad of the moment." I am afraid that student protesters, bumper stickers, and all the rest of the trappings of modern-day hoopla may make this whole problem a sort of "flash in the pan" type of thing.

It is important, of course, to arouse not only the American people but people all over the world to just what may confront humanity in the years immediately ahead. To this end, any kind of publicity serves a purpose. But this is one case where, after we wake up, we have to remain aroused and active or we can lose the battle.

On the question of pollution, it takes more than a month-long or even year-long propaganda effort. It should be much more than a political football for aspiring office-seekers or office-keepers. It certainly must be more than a liberal club to beat business and industry over the head because some sources of air and water pollution result from industrial production.

Let me raise a question. Suppose you, the average citizen, want to do something to help. How would you "Pounce on Pollution"? About the only way the average person can do any pouncing right away would be to voice his concern to his neighbors, or express it in letters to the news media, or start pressuring his representatives in the state assemblies and Congress on behalf of remedial legislation.

This is a big problem. It is also highly complicated. It is intricately woven into the fabric of leisure and comfort which go along with a high standard of living.

For example, it is possible to visualize the prospect of the American people having to make some unhappy and large-sized sacrifices in order to preserve their environment.

Take a small town where the economy is supported by one industry which gives off smoke pollution for the lack of adequate equipment to avoid spewing noxious gases into the air. Then suppose that a group of concerned citizens forces that industry to spend the money required to end the pollution. In some instances this would be just another way of forcing that industry to shut down because of its limited financial competence to meet competition, turn out an acceptable product, as well as spend large amounts for smoke abatement devices. In such a community, the problem of ecology gets all mixed up with that of economy, and the question becomes whether the local citizens want the continued employment which such industry provides or whether they want a completely clean atmosphere.

In another context, it is important to ask how the American people would react if it becomes necessary to slow down and complicate their means of self-transportation. Suppose the pollution problem becomes such that we have to forego the continued production of gasoline-burning automobiles and settle instead for a more expensive and less efficient conveyance with a different driving force. Suppose it becomes necessary to sacrifice the speed and maneuverability and the economy of gasoline-burning cars in the search for cleaner air.

The question of comfort figures immensely in the pollution equation. Suppose, in another application of hypothetical discussion, it becomes necessary to crack down on the pollution which comes from our coal-burning electric power companies. Suppose it becomes necessary to sharply reduce the amount of electrical power available to the American homeowner in return for a less dangerous environment. Here, of course, we run into the problem of whether we can support in terms of electrical power the amount of air conditioning which a growing population is demanding every summer. The entire question of limiting electrical power cuts across almost every area of human endeavor in modern-day America, and this is only one facet of the environmental problem.

President Nixon correctly describes the problem as one which is too big for government alone. He claims the tasks that need doing require money, resolve, and ingenuity and call for fundamentally new philosophies of land, air and water use; for stricter regulation; for expanded government action; for greater citizen involvement and for new programs to make sure that everyone concerned is called upon to do his share of the job and pay his share of the cost.

The President has proposed a multi-billion-dollar program involving 23 major legislative proposals and 14 new measures to be taken by administrative action or executive order. He sees the environmental problem as one that involves (1) water pollution control, (2) air pollution control, (3) solid waste management, (4) park lands and public recreation.

The President is to be commended for assuming leadership in this highly complex and all-pervading problem. Because of its enormous ramifications, only the President can assume such leadership at this time. It might help us to get some concept of what is involved when we consider:

America alone pumps approximately 175 million tons of pollution and poison into the air every year.

No body of water—no ocean, lake or river—is free from pollution.

Scientists believe that every part of the Earth's surface, including the continent of Antarctica, has been contaminated by insecticides that threaten various forms of life.

The world's population doubles every 35 years, thereby increasing by geometric progression man's demand on the resources of the Earth, man's pollution of the closed system in which he lives, and man's threat to all earthly life including his own.

In these United States we have one huge example of man's enormous destructive ability in this regard. He has, to all intents and purposes, killed Lake Erie, once the thirteenth largest lake in the world.

Scientific experts tell us that Lake Erie no longer exists; that a lake is a body of water containing complex, interdependent and varied life systems. Today, Erie is a 10,000-square-mile body of liquid from which all life forms have vanished except worms living in the mud of the former lake bed and a mutant carp that has learned to thrive on poisonous industrial waste.

In light of such a negative achievement, it is scarcely possible to claim that man's ability to destroy his environment has any serious limitations. There is no longer any reason to question whether the threat is real. The only questions left now are how much time do we have and how much determination can we bring to the job. Experts believe that in the end the success or failure of man's efforts to rescue his environment will depend upon whether he, as a species, is able to conceive of the emergency as genuine and personal—not at some distant time in the future but in the impinging moment of the present.

In other words, the major questions are the following:

Will man be able to curb his lust for material luxury?

Will man bring himself to accept a substitute for the internal combustion engine, if that proves necessary, or at least a more expensive, less efficient fuel?

Will man be willing to restrict the consumption of electrical power until he is safe and a nonpollution means of production is found?

Will man forego, or at least control, his huge appetite for such conveniences as nonreturnable bottles, indestructible drinking cups, poisonous insecticides and animal skins?

Will man, in the interest of the future of his own kind, surrender his right to unrestricted parenthood?

What is required is a rapid and drastic course in adult education with an inspired and effective leadership which can pay allegiance to no partisan political endeavor and no special economic interest.

The first step in this direction, I believe, may have been taken on March 3, 1970, when the Senate passed and sent to the President a bill to establish a "Commission on Population Control and the American Future."

If it does no more than concentrate public attention on the problem of population control as it relates to the nation's future, it will be providing valuable assistance. Because this is an issue with which we, as a people, must come to grips. Government can be of help. Government can lead the way. But the problem is such that it takes more than government by itself can contribute.

The United States in recent years has begun to fall into step with many of the nations that are suddenly beginning to realize the dangers inherent in overpopulation of the globe.

Demographers estimate that, at present growth rates, the population of the world will hit seven billion by the turn of the century. So far, science and technology have kept us ahead of the so-called Malthusian theory of population outstripping the means of subsistence. Even so, some estimates claim that nearly two billion of the world's three and a half billion people are underfed today. I personally believe that these figures have been greatly exaggerated or, at the very least, need a great deal of explaining. But if only a fraction of that number go hungry today for any reason whatsoever, there is significance in the fact for all those who believe in the brotherhood of man.

Because of the tremendous growth rate in population, the question of feeding the world's people becomes far more than just a problem in logistics requiring cooperation among nations to guarantee adequate distribution of available supplies to those in the greatest need. Ecologists now believe that just to produce the essentials for subsistence of our growing population could exhaust our present resources and bring about irreparable changes in the air, ocean, weather—in the life systems that sustain us all.

Estimates place the United States growth rate at about one percent annually. This does not sound like much, but it means that our population will grow from 204 million at present to over 300 million by the year 2000. These figures take on additional meaning when you understand that we are today faced with nearly insurmountable problems of garbage and sewage disposal. Those who like to console themselves with the thought that there is a lot of room in this country still unused must come to understand that much of the land they refer to is unproductive, mountainous, and not readily usable by a technologically oriented, urbanized society.

But even parts of this rugged terrain have felt the heavy hand of man in competition with nature. It is relatively easy—in the heavily populated metropolitan areas and in the tidewater sections of the country—to see the inroads made by pollution. The city residents have only to look to their skies to see the smog results of our stepped-up industrial production and automobile usage in connection with tricky weather inversions. Along the coastal regions and in the tidewater, oil slicks, dead fish and human refuse make the problem all too clear.

But now let me transport the reader for a moment to one of the wonders of the world, one of the remotest, most seldom-visited areas of North America, to show you how the problem of ecology has reached even there. My reference, of course, is to that great love of mine, the Grand Canyon. When I first went down the Colorado River as part of a crew which negotiated the entire length of the Grand Canyon in 1940, I believe I was about the seventieth person ever to make this trip. Deeply etched in my memory were the scenes which greeted us on either side of the turbulent, frisky Colorado River. I recall a great abundance of small beaches all covered with clean sand. My memory dwells fondly on the ease with which we built our evening campfires with the superabundance of driftwood which littered our route. There was no need for us to pack canteens in the old accepted Arizona custom going back to the days when Tombstone and its famous newspaper, *The Tombstone Epitaph,* were symbolic of this vast region in the Southwest. No, it was not necessary to carry water with us because the water of the Colorado River—even in spots where it had been made sandy and muddy by the rush of the torrents—was perfectly safe for humans to drink. As I say, these are the memories I have of that great trip 30 years ago. They are the memories I carried with me when I went down that same Colorado River and covered the same territory just five years ago. Many things had changed. Man had been there in comparatively large numbers and left his imprint.

For one thing, he had built the celebrated Glen Canyon Dam behind which are stored the beautiful waters of Lake Powell. But as a result, the flow of the Colorado River is now controlled. No longer are there occasional floods brought on by sudden cloudbursts—floods that roared through the Canyon, cleaning it of excess driftwood and nature's own debris; floods which deposited additional sand on the canyon beaches and cut the canyon a bit deeper into Mother Earth. Instead, the flow of the river is now regulated and no floods rush through. The immediate result which I could see was a rapid deterioration of the beautiful beaches, and I prophesy that within another five to ten years there will be no sand beaches left at all in the Canyon.

Even though the Little Colorado continues to deposit silt along the way, the regulated flow of water, which now never goes above 24,000 second-feet, prevents deposits on the rocks higher up in a way that would enlarge existing beaches and preserve the ones already created. In the days of the old, uncontrolled river flow, floods sometimes reached as high as 300,000 second-feet.

And the great movement of tourism in the wake of American affluence has had its effect in the Grand Canyon. Where I was perhaps the seventieth man to make the trip down the Colorado in as many years, there were an estimated 5,000 people who went through the Canyon last year. And the number grows with each passing month. The result of the increased traffic has had its effect. The water, although it is clear and cool, is not safe to drink because of the amount of sewage and garbage that gets dumped into the river. What little driftwood there used to be has now disappeared. People who make the trip down the Colorado today must carry their own stoves and feed them with manufactured fuel. And the sand which used to be enough to handle the normal problem of sewage created by a limited number of travelers is no longer equal to even a small portion of the task. There is no way in the world for nature to handle the sewage created by 5,000 people, unless we resort to the expensive process of digging latrines in rock formations which are among the oldest and hardest known to man. Garbage must now be placed in plastic bags and carried the entire length of the river trip so that it may be disposed of by modern, man-made methods.

As this chapter heading indicates, the problem is worldwide and not just confined to the United States. But it falls upon us, as the most powerful and enlightened nation in the world, to set an example and to do this by taking intelligent steps toward population control. The law enacted March 3 created a 24-member commission composed of citizens in public and private life. Their job will be to recommend legislative and administrative means for meeting the immediate challenge of the population explosion. The emphasis will probably be placed on efforts to bring family planning service to an estimated 50 million women who today do not have access to this information—and who are creating new population at a far faster rate than they are prepared to provide for. In this connection, the disappearance of the family-owned small farm from the American scene—a phenomenon of the last 30 years—is a relevant factor. The days when every family needed several sons with strong backs to help with the day's plowing are over.

Today man's population expansion is beginning to put genuine pressure on his means of survival. In the old days wars and plagues took care of the overpopulation menace in many areas. Today we have nearly eliminated plague and are striving mightily and with growing success to reduce the threat of war.

And human nature being what it is, modern man seemed to couple his control over disease and the causes of death with a belief in growth of all kinds for the mere sake of growth. Thus, population gains became something in the nature of a blessing, and technological advances were hailed with almost as much enthusiasm.

This attitude grew naturally from the pioneer days when we were pushing our national frontiers westward and needed additional population for the settling of vast land areas never before inhabited by anyone except the American Indians. The advances in technology, such as the development of the railroad and its extension into a continent-girding system; the invention of the telegraph, and later the telephone; the advent of the automobile and the airplane—all these technological changes helped man to overcome the rigors and the hardships of this pioneering and thus were equated with the development of what is regarded as good.

In light of today's pollution, one wonders at our former measuring rod of progress. When we survey the results of the population explosion and the industrial and scientific advances which it engendered, the question naturally arises as to whether we have not pushed our progress to the point of possible extinction. Is such progress something to be desired? Is this the result people have worked and strived to achieve?

Regardless, the problem is upon us and it is enormous, both in its ramifications and in its implications. I get the distinct impression that some people, especially the liberal Democrats, believe it is a problem which can be solved through the medium of rhetoric alone. Those who today like to accuse President Nixon of preempting pollution as a public issue which the administration is determined to embrace would do well to ask themselves why this is necessary. Democrats who believe that Nixon is a "Johnny-come-lately" to the battle for rescuing our environment might ask themselves what their political party did about prevention and correction of pollution problems during the three and a half decades in which it held undisputed control of the Federal Government and the Congress of the United States. If the President is newly arrived on the scene, why is it necessary for him to devote a special message to the Congress on this problem and present a 37-point program in what he termed "a cause as fundamental as life itself"?

Why is it that only in recent months are we reading in the newspapers about Justice Department actions to obtain grand jury indictments against large corporations accused of dumping waste in our waterways and poisonous gases into the air we breathe? As this is written, the papers tell of a special grand jury in Chicago reporting a true bill of indictment against the U.S. Steel Corporation and one of its Chicago plant managers. The allegations, which charged the company with dumping waste from its blast furnaces into Lake Michigan, were only the latest move in a long string of prosecutions and lawsuits aimed at persuading industry that the Nixon Administration is serious about combating pollution.

The point I am making here is that the process of pollution in Lake Michigan is not new. It has gone on for a long time. The only thing new in the situation is that we finally have in the White House a President who is determined to do something about it.

But it is important for us to remember that there is no easy answer to this tremendous problem nor is any one company, one industry, or one group of special interests in the United States solely responsible.

I happen to be one who has spent much of his public life defending the business community, the free enterprise system, and local governments against harassment and encroachment from an outsized Federal bureaucracy. Thus it is that my attitude on the question of pollution seems to have caused more than customary interest. I am very frank about how I feel. I have discussed it with newspaper reporters, in speeches, and on nationally televised talk shows. I feel very definitely that the administration is absolutely correct in cracking down on companies and corporations and municipalities that continue to pollute the nation's air and water. While I am a great believer in the free competitive enterprise system and all that it entails, I am an even stronger believer in the right of our people to live in a clean and pollution-free environment. To this end, it is my belief that when pollution is found, it should be halted at the source, even if this requires stringent government action against important segments of our national economy.

Pollution today, of course, is the most popular "totem" in all areas of public discussion and demonstration. To be against pollution today is like being against war, against disease, and in favor of mother love. Led by the politicians, many of whom see more votes than danger in the situation, the subject of pollution has been taken up by almost every group of concerned citizens in the nation. And it happened almost overnight. I just want to point out here that my stand for strong action to end pollution, regardless of whose toes might be stepped on, is not a new position. In the presidential campaign of 1964, I repeatedly raised the broad political issue of the deterioration of the "quality of life" in the United States. And the quality of life issue, of which pollution is a major factor, now concerns citizens from one end of this country to another.

But lest I be mistaken, let me hasten to say that pollution is not a problem confined to a few corporations who happen to dump waste in our rivers and gases in the air we breathe. Pollution is everybody's business. It affects the citizen who shouts "stop pollution" while he lowers the window of his automobile to throw out an empty cigarette package. It is the business of people who carry bumper stickers against pollution on automobiles from which foul exhaust spews out of their broken tailpipes or mufflers. It might help to understand the true scope of the problem I speak about to consider a report put out by an organization called the "Crusade for a Cleaner Environment." This report says that in a one-mile stretch of two-lane highways in Kansas, investigators found: 770 discarded paper cups; 730 used cigarette packages; 590 empty beer cans; 360 pop, beer and whiskey bottles; 90 discarded beer cartons; 90 old oil cans; 50 livestock feed bags; 30 paper cartons; 26 magazines; 20 maps; 16 coffee cans; 10 shirts; 10 worn-out tires; 10 burlap bags; 4 automobile bumpers; 4 shoes (without mates); 2 undershirts; 2 bedsprings, and 270 miscellaneous items.

This mess could not belong to industry alone. And it won't do for the American people to shrug off their personal responsibility on giant scapegoats. As an especially observant newspaper columnist—Nick Thimmesch of the Newsday Newspapers—recently wrote:

"It's true that government, business and industry have been laggard in preventing pollution. The utilities deserved the hell they caught on this question, and the auto companies should have developed emission-control devices for those millions of cars years ago. . . .

"But preventing pollution amounts to an act of individualized decency. Making industry obey the many anti-pollution laws is much easier than policing the 200 million of us who shove forbidden materials down incinerators, burn leaves, let our broken mufflers go and generally behave like pigs on the road."

Pollution is a nice word to attack in a society which lately seems to prefer slogans to personal responsibility. And until the Nixon Administration took over in Washington, pollution was only a word. It wasn't as though the Democrats were unaware of the problem. Just a couple of years ago, Representative Robert A. Taft, Jr. (R-Ohio) issued a report on behalf of the Republican Coordinating Committee which lit into the Johnson Administration by charging that 237 Federal installations discharged waste into United States waterways; that the Potomac River was badly polluted; and that Federal buildings, including the National Institute of Health, were adding to the pollution problem in the Washington area. Nothing much got done, however.

President Nixon, in sending his pollution recommendations to Congress, very wisely pointed out that the government is not conducting a search for villains. He added, "For the most part the damage done to our environment has not been the work of evil men, nor has it been the inevitable by-product either of advancing technology or growing population. It results not so much from choices made as from choices neglected: Not from malign intentions, but from failure to take into account the full consequences of our actions."

What has happened to our environment grew almost unnoticed in the feverish rush to attain more and more material benefits and human pleasure. The process of polluting our environment had its actual beginning with the development of a period we have long looked upon with pride—the Industrial Revolution. It was during this revolution that man developed formidable new skills in the exploitation of nature. He also developed formidable new reasons for deploying these skills as widely as possible. Technology grew rapidly; and as it did, the need for sources of energy to supply it also grew. And these technological advances raised living standards to a new high level and produced the kind of affluence which promoted additional population. Thus, man began to overpower his natural environment, not only with technological skills but also with a sheer force of numbers.

Stanford biologist Paul Ehrlich claims that the world population, which stood at about 500 million in 1650, had reached the one-billion mark by 1850. He further claims that our population doubled again in the next 80 years and now appears to be doubling at the rate of every 35 years.

So far as America is concerned, the problem seems to be that we have run out of frontiers to cross and new land masses to populate.

In the nineteenth and twentieth centuries our nation was a burgeoning, dynamic continent which was busy assimilating settlers from many European countries. It was bent on pushing lines of transportation and communication westward toward the Pacific and on settling transcontinental routes. The essence of American activity in those days was change of the most radical nature, and it was change that had all the earmarks of being beneficial.

The individuals and groups that participated in the dynamic growth of America in the nineteenth and twentieth centuries had almost unparalleled opportunities to exercise their individual and collective skills and capabilities. Indeed, the outlets for emotions and activities which had been stifled in the Old World were unlimited in the vast reaches of the North American continent. The accomplishments which grew out of this freedom can be seen everywhere—in vast communications systems, interstate highway systems, huge agricultural developments, the whole spectrum of technology, to mention only a few. This was the result, we are now led to believe, of a situation in which our people were able to give expression to all the psychic and muscular syndromes which go with vast change. So it is not without solid justification that Americans generally have been led to believe that change is synonymous with good. For years on end they were confronted with a vastness, much of it wilderness, which could be tamed and made habitable and friendly only through great change. Such being the case, they set about in the earliest days of our country to wreak that change with their own hands and with tools made by their own hands. They succeeded beyond the dreams of all mankind, and this finally became the basis and the underpinning for American optimism.

This optimism was based on genuine cultural experience. And for this reason, Americans until recently were almost constitutionally unable to accept the concept that change in some circumstances can be both painful and destructive. The scholars of our times regard this as one of our "cultural biases" which still exists even though conditions and internal events (such as pollution) now strongly suggest that unlimited American optimism is based on some doubtful premises.

A saying which prevailed among government planners and

other American citizens during the challenge of two world wars went something like this: "The United States will bungle through —we always have."

The whole idea seemed to suggest that our resources and our "know-how" were so unlimited that even though we started late in both world conflicts, we eventually would win out. That sentiment is still fairly prevalent in this country. Our resources, while a lot smaller than they used to be, are still tremendous in most categories. However, I don't think it ever occurred to any of our planners— until recently—that the time will soon come when we will be in danger of exhausting the most important resource of all—our environment.

This being the case, one possible remedy for future eras may lie in the outer regions of the universe.

Think about this for just a moment. We have already landed on the moon and proved that we have or can attain the mechanical and technological ability to travel through space and explore other planets. To people who 20 years ago considered the idea of man's walking on the moon in the category of space science fiction, the idea that man may actually reach the point where he would seek to colonize other planets is something less than sheer fantasy.

The problem of space and the opportunities and challenges it holds for future generations of Americans is a question to which I have been devoting a great deal of time since my return to the United States Senate. As a member of the Aeronautical and Space Science Committee, I have made the point of questioning every expert who comes before that committee about what he thinks the future in space holds for mankind. Some of the answers are quite naturally the stuff that dreams are made of. And every time I hear such predictions for the future, I am reminded of a quotation attributed to Dr. Robert H. Goddard, American rocket and space pioneer, who launched the world's first liquid-fuel rocket 46 years ago at Auburn, Massachusetts. Here was a man who was so far ahead of his contemporaries that one line of his high school oration read as follows:

"It is difficult to say what is impossible, for the dream of yesterday is the hope of today and the reality of tomorrow."

Along this line, it might be well for us here to consider one of Dr. Goddard's dreams of yesterday. Astounding as it may seem, this amazing man suggested in 1908 that it might be possible to send a camera around distant planets guided by the "intensity of gravity at predetermined points of its path" which could be returned to Earth. Now we are just beginning to hear the details of what NASA administrator Dr. Thomas O. Paine has referred to as NASA's "Grand Tour Missions" to explore the outer gaseous planets via gravity fields.

As so often happens with scientific prophets, this recent-day counterpart of Jules Verne was roundly ridiculed in 1919 when he suggested, in a report to the Smithsonian Institution, that a rocket could be used for scientific purposes in exploring higher altitudes than could be reached by airplanes and balloons and that the moon itself could be reached by a larger rocket. Of course, Dr. Goddard was immediately labeled as the "Moon Rocket Man" by an unbelieving American press. Thereafter, Dr. Goddard was always reluctant to discuss publicly his thoughts concerning space exploration.

So it was that the nonbelievers of 1919 prevented this rocket pioneer from possibly making much greater contributions to the whole concept of space travel.

I have mentioned here the possibility of stretching our imaginations to the point of crediting the possibility of colonization efforts in outer space. If any endeavor comes about in future years, a very probable forerunner will be the NASA Grand Tour Missions. These, of course, would be designed primarily to obtain information. They would be unmanned ventures aimed at scientific exploration via instruments.

In dealing in this chapter with the rescue mission to save man's environment, it seems to me Dr. Goddard's example has two important applications. First, young Americans need to appreciate that what appear as unsolvable problems today are not new to man's experience. Dr. Goddard's lifelong labor should prove to be an inspiration to new generations of young Americans as they grapple with the problems of their day and their dreams of a better world tomorrow.

The second application involves the whole concept that space exploration may prove to be mankind's new "bootstrap" by which he can pull himself up to a fresh level of greatness. It perhaps would prove to be the longest bootstrap in history, but I believe it's fair to say that the vast reaches of space in a dynamic universe offer mankind its greatest opportunity to again achieve, through explora-

tion and change involving new frontiers, new lands to conquer and
new civilizations to build.

Now is such a thing possible? Or is it all a dream? Even a few
years ago, I might have been inclined to doubt the possibility that
man would ever use outer space in the bootstrap fashion I have
described. However, my membership on the Senate Committee on
Aeronautical and Space Sciences has been something of an eye-
opener. Because in our sessions with the men who know these problems best, we are treated to considerable stretching of the imagination. For example, from these sessions it is possible to see how far
we have come in a very short time in the field of space exploration.
America's first dozen years in space, for example, saw our orbital
payloads increased 10,000 times, from 30.8 pounds to 300,000
pounds. Our speed record increased 13 times, from 1,900 miles per
hour to 25,000 miles per hour. Our flight altitude record increased
10,000 times, from 126,000 feet to 248,000 miles.

American astronauts, prior to the flight of Apollo 13, had
logged a total of 5,843 hours in space, safely flying more than 66
million miles in the Mercury, Gemini and Apollo programs. Twelve
Americans had orbited the moon; four had left their footprints on
the lunar surface.

Between the time when America's first satellite, Explorer I,
was launched twelve years ago, and Apollo 13, the United States
had also successfully launched 154 unmanned spacecraft, 23 of
which were launched in cooperation with international programs.
The sum total of our space activities over the past decade has returned to mankind tremendous amounts of new, practical and
scientific data of great value. Observations made in space of the
Earth, sun, moon, planets, stars, and the fields and particles of in-
terplanetary space have yielded impressive benefits which are only
beginning to be realized. Special benefits have been realized from
experimental and operational weather, geodetic, navigation, communication and other global applications of satellite systems. Even
though worldwide TV coverage of American space adventures laid
out our dramatic achievements before the largest audiences in
history, the full ramifications of these achievements haven't even
begun to sink in on a majority of the spectators.

The spectacular achievements such as the lunar explorations
have made tremendous contributions to technologies of all kinds.

However, some less dramatic but equally important benefits are being realized from other portions of our space program.

No matter how tempted the average taxpayer might be to deplore the vast expenditures of public money which it takes to launch lunar explorations and similar projects, the fact remains that space is the new frontier in every possible sense of the word. It is the new frontier for possible exploration and colonizing. It is the new frontier for our transportation and communication efforts. It is the new frontier in all branches of research having to do with the human being and his ability to live and thrive, comfortably and luxuriously, in every conceivable kind of condition. Thus, our space efforts are having and continue to have a tremendous impact on every phase of human society, human technology, industrial economy and planetary environment. Benefits will be especially pronounced in the areas of science, meteorology, communications, transference of technical information and management of our socio-economic system.

Many of the witnesses, perhaps the majority, who come before our committee are technicians and scientists employed by the National Aeronautics and Space Administration. By the nature of their work, they are necessarily scientific-minded men who express themselves in highly technical terms. However, the tremendous events that they have participated in sometimes move them to statements of wonderment and awe. Committee Chairman Clinton Anderson once observed that the space accomplishments of the last decade "have moved the minds of men around the globe." To this I would add not only has it moved men's minds around the globe, but it has caused men to cast their minds into the vast, outer reaches of space and realize that we at long last are on our way to discovering what exists in other galaxies and other parts of the universe and to applying this knowledge to our earthly life.

Almost unnoticed, our space program has changed the world in which we live. This can be grasped through the realization that since we first began our exploration of space in 1958, over a billion children have been born around the world into what will be known in the future as the "First Space Age Generation."

Because of the accomplishments of our courageous astronauts and the achievements of our determined scientists and industries, these children will learn a new science, a new cosmology, and a new view of man and his possible destiny in the universe, if not in eternity. The dramatic United States flights to the moon's orbit and to the moon's surface appear to us now as a revolutionary victory for mankind over the Earth's gravitational pull and the vacuum of space. They are viewed as a victory of liberation over the forces which previously had confined life to our home planet.

But you might give your imagination free reign right at this point and try to figure out what these moon flights will seem like to the children of the First Space Age Generation when they reach maturity. Even now, the Apollo flights are turning the tremendous adventures of flights to the moon into something of a scientific commonplace. Thus, today's infants and small children can look ahead expectantly to tremendous new challenges and new opportunities. And they can look ahead, because of what our space program has accomplished, with some real confidence that great, new history-shattering strides will be made by man in the 21st century.

When the space-age children reach their thirties and forties, they will have a unique opportunity to view the Earth as a whole—as a single unit—for the first time. They perhaps will deal with technology, with science and with philosophy in a unified way, projecting an experience common to all men of all races, colors and creeds who hold residence on the blue-green planet we call the Earth.

The consequences of such human capabilities cannot be understood or even guessed at in an educated way. We can only obtain a hazy idea that there will be vast changes in the human experience as well as in the human condition in the decade ahead.

Dr. Thomas O. Paine, NASA administrator, has drawn the situation into its true perspective by asserting that there is no way to express in monetary terms "the human values involved in new horizons and new hope for a better world that have resulted from the space program's demonstration that free men of competence and good will can work together within our institutions to achieve an almost impossible goal."

There is no denying the truth of that statement, and I believe it stands as a competent and adequate answer to many shortsighted critics who run around complaining about the cost of our space program while demanding to know "what good it did us to land on the moon."

These narrow-minded observers would never be satisfied with a full and complete answer to that question. The elements involved in the human values of new horizons and new hopes do not translate for these people. Nor do the developments of vast, practical "spin-offs" from space research and technology. Such critics, I sometimes feel, would only be satisfied if the first astronauts to land on the moon had discovered a mountain range of solid gold and a landscape littered with diamonds and other precious gems.

I admit it is not easy for the layman to get a true picture of the potentiality that exists in our space efforts. I believe it is wasted on him to point out that the space effort continues to act as a spur to other parts of our society, providing an essential challenge and a yardstick by which to measure human achievements in other areas.

United States spacemen have shown us how to create a uniquely American blend of governmental, industrial and academic research, competence and achievement.

NASA officials like to point out that we have learned to forge these dynamic elements, using new methods but without changing our viable system of private enterprise and government direction.

No one who has seen an Apollo moonshot and watched an effective team of Americans representing many lines of endeavor directing their creative talents and energy in one splendid direction can doubt this. If you want to put it in the vernacular of today, NASA has proven that Americans can, when they want to, "get it all together" and make it work. I like to put it in abbreviated, if old-fashioned terms—"you can't argue with success."

One current phrase is becoming a bit hackneyed from frequent usage, but I believe it stands as a constant challenge to all mankind in the rescue mission to save the Earth. And that phrase is, "Any people who can send men to the moon and bring them back can measure up to any of the human and environmental problems which today plague our society." If the space program provided nothing more than this rallying cry to draw men out and to force from them greater effort, it would have been worth all the billions we spent on the lunar mission. I sincerely believe this and I also feel very strongly that it serves no useful purpose to argue that if we hadn't extended our space exploration, we would have had much larger sums to expend on domestic problems such as the eradication of poverty, the development of new and bigger and better health, education and welfare programs, etc.

The positive approach is not to do less in space, but to do more on Earth and to do it better. The positive approach involves making sure that we utilize to the fullest extent the lessons and technology and resources growing out of our space efforts to facilitate the handling of problems closer to home. We must, as Dr. Paine has repeatedly urged, continue our progress in space, while at the same time applying ourselves to other United States needs.

America's space achievements increase rather than detract from our hope, our ability, and our national resolve, to face and overcome the new and chronic problems which afflict the Earth.

Throughout our history as a nation, the two greatest spurs to periods of vigorous, successful scientific and technological advances have been either the open frontier or the challenge of a major war. We, of course, have run out of frontiers in this country and the resort to war is not worthy of consideration.

Thus, it behooves us to turn to the endless physical, psychological, and technical and scientific frontiers of space. Our attention to this frontier has already stimulated development of entirely new systems of transportation, communication and management. These can be seen in items such as: manned and automated spacecraft, data lengths, ground support facilities, and new local institutions to manage them.

And who knows what the unified approach of future generations might mean in the family of nations? Space has given both the United States and the Soviet Union unique opportunities to demonstrate before the entire world their national will, the strength of their institutions, the quality of their people, and the vision of their leaders.

In this direction I believe lies the road to a better understanding among the nations. If a stabilizing force in world affairs is possible to achieve, I believe it can best be found in human attempts to understand and explore vast reaches of outer space and the universe. Such endeavors certainly would seem to dwarf the whole idea of military exercise and confrontation for the purpose of demonstrating to the world relative national power.

Space flights have already made the world seem smaller, more fragile, more luxuriant, and more precious. Perhaps further effort in this sphere will also make it more manageable.

CHAPTER

XI

The Great Challenge

WHETHER YOU VIEW THE FUTURE AS THE NEXT 200 YEARS OR THE three decades separating us from the 21st century; whether you see the future as a period of tremendous promise or a period of enormous peril—the one thing that will transcend all other considerations is the element of challenge.

There can be no doubt that our nation stands on the brink of its greatest challenge, perhaps the greatest challenge ever faced by the inhabitants of any nation since the beginning of time.

In purely physical terms, our task will be to meet and overcome the tremendous problem of world overcrowding and all that this means in the material sense of food, shelter, pure air and clean streams.

In philosophical terms, our challenge is equally enormous in scope and significance. By its very nature, this challenge is conservative—it is the challenge of retaining individual freedom in a world where population explosions and technological revolutions converge. It will be the challenge of making the very best possible use of every single lesson that mankind has learned to his benefit from the very beginning of recorded history. It will require experience and know-how based on solid assumptions and proven fundamentals. These are the essential tools for our enormous task, and there is no substitute for them.

The challenge of the future not only involves the negative aspects of a population crush, but it also includes problems presented by too much leisure time, too great an abundance of material goods, and a vast multiplicity of mechanical gadgets. These will produce an impact on our civilization which must be foreseen and planned for if we are to survive as a free people.

There are two ways to look upon the future. You can assume, and correctly, that we may be entering upon an extended period of vexatious and troublesome problems produced by a too-rapid rate of change without proper planning. Or you can believe in the predictions that we are headed for a period of supreme human achievement, leading us into an era of unparalleled abundance, prosperity and well-being.

A pessimist could easily see the road ahead as leading our rapidly growing numbers down a smog-covered, congested and trash-littered road to a virtual "hell on Earth."

But it is just as easy for the supreme optimist to envision man rising to new heights of moral responsibility, mechanical and technological achievement, and inheriting a virtual land "flowing with milk and honey where the streets are paved with gold."

If one observer, who is deeply interested and gravely concerned, is allowed to make a prediction, I confidently forecast that our American people will rise to the occasion, meet all challenges courageously, and lead the world in overcoming the obstacles which might prevent it from inheriting a magnificent tomorrow.

In the previous chapter I dealt rather extensively with the whole problem of saving the Earth from man's own excesses. In this chapter I should like to dwell on the positive aspects of a future I believe is the most exciting and adventuresome and thrilling ever faced by any generation of human beings.

And I believe we will tackle this journey with more freedom of conscience than would have been possible at any other time since the end of World War II.

At long last, I suggest the American people have emancipated themselves from the prolonged and paralyzing fear of nuclear catastrophe. It has taken us many years to learn to live with the specter of the mushroom cloud. There are still, of course, many alarmists among us who continue to dig backyard shelters and convince themselves that a nuclear holocaust is just around the corner. While I do not want to be placed in the position of saying that all-out nuclear war could never occur, I think it is worthy of note that the whole problem presented by the development of nuclear fission has finally been drawn into a better perspective.

I believe more and more people are beginning to understand

that the leaders of the world know full well what the problem is and that they will exert continued restraint.

I know of no leader in any nation who is tempted to make use of nuclear weapons to pursue either his personal or his national aspirations. It is easy for those who want to keep the world's population in a continual state of abject terror to envision a madman gaining control of a nation with nuclear arms and precipitating an enormous nuclear confrontation that would result in the deaths of millions upon millions of human beings.

I believe the nearest thing to such a figure that the world has seen in my time was Adolf Hitler. However, it must be remembered that even Hitler's insatiable desire to rule the world did not lead him into the use of poison gas. This frightful weapon, first used in World War I, was the forerunner to nuclear weapons in terms of horror. The abstention of Hitler in the use of poison gas, I believe, stemmed from his realization that if he put such a weapon in motion, it would be used very rapidly against Germany in retaliatory action by other nations.

Then there is the whole psychological aspect of human beings becoming accustomed to a threat that has been held over their heads for years. In other words, the liberals have shouted so long about the possibility of nuclear disaster that people have become accustomed to taking it in stride. It is a basic human trait that man can adapt himself to live with almost any idea, no matter how frightful, if it is premised over a sufficient period of time without actually happening.

So we find ourselves facing the great challenge of the future somewhat less encumbered by our fears. I believe more people are today concerned, not so much for the continuation of life on this blue-green planet, but with the quality of that life. If an overriding fear accompanies free men on their journey to the land of milk and honey, it will be the fear that their own excesses may poison the environment before they get there. And unlike nuclear fission, this is a problem that all men can understand. It is also a problem that all men can do something about in their own personal actions.

Tremendous strides would be made in the direction of free air, unpolluted streams and unlittered landscapes, if men individually decided that they would make sure that their actions and their activities would not add to the problem of pollution. Of course, it isn't all that simple, but, as I say, ecology and pollution are obstacles to an abundant future which man can not only understand

but which he can do something about in his personal life and demand and urge his neighbors to do likewise. He can also be the
instrument which can help force action at the industrial and governmental and commercial levels of our society. An individual who is
seriously concerned about the quality of life, not only for himself
in the years immediately ahead but for his children and his grandchildren in the distant future, would be much more receptive to
the kind of restraint and limitation which may have to be enforced
upon individuals to insure the quality of that life. For example, such
a concerned person would not be hard to convince that he should
forego the use of a fast, high-powered gasoline-driven automobile in
the interest of cleaning up the atmosphere. He might even lend himself to the idea that he can do without some of the gadgets which
require electrical power produced through the burning of pollutants.

It is not difficult to envision the energetic, inventive human
being who has managed to journey to the moon overcoming the
problems of contaminated environment. Nor do I credit any of the
current suggestions that a sizable number of frustrated malcontents
in this country are bent on a violent war against United States society,
which could wound us irreparably for the future. I am aware of all
of the arguments wrapped up in this contention. And I suggest that
they aggravate and compound all existing problems of our society
and attempt to magnify them into a crusade of destruction aimed at
what is loosely called "the Establishment."

The number of bombings of government buildings, business
offices and city skyscrapers has escalated rather sharply over the past
year. And this trend toward the violent resolving of grievances, real
or imaginary, is not to be taken lightly. It has very serious ramifications which grow out of a long period of liberal permissiveness,
which has led many of our citizens to believe that the rules of society
were made to be changed by them, any time they please and by any
method that might come to hand. The whole idea of aggrandizing
civil disobedience and mass demonstrations of disregard for laws
that were passed to protect a majority of our people—but which a
minority feels are not moral—has brought this about. It is not possible
to convince militant revolutionaries that they may violate certain
laws with impunity, but that they must obey other laws. This whole
approach lacks consistency, and it provides a rationale for lawlessness
that finds no barrier to violence.

The real danger, of course, is not to the nation. This violence,
which risks thousands of innocent lives, will not be tolerated in a

free society. It will be brought under control and stamped out with the complete approval of the vast majority of Americans, no matter what methods might be required.

Some discerning observers believe that the greater peril would come from the provoking of a massive backlash from Americans who may become fed up once and for all with the use of violence and force to bring about social changes. This theme was pointed out with particular force in a column written earlier this year by Roscoe and Geoffrey Drummond which appeared in the *Washington Post*. It envisioned a possible backlash from the bombings which might provoke a majority of Americans to say in effect, "If this is what comes from all we are doing about poverty and racial justice, it's time to stop."

There are, of course, some radicals who are attempting to convince the American people that our society as it now exists must be completely destroyed before any social justice can be achieved. Adding to this line of thinking was a Louis Harris poll published by *Time* magazine in late March of 1970. It contained this arresting statistic on attitudes of black Americans as turned up by the Harris poll—a statement that 63 percent of American Negroes agree that the political "system is rotten and has to be changed completely for blacks to be free."

This product of the Harris poll has done a lot to increase my suspicion that our polls are less and less reflective of public opinion. In fact, I agree with an editorial which appeared in the *Washington Evening Star* on April 4, 1970. It called attention to the *Time* magazine report of the Harris poll and said the following:

> *Perhaps the most arresting statistic turned up by the Harris pollsters—the one that understandably received most attention in the news stories about the sampling—is the statement that 63 percent of American Negroes agree that the political "system is rotten and has to be changed completely for blacks to be free."*
>
> *That, on the face of it, is a frightening statistic. It means—or seems to mean—that some 15 million blacks have given up on the system and are prepared to tear it down by any means available. It is a statistic that will be repeated for years to come in the councils of the black militants and of the white supremacists.*
>
> *It is also a pointless statistic. The question is so ill de-*

fined and open to such a variety of interpretations as to make the answers meaningless. Even the generalized despair that the result appears to reflect is effectively contradicted by other, more specific questions in the sampling.

It does not jibe with the observation that "the vast majority want to work through the existing system—economic and political power—for further improvements." It cannot be reconciled with the findings that the most respected civil rights organization is the NAACP and the least respected the Black Panthers; that the most respected Negro leaders are Carl Stokes and Ralph Abernathy, the least respected Bobby Seale and Elijah Muhammed; that 97 percent believe that the road to progress lies in better education; that 9 percent consider themselves revolutionaries and advocate violence.

But the fundamental fault in such a poll is not in its specific findings. A careful reading will provide something encouraging and something disturbing for just about everybody, which seems fair enough. Even the general conclusion that black expectations and frustrations are both on the rise cannot be faulted—except for the fact that it is so obvious that an expert sampling and a computerized projection hardly seem necessary.

The real trouble is that such a poll tends to solidify a dangerous concept of contemporary thought: The belief that there are two Americas, one white and one black, and that the two are in inevitable conflict. . . .

It would be foolish to deny that differences exist, or to insist that inequality is a myth and that there are no areas of friction. It is, however, a tragic mistake to accept the divisions as inevitable and permanent.

I have dealt here with the questions of population, pollution and social unrest primarily to show that the things which stand in the way of our full and complete realization of a bountiful tomorrow are known and manageable. It perhaps is easier to envision the troubles that lie ahead than to see the vistas that will be opened up through our expanding economy and burgeoning technology.

Envision, if you will, an economy which has a Gross National Product which exceeds two trillion dollars; an output of goods and services rising four times faster than the United States population;

an average work week of between 20 and 30 hours. Let your minds wander over the possibility that fast-moving and busy Americans will soon be able to substitute food pills for time-consuming meals. Or spend the day with a budget-minded housewife who will prepare dishes that look and taste like meat but which actually will have been created from the protein of soybeans or algae at a fraction of the cost and twice the convenience. She may well be a housewife who doesn't worry about vacuum sweepers and dusting cloths but who relies on central air cleaning systems which eliminate all individual effort. She may well be a housewife who does her browsing through the shops, as well as her shopping, via "picture-phone" facsimile transmission. And only occasionally will she visit a kitchen with an automated food preparation system, where one section would store freeze-dried and frozen foods, and another would hold an instantaneous microwave oven cooker. She might be able to order a complete meal merely by punching out a few instructions on an electronic computer. The food would then be transferred from the storage compartments to cooking units and heated so that every item would be ready for serving at the correct time. Pots and pans will be a thing of the past.

What the future holds in terms of household gadgets and improved implements with which man will surround himself literally defies the imagination. Even today, improvements and advancements are being perfected which will make the popular implements of the present seem like relics of the "horse and buggy" era. How soon these developments will reach the market and how soon they may reach the stage of generalized use by our citizens are questions which are obscured by economic, marketing, distribution and similar considerations. I believe it is sufficient to say that almost everything we use today in our daily lives, whether it be our methods of transportation or new techniques of learning, will be radically changed, some of them even revolutionized.

These are the inevitable, common, everyday results of an accelerated pace of research and development in the mechanics of living such as we have never seen before. Our drawing boards are literally covered with plans for new and different and radically improved devices for all parts of our houses, for all kinds of transportation, for all kinds of health care. And the rate of progression from drawing board to production is moving at a swifter and swifter pace.

Space does not permit me here to even scratch the surface of the material future of this country and of this world. However, I believe it does us all good, when we consider the problems that afflict our society today, to try and visualize something of what the future could be like.

Take the question of our cities, for example. At the present time, the problems growing out of overcrowded conditions and ghetto-type slums hold the national spotlight. These are grave problems, which must be attacked with every means at our command. However, we should not allow the problem of the innercities to completely obliterate developments taking place on the urbanized outskirts. At an ever-increasing rate, houses, businesses, schools, churches and swimming pools are spilling over the American suburbs. The metropolitan outskirts are growing more and more remote as the central city buildings grow higher and higher.

Actually, our citified society is developing an urban sprawl which is not about to let up anytime in the near future. A new name is beginning to emerge from the growth of suburban sprawls, and the word is "megalopolises." It is used by planners to describe immense, greater-city metropolitan areas which are now just beginning to develop. In 30 years, some experts say there will be unbroken stretches of urban civilization that may run from just above Boston to a point far below Washington, D.C. This megalopolis would thus encompass some 480 miles. Other such urban sprawls may easily cover the entire 250 miles which now separate Chicago from Detroit and the distance which separates Cleveland from Buffalo. And the megalopolis development is not expected to be confined to the Eastern half of the nation. Western planners envision an urban sprawl from a point north of Los Angeles down to the Mexican border.

And the great migration from the central cities, most of which have been losing population in recent decades, may have beneficial effects over the long haul. As the movement out of the cities continues, pressure may be expected to be eased in the innercity sections and facilitate the rebuilding and renewal of these population areas. Eventually, some future planners believe the central cities will become attractive enough to draw back many of the former residents who fled their precincts to build a life around some suburban shopping center far removed from the previous dirt and traffic and noise of downtown metropolitan sections.

Of course, unless there is a radical drop-off in population statistics, the suburban areas will continue to grow as well. According to William L. C. Wheaton, a professor of planning at the University of California, "by the 1990's our cities will be exciting enough to be drawing people back in, causing many with homes in the country to take up apartments in the cities."

City dwelling bids fair to show vast improvement under the most advanced rebuilding plans which are being thought of today. There is the fascinating modular concept of prefabricated and easily assembled parts for a whole city to be housed in one huge building. Such a development was part of a concept presented in great detail last spring by Paulo Solari, an architect with an appreciation for ecology, who foresees a complete change in our way of life in the cities. Actually, such a plan might call for the rebuilding of our prominent cities like New York, Philadelphia, Baltimore and Detroit—to name just a few. Eventually, we may well find all business being conducted beneath the city, and we might well find ourselves living in a world where the hustle and bustle of city life would be concentrated in protected areas equipped with special kinds of lighting and air conditioning.

Mr. Solari presented his plans for a pioneer city along these lines in the Arizona desert for display at Washington Corcoran Gallery. The pioneer city would be called "Arcosanti" and would literally be a city under a roof where it would be possible to regulate the weather for city dwellers at all hours of the day and night.

Mr. Solari has been called a "prophet in the desert," and there can be no doubt that he is a man whose work will have great impact on our future. At the moment, he offers some fascinating and almost fantastic answers to the twin problems of city building and pollution control. More and more I believe our planners will be required to look to such men as Mr. Solari for concepts and ideas if we are to save any semblance of city life. For unless something is done to revitalize and reconstitute our innercities, I hate to think of what our present-day metropolitan areas will look like in 25 or 50 or 100 years. In my lifetime these areas have not improved despite all the public expenditures on employment, housing and similar activities. In fact, the congestion and the pollution and the filth of the innercities have gotten steadily worse in my years on Earth.

Perhaps we who live in the West are more sensitive to these things. We have become perhaps too accustomed to wide streets and clean air and the other advantages which have so long been features of the process of living in "the wide open spaces." I think it would serve us well in the West to look carefully at the mistakes in engineering and planning that were made by large Eastern cities as their population grew year after year. Perhaps we can avoid these pitfalls as the West receives hordes of new residents and watches cities like Phoenix and Los Angeles doubling and tripling their populations every other census.

Some Westerners appear to think that our space will last forever. However, I believe the smog blanket, which is becoming a landmark of the Los Angeles horizon, and repeated instances of "smust" (smoke and dust) even over the Arizona desert, are beginning to bring home the fact that the cities of the West must think ahead and plan for a radically different and heavily populated future.

All you have to do is look at our Eastern cities and figure out little devices in your own mind that could have been accomplished by adequate advanced planning but which are almost impossible to achieve today without a complete process of rebuilding. It always occurs to me, for example, as I am driving in Eastern cities what a wonderful thing it would be if all the cities in the country could ban left-hand turns and take other obvious steps to speed the flow of traffic. In our capital city of Washington, I often think about those tree-lined circles which look so symmetrical and beautiful from an airplane but which complicate the movement of traffic in an almost unbelievable fashion. If these were eliminated and thoroughfares which converge on them made through-streets, at least twice as much traffic could move around our capital city with greater ease. All truck deliveries could be made at night, and this would further relieve congestion.

Even without missiles and spacecraft, we can be assured that in the immediate and distant future we will be an extremely fast-moving population—at least by comparison with today's standards. To gauge the true image of American transportation and what lies ahead of it demands that we exercise our imagination and credit what only a few years ago we might have regarded as science fiction. We are headed for an amazing, hard-to-believe era of faster and easier travel in all areas of transportation.

There are many problems, but I am confident that the private aviation industry, with the help of a streamlined and modernized government policy, will be able to take them in stride.

Perhaps the most fascinating area of transportation planning for the future is the one aimed at the mass movement of workers, shoppers and other commuters around the "urban sprawl" sections which will dot the landscapes. All kinds of methods for short-haul innercity passenger movement are being explored. Some involve the use of helicopter-type planes which would lift full buses and carry them from outlying residential areas to tiny landing fields in the downtown section, from which the buses could begin their rounds.

Another mode of transportation being explored is the so-called "air-cushion" vehicle that would shoot through tubes at speeds up to 600 miles an hour, thus connecting all areas of the planned "megalopolises" of the future. Laboratory models of such tube vehicles have already been built at the University of Manchester in Britain and at Massachusetts Institute of Technology in this country. And the Garrett Corporation, a Los Angeles subsidiary of Signal Oil Company, has a Federal contract to study the feasibility of the air-cushion system.

The system would operate on electromagnetic energy from a power source sunk into a concrete roadbed, which would pull the wheelless vehicles along at enormous speeds. When at rest, or when slowing down, the cars would settle onto the roadbed, but at other times they would travel inches above the surface. They would blast jets of air against the walls of the tube in order to keep centered above the roadbed and on course. And, naturally, the tube would muffle noise from the vehicles that otherwise might disturb residential areas along the right-of-way. While most planners believe the tube system is perhaps 20 years away, most agree that such a system would greatly ease the problems of our overcrowded cities.

But it is in the field of air transportation that the most exciting possibilities exist for the near future. The supersonic transport (SST) is a much debated project which is receiving top consideration from the new administration and which undoubtedly will become a reality in the next few years. The SST, a transport jet designed to travel 1,400 to 1,800 miles an hour, can take to the air as early as the late 1970's if encouraged. Aircraft experts believe there is still a question as to whether the SST will ever be able to fly over land because of the grave problem created by the sonic boom. Some of them believe the supersonic transport, at least in its initial stages, will be used almost exclusively over water. Others, however, insist that the problem created by the boom resulting from a run through the sound barrier will eventually be greatly reduced or solved, at least to the extent of making this a surmountable problem in populated areas. It is interesting that some aircraft engineers are intrigued with the fact that missiles going straight up through the sound barrier do not create a loud explosive sonic boom. This leads them to believe that some design of the SST may eventually have to be developed that would achieve a vertical take-off until the sound barrier had been pierced. At the present time such models of the SST would seem to be some distance from even the drawing board stage; but the way this industry is moving, anything is possible for the future.

While our supersonic transport has yet to fly, the aerospace industry is already talking about a hypersonic transport. The HST could conceivably be put into operation in the 1990's. It would, according to some advanced planners, travel 4,000 to 6,000 miles an hour and carry 250 passengers. Such a transport, of course, could get you from New York to Paris in about one hour, and it would be extremely convenient for long distance flights to the Orient, to Australia and other far-distant points on the globe. In fact, it could get you from the Atlantic Ocean to the Pacific Ocean, or vice versa, in the time it now takes to get from Dulles International Airport into the nation's capital.

Of course, the HST is regarded as the ultimate in long range air travel in this century. But it would not replace other types of supersonic and even subsonic jets. The SST would perhaps be the most popular long distance conveyance within the continental limits of the country, while slower and cheaper subsonic jets would still have a place in the air transportation picture in future years. Mammoth versions of the subsonic jets which fly today will in the future probably hold a place equivalent to the motor bus in today's ground transport system. By this I mean the subsonic jets would be the cheapest means of air travel. They would operate profitably by offering cut-rate fares.

Some planners, for example, believe that by the late 1970's it may be possible to fly round-trip from New York to London for as little as $150 per person. This would open up foreign travel to an entirely new segment of the traveling public. It would almost overnight strain to the breaking point all the air travel facilities which exist today.

Just think how far we have come in a few short years. It wasn't long ago that new airports such as the National Airport in Washington, D.C., were being described as white elephants with runways that would never be fully utilized. Today the air traffic problem at Washington's National Airport, coupled with weather, keeps incoming planes stacked up sometimes for as long as two and three hours. Its congestion problem continues even though some of the jet traffic has been drawn away to Dulles International Airport. And today, strangely enough, Dulles Airport is still being described by some people as a white elephant which does not have sufficient business to keep it operating at a normal rate, and in my opinion all airports should be built along similar lines as Dulles. I have no doubt that within a very short time the facilities at Dulles will prove as inadequate as those at National Airport. But when that happens, there will be plenty of room for expansion in all directions.

But there is in the development of new planes considerable reason for optimism on this score. The greater size and speed of tomorrow's planes should mean that the number of planes aloft will not grow as rapidly as the number of passengers and the volume of cargo. At a conservative estimate, the airlines' passenger business may increase as much as ten times as capacity climbs and rates decline in future years. But even with the larger and faster planes, the congestion in the skies over America will require elaborate new systems for electronic control of aircraft movements. Airports will have to be completely revamped, and this is the most important element in the whole problem of congestion. New arrangements will be needed for channeling passengers, handling baggage, etc. I have often said that Dulles is the only truly modern airport in the United States and that we should plan on bulldozing all the others.

Now, if you are surprised at the developments which in two generations have brought us from the horse and buggy era to our first landing on the moon, you haven't seen anything yet. There are even people in this nation today who are toying with the idea of using rockets to move mail and people at speeds in excess of 10,000 miles an hour. Of course, practical considerations at the present time rule out this possibility because of the limited demand for such flights. What's more, rocket experts in the aerospace industry claim that civilian passengers couldn't be expected to endure the discomfort of high acceleration and deceleration necessary for such trips.

Regardless of what changes and innovations are wrought in our way of living and traveling in the future, one revolutionary development is bound to transcend them all. It is the rise of the computer as a powerful, important and constantly changing force in the operations of mankind. More than any other development, the rise of the computer—the mechanical thinking device—contains not only a high quotient of promise but also a heavy element of peril. Within the next decade, or even sooner, it is possible that many services now conducted by human hands and human minds will be replaced by what has been termed a "mechanical genie."

The problem is illustrated by an example cited by *Wall Street*

Journal writer Stanley Penn in an especially fine article on the computer revolution. He put it this way:

> *It's 1980. A motorist is barreling along an eight-lane freeway. Traffic is light, so he nudges his car five, ten, then 20 miles an hour over the speed limit. No police car with flashing light or screaming siren appears on his tail, and he arrives at his destination without a care in the world.*
>
> *The next day he is notified by the police that his car was involved in a speeding violation and that whoever was driving it was due in court. The infraction had been observed by an electronic device that measured the car's speed, noted the license number and flashed the information to a police computer. The computer plucked the name and address of the license-plate holder from its memory and printed it out, along with the details of the offense.*
>
> *Certainly this is fast, efficient law enforcement—and entirely within the realm of technical feasibility. But the prospect of being nabbed by an all-knowing assemblage of transistors and circuitry has disturbing aspects for some people. Their doubts about computerized cops suggest something of a general mood of ambivalence often found among those who have pondered the role of the computer over the next few decades.*

Mr. Penn's example points out dramatically the whole question of individual freedom versus mechanical advancement. There can be no doubt that computers will bring great benefits. Many of them will be labor-saving devices that will increase the ease and efficiency and productivity of factories and plants and offices. Others will have a tremendous impact on educational techniques and all kinds of scientific research. The effect on medicine alone, where computers could provide instant access to any bit of needed information to thousands of widely scattered people, would be tremendous. In the laboratories of the nation, solutions that once took many man-hours of concentration and figuring and testing will be provided with the speed of lightning.

But like in most remarkable advances, the negative aspects of a computerized society are growing more obvious every day. The tendency toward impersonalization and the reduction of individual human beings to statistical units or punchholes on a computer card occur at perhaps the most unfortunate time possible. The ability to accomplish such impersonalization coincides with the population explosion, which is making it more difficult every day to provide human beings with individual treatment, concern and even love. The trend is toward mass treatment. College classrooms are no longer small enough to allow instructors to draw out the particular characteristics, capabilities and traits of individual students. And in universities where enrollment runs into the tens of thousands, the use of mechanical equipment is becoming almost an essential requirement.

The computer population of the United States is now beginning to keep pace with the demands of an increasing population. These highly complex machines are multiplying at an ever-increasing rate. In 1956 there were less than 1,000 computers in the entire United States of America. Eleven years later, 30,000 of these machines were functioning, and spokesmen for companies which make computers, like the Radio Corporation of America, predict that the total number of computers will be approaching 90,000 by 1975, 170,000 by 1985, while 220,000 will be on hand to inaugurate the 21st century in the year 2000.

From what we know at present, individual frustrations can be expected to grow even more rapidly than the mechanizing process. Such a situation exists on a minor scale today. Take, for example, the wage-earner who is hauled up for a complete auditing of his Federal income tax because a machine located somewhere in West Virginia started blinking particular lights when his form 1040 was processed. Many of us have run into angry customers who found themselves improperly billed by a department store struggling to install a new, computerized bookkeeping system. And as Mr. Penn pointed out in his example, "How do you explain to a police computer that you were speeding because a passenger was suddenly taken ill and needed immediate attention?"

For government, however, and for the people, the big problem which must be faced involves the right of the individual citizen to a life of privacy insofar as that life does not unduly infringe upon the rights of his fellowman. This poses an ever-growing problem for government agencies and institutions and businesses which base many of their operations on information about individuals. It has been pointed out that already in this complex society of big government, big business and big labor considerable amounts of information on private citizens—information on their incomes, bank balances, tax payments, credit ratings—have been accumulated in government and commercial computer banks. And the ever-reaching quest for more data to feed more machines is accelerating at an enormous and frightening rate of speed. One Federal commission is understood to have proposed a nationwide employment service that would use a computer to store information on job openings and match that data with detailed information on the characteristics of people looking for jobs. The *Wall Street Journal* has reported that the Budget Bureau is considering a computerized national data center that would collect information on millions of Americans from the Census Bureau, the Internal Revenue Service, and other United States agencies.

There can be no doubt that such an operation could offer tremendous advantage in producing more employment at an ever-higher rate of productivity and production. By the same token, however, it could constitute the greatest mass invasion of individual privacy ever conceived. The power represented by such information stored by computers would be almost impossible to calculate. And mankind has no assurance that the people who have access to such computerized dossiers will be steeped in brotherhood and goodwill and inclined always to use this power for benevolent purposes.

Here again is a place where the requirements of continued freedom must be held paramount and even superior to the possibilities offered by a computer revolution.

The nature of man has not changed despite all of the enormous strides which he has made in the fields of science and technology. His nature still encompasses both the good and the bad and he can be expected to perform in many different ways. Some human performances will equal the nobility established by many good, fine, God-fearing men and women of past generations and ages. But some others will seem like the incarnation of evil itself—men of greed and avarice bent on persecuting and enslaving their fellow human beings. In the hands of such power-mad men, the great implements of the future could be the instruments of a worldwide nightmare.

However, as I look into the future, I like to think that I detect the emergence of new and responsible generations that will study carefully both the benefits and the liabilities of the technology we pass on to them.

And I predict that they will use the enormous mind-challenging developments of our times to increase the welfare of man everywhere on Earth.

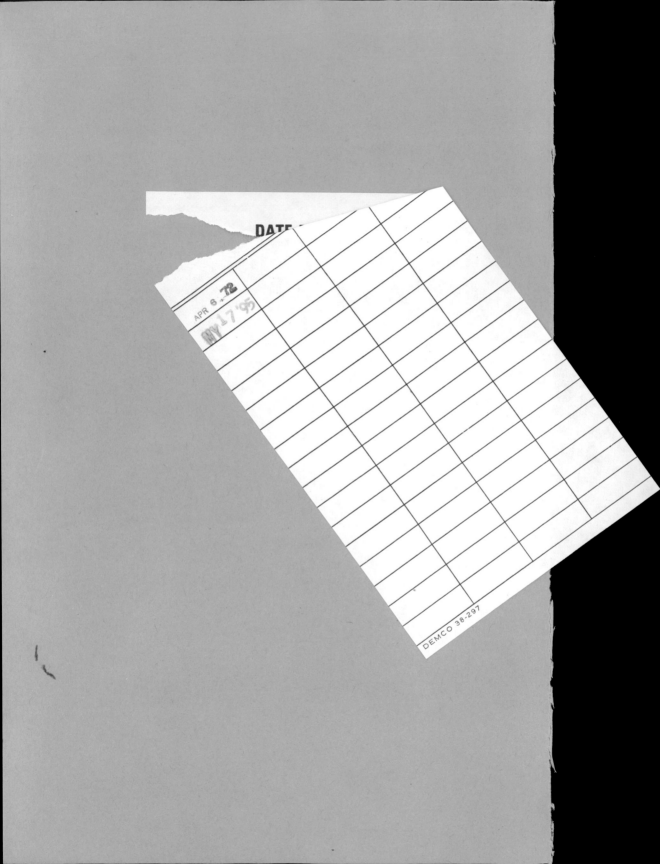